Quispamsis
A Historical Sketch

by

the Quispamsis Historical Committee

QUISPAMSIS FLOREAT

2008

DREAMCATCHER PUBLISHING
Saint John ● New Brunswick ● Canada

Copyright © 2008 Town of Quispamsis

First printing - November 2008

All rights reserved. No part of this publication may be reproduced or transmitted in any form or by any means - electronic or mechanical, including photocopying, recording or any information storage and retrieval system - without written permission from the Town of Quispamsis, except by a reviewer who wishes to quote brief passages for inclusion in a review.

DreamCatcher Publishing acknowledges the support of the Province of New Brunswick.

Title: Quispamsis, A Historical Sketch

ISBN: 978-0-9784179-5-6

FC2499.Q84S66 2008   971.5'41   C2008-905834-8

Printed and Bound in Canada

Typesetter: Michel Plourde

Editor: Quispamsis Historical Committee

Cover Design: Doug Belding

55 Canterbury St, Suite 8
Saint John, NB Canada
E2L 2C6
Tel: 506-632-4008
Fax: 506-632-4009
www.dreamcatcherpublishing.ca

Quispamsis, A Historical Sketch

© 2008 Town of Quispamsis. All Rights Reserved. No part of this publication may be reproduced or distributed without the prior written permission of the Town of Quispamsis.

Town of Quispamsis
12 Landing Court
P.O. Box 21085
Quispamsis, NB
Canada, E2E 4Z4

Foreword

This project was launched during the summer of 2005, when it was recognized that up to this time, the Town only had bits and pieces of its history. Many requests had come in over the years from people interested in the community's past, which emphasized our need to put to pen what history we could gather from all available resources.

Town Council, on March 15, 2005, accepted a recommendation put forth by the Mayor of the day, Ron Maloney, to appoint a Historical Steering Committee, made up of Councillor Beth Thompson and Town Clerk, Catherine Snow, who, through the assistance of university students, began the task of exploring Quispamsis' past. Initially, the goal was to post a history page on the Town's web site, but as the project developed, it became obvious that the wealth of information that was being gathered warranted its very own publication, in book form. The most important resources were our older residents and individuals who had a long association with Quispamsis. Many interviews were conducted over the course of two years, coupled with extensive research at the Provincial archives, libraries and historical museums.

This publication is the beginning of a journey through our Town's history. We do regret that there are gaps in the chronology of this compilation that will hopefully be filled in with a future edition. History is always in the making, and is never complete.

The Town of Quispamsis would like to express its sincere gratitude to all those who have given so willingly and generously of their time, memories, and photographs. A major portion of this historical sketch of our Town would not have been possible without their help.

We anticipate that this account will accurately depict the Town as it has changed over the years. By reading this document, we hope it will bring back fond memories to those who remember, and give insight to those who do not. This history is dedicated to all of the past, present, and future residents of the Town of Quispamsis who lived, are living, or will live in our great community.

former Mayor Ron Maloney
Town of Quispamsis
{Mayor, 2001 - 2008}
{Deputy Mayor, 1997 - 2001}

Mayor G. Murray Driscoll
Town of Quispamsis
{Mayor, 2008 - }
{Deputy Mayor, 2001 - 2008}

Quispamsis Historical Committee:
Catherine Snow & Beth Thompson
Town of Quispamsis

Acknowledgements

An acknowledgement and very special thank you is extended to Petra Kalverboer, B.A., B. Ed., considered the first author of this compilation, who was a university student at the time, and worked extensively for the Town for two summers researching and interviewing people to compile much of the information contained in this publication.

A further acknowledgement and thank you to Amy Cook, who was hired during the summer of 2006 to assist Ms. Kalverboer in the fine tuning of this compilation. Both Petra and Amy are currently English teachers, with Petra teaching abroad.

A special thank you is also extended to Nita Driscoll and Joe Thompson for their part in reviewing and editing the draft manuscript.

And finally, an acknowledgement and thank you to the Historical Steering Committee members, Councillor Beth Thompson, and Town Clerk, Catherine Snow, for their dedication in co-ordinating and overseeing this project from its beginning to end ...

A Special Thank You to the following Individuals & Organizations who made this publication possible:

Petra Kalverboer
Agricultural Museum of NB
Iris Bettle
Phyllis Bettle
Dave Buckland
Murray Joseph Howard Carpenter
Lolly Chamberlain
Dwight Colbourne
Amy Cook
Catherine Crowley
Ruth Crowley
Janet Cunningham
John Darling
Phyllis Darling
Dorothy Dearborn
Muriel Delong
E. Louise Dickson
Louis Dixon
Donna Dobbin (Warden at St. Luke's Church)
Nita Driscoll
Brenda Dunsmore
Valerie Evans
Betty Fleet
Irene Flower
Gordon Friars
Chief Larry Greer (Rothesay Regional Fire Department)
Donna (Buckley) Harriott
Hugh Harriott
Evelyn Haslett
Annie Hickie

L. J. Hickie Bartlett
Bertha Horgan
John Hughes
8th Hussars Regimental Museum
James C. Irving (Telegraph-Journal)
Cecil Johnston
Doug Jones
The Family of the Late Eleanor (Nelly) Jones
Garth R. Jones
Hope Jones
Shirley Jones (Saunders)
Duncan Kelbaugh
Peggy Kelbaugh
Alan Kelly
Doreen Kelly
Karen Kalverboer
Kennebecasis Public Library
Kings County Museum & Archives
The Late Clara Laming
Marion LeMesurier
Robert Love
Jean Lovegrove
Megan Lucas
Ron Maloney
(for his encouragement of the project)
Peggy Martin
Hailey Matthews
Barbara Maybe
Barb McBean
Chief Stephen McIntyre (Rothesay Regional Police Force)
Betty McLaughlin
Roger Nesbitt
(President of Kings County Retired Teachers Association)

Emil T. Olsen
Deputy Chief Stephen Palmer
(Rothesay Regional Police Force)
Guilford Roberts
Rothesay Living Museum
Royal Canadian Legion Branch #58
Fred Saunders
Otty Sherwood
Reverend Peter Smith (Quispamsis United Church)
Catherine Snow
(Quispamsis Historical Steering Committee)
Vera Stephenson
George Teed
Beth Thompson
(Quispamsis Historical Steering Committee)
Gerald G. Thompson
Joe Thompson
Ann Titus
Doris Tonge
Ann Waddell
Jean Watson (The Kings County Record)
Paula White (KV Style)
Jean Wilson

Table of Contents

Origins of Quispamsis...............13
Names within Quispamsis...............16
Names That Have Changed or Vanished Over the Years...............27
Acadians...............29
Loyalists...............30
Other Settlers...............34
First Nations...............36
Distinguished Residents...............47
Visitors...............62
Cottages...............65
Churches & Cemeteries...............69
Businesses, Hotels, & Stores...............84
Post Offices...............104
Older Homes...............105
Stoneycroft...............125
River Scenes...............137
Bridges...............141
Transportation...............160
Transportation by Water...............160
Transportation by Coach...............186
Transportation by Railway...............186
Transportation by Bicycle...............154
Transportation by Automobile...............195
Transportation by Bus...............197
Schools...............199
Community Halls...............234
Recreation & Culture...............240
Beaches...............250
Entertainment...............259
Special Occasions...............275
Family Life...............278

Table of Contents (cont'd)

Doctors and Homemade Remedies 279
The Depression Years 282
Involvement in the Wars 283
Taxes 309
Election 309
Weather 312
Environment 315
Road Maintenance 321
Views of the Area 323
Mayors and Councillors 326
Amalgamation 352
The Town Crest 355
Development of Quispamsis 359
Emergency Services 368
Services 381
Communication 382
The Supernatural and Legends 383
Capturing What Life was Like Through Art and Poetry 387
In Their Own Words 395
References 401

A Note from the Town of Quispamsis -

It is important to acknowledge all those individuals who have contributed to this history compilation. Without their dedication to this project, the collection would not be in the stage it is now. If an effort is not made to continue recording our history, cherished memories and details of pivotal events will be lost. For this reason, it is anticipated that this project may arouse a desire within the community to continue researching the evolution of Quispamsis. As this is a work in progress, the history will continue to blossom and grow with the help of the entire community.

Origins of Quispamsis

The Mi'kmaq (mic maq) and the Maliseet were two of the major First Nations groups that existed in New Brunswick when the French first explored the area in the early 16th century. The Mi'kmaq, also referred to as the Souriquois by the French, occupied the eastern portion of the province from the Restigouche River, extending north to Gaspe, and into Nova Scotia. The Maliseet inhabited the Saint John Valley and the southwestern portion of the province. Both the Mi'kmaq and the Maliseet were a part of the Algonquin Federation, and at that time they coincided in peace. The first inhabitants of the area now known as Quispamsis were members of the Maliseet tribe known as the Etechemins.

There are numerous communities in New Brunswick that are named in honour of these first inhabitants including Quispamsis, Mactaquac, Shubenacadie, and Restigouche. There are a number of roads in the area surrounding Quispamsis that are also named as a reminder of the First Nations groups who occupied the area including Maliseet Drive in Rothesay. An interesting project for the future would be to catalogue and photograph the First Nations artifacts that have been uncovered over the years in this region and to write an account about the First Nations of the area. There are numerous stories of First Nations people who inhabited this region. One individual in particular was Louie Morris, better known by residents of Quispamsis as Laughing Louie. He was a First Nations individual who lived and socialized with several of the residents of the Quispamsis area. Refer to the section entitled First Nations for more stories and details about the First Nations' individuals who lived in this area.

Presently, with the research that has been conducted by the Town of Quispamsis, it is unclear if the Maliseet possessed any year round residences within Quispamsis. What is certain is that the Maliseet used this area for hunting, trapping, and fishing due to the abundance of fish and game. The forests of the Kennebecasis Valley were also a rich source of Ironwood, Oak, and Ash trees which were the Maliseet's preferred woods for constructing axe handles, baskets, and other wood based products.

Quispamsis is bordered by two rivers the Kennebecasis River and the Hammond River. These two rivers were the main canoe routes used by the First Nations who inhabited the area. Early settlers later used these river systems as a means of transportation. Refer to the subsection entitled Transportation by Water in the section entitled Transportation for more information on how the rivers have been used over the years.

In the days of the French conquest of Atlantic Canada, the relationship between the French colonists and the First Nations groups of the Maritimes were generally described as friendly. The first documented contact between a First Nations group and the French in the Maritime Provinces was recorded as June 30, 1534 when Jacques Cartier sailed his ship along the shores of Prince Edward Island. Heavy winds prevented Cartier and his crew from going ashore to greet the First Nations' individuals who were spotted along the seaboard. Eventually, on July 7, 1534, Cartier and his crew made it ashore and began trading with this First Nations group. Soon European influence had spread throughout the Atlantic Provinces and to the Maliseet tribes who resided in Saint John, Kingston, and the Kennebecasis Valley.

As the Europeans began to colonize the Atlantic Provinces, they also established trading alliances and small military reserves. Over time, as more settlers came to the Province, Indian reserves were created. However, small bands continued to wander and camp on private property. Many residents did not mind because the First Nations groups were generally characterized as honest and harmless. For many years, the First Nations were reported to have camped near early towns and summer resorts engaging in trade with the settlers.

Settlers were slow in coming to this area and much of the land in the 1600's and early 1700's was associated with Seigniories from Quebec who were granted tracts of land. In 1689, during the French colonial period, a Seigniory, a title and authority over a particular section of land, was granted to a Pierre Chesnet Sieur de Breuil. The land granted to Sieur de Breuil consisted of the territory on the south shore of the Kennebecasis River, between what is roughly present day Meenan's Cove and Hampton. Six years later, in 1695 another grant was issued to Sieur de Plenne. This land was to the west of the earlier land grant, which was issued to Pierre Chesnet Sieur de Breuil, and consisted of the remaining territory of the Quispamsis area. Together these two land grants comprise what is present day Quispamsis.

It is unclear what Sieur de Breuil and Sieur de Plenne did with their land grants; however it is known that in later years the land was reissued to residents who settled in the area. English settlement in the Valley began after the Seven Years War, but it was the coming of the Loyalists in 1783 that greatly increased the population of the Kennebecasis Valley. By the 1820's individuals who owned land in the Quispamsis area included Joseph Bailey, Nathaniel Warren, Caleb Wetmore Jr., James Wetmore II, James Kierstead, Caleb Wetmore Sr., Ezrahiah Wetmore, and John Harris Wright. For more information on these people and their accomplishments refer to the sections entitled Acadians, Loyalists, and Stoneycroft.

Names within Quispamsis

Long before Quispamsis was established as a town, or even as a village, it was associated with the surrounding territorial areas of Rothesay and Hampton. Quispamsis was originally a part of the Parish of Hampton but in 1870, when the Parish of Rothesay was created, it became part of the Parish of Rothesay.

The Quispamsis we know today was formed through the joining of a number of smaller communities and their surrounding area. The Quispamsis area has a history of names and locations, many of which predate the official formation of Quispamsis. Some of these names and locations include Blair Siding, Gondola Point, Ritchie Lake, Lakefield, Model Farm, Otty Glen, Stock Farm, Meenan's Cove, Jubilee, and Hammond River. The Town's boundaries have changed over the years as the community has grown to include some of the smaller outlying areas, many of which still maintain their individual identities.

The following map from 1885 illustrates the different communities that existed and have now combined to make up Quispamsis. Quispamsis is actually spelled Guispamsis on the map.

In the following paragraphs you will find some of the older names of places that joined together to form Quispamsis. You will also be able to note how the name has evolved and changed over the years.

Quispamsis:

The European and North American Railway gave Quispamsis its name in 1857. The name was derived from the Maliseet word Quispem Sis. When translated into English this Maliseet word means "little lake" in reference to Ritchie Lake. The area, before being named Quispamsis, was known as Wetmore's, Gondola Point Road, French Village, and Lakefield.

Hammond River:

The area, Hammond River, was named in 1783 in honour of the

CUMMINS RURAL DIRECTORY MAP

HOW TO OBTAIN OTHER FREE MAPS—SEE BOTTOM OF THIS MAP

PARISHES OF
ROTHESAY & HAMPTON
KINGS CO. N.B.

1 SMITHTOWN
2 TITUSVILLE
3 NAUGEWAUK R.E.
4 HAMPTON
5 FRENCH VILLAGE
6 SMITHTOWN R.E.
7 HAMMOND RIVER
8 CITY GLEN
9 ROTHESAY
10 GUISPAMSIS
11 GOLDEN GROVE
12 GONDOLA PT.

Lieutenant Governor of Nova Scotia, Sir Andrew Snape Hammond. This is the same Major Hammond referred to by H.L. Smith in "A Rambling History of the Hammond River Valley." In this history, H.L. Smith is assumed to be using Mr. Hammond's rank at the time Hammond River was officially named. The translation of the name Hammond River by the Maliseet in their Native language was Nahwiejewauk and by the early Acadians in 1786 as Petit Nachouac. Hammond River, or Little Kennebecasis, nestles on the eastern boundary of Quispamsis. Between 1852 and 1885 Hammond River had its own Post Office. At one point Hammond River was called Jubilee, which also had its own Post Office from 1901 until 1916. For more information on the Loyalists of Hammond River refer to the section entitled Loyalists.

Kennebecasis River:

To distinguish the Kennebecasis River from the Hammond River, people often referred to the Hammond River as the Little River. It is thought that the Kennebecasis River derived its name from the Mi'kmaq name Kenepekachichk meaning "little long bay place." Kenepekak is believed to be the original Mi'kmaq name for the Saint John River. Other derivations for the word include "long river," "deep river," and "snake," but they all allude to the Kennebec River in Maine. In grants that date back to 1765, Kennebecasis is written as Canabecasius. A folk tale surrounding the origin of the name Kennebecasis suggests that the name originated from a situation where one man stated to another upon sighting a light on a stormy night during a canoe trip: "Can it be Case's?"

Gondola Point:

Gondola Point is approximately 6.5 kilometers (4 miles) north of Rothesay. The name Gondola Point is composed of two words with significance to the community. The word 'Gondola' describes a dugout similar in shape to a canoe and was used for transporting people along rivers in New Brunswick, including the Kennebecasis River. The word 'Point' was derived from a section of land that extends into the Kennebecasis River. There are references to gondolas being used in New Brunswick dating back as far as 1768. A gondola is reported to have sunk in the vicinity of where the current ferries at Gondola Point operate. The present two ferries commute between Gondola Point and Reed's Point on the Kingston Peninsula. Refer to the section entitled Transportation for more information regarding the ferries.

Blair Siding:

Blair Siding was named after Winifred Blair of Saint John, New Brunswick who in 1922 became the first "Miss Canada". It is rumored that the train carrying Miss Blair had stopped along the railway tracks at a train station between the Quispamsis and the Model Farm Train Stations. This train station eventually became known as the Blair Siding Train Station. Heading towards Hampton, it was located on the left hand side of the railway banks beneath the CNR overhead bridge (now known as Blair Bridge), near the Hampton Road intersection with the Gondola Point Arterial. Refer to the section entitled Transportation to obtain more information about the railway stations in the area.

Stock Farm Road:

The Stock Farm Road received its name when it became the location of the Provincial Stock Farm in 1882. The Provincial Stock Farm was a project designed to investigate methods to improve farm livestock, with an emphasis on cattle. The Stock Farm was also referred to as the Model Farm. The Otty family originally owned the land and rented the land to the government who in turn set up and developed the Model Farm. The following excerpt was written on the Stock Farm in a Clifton Newspaper under a section titled "Linking the Past with the Present," on January 10, 1930. The title of the article is The Legislature and The Otty Farm When It Was A Provincial Stock Farm. The author of this article is listed as "BY OBSERVER".

THE LEGISLATURE AND THE OTTY FARM WHEN IT WAS A PROVINCIAL STOCK FARM

When writing of the Hanington family yesterday I noted the keen interest of Honourable D. L.

Hanington when a member of the Provincial Government under the leadership of Premier John James Fraser from 1878 to 1882 in the encouragement of agriculture, and to that end the establishment of government farms where it was intended to introduce better breeds of cattle which could be sold to the farmers direct or through their agricultural societies. When Hon. Mr. Hanington became Premier in 1882 the Provincial Experimental Farm was nicely established. The fact that there was a deficit of a thousand or two every year was disturbing to the members who knew that the great majority of their constituents were farmers and the keenest criticism would come from them.

The Agricultural Department had engaged a Mr. Barker for "manager," and he had to be paid a fair salary. The rental of the Otty farm, which for a time became known as the "Model Farm," (not to be confused with the Model Farm Road), was considered generous - $940 per annum - and there were constant amounts necessary to enlarge and improve the farm buildings, as well as to erect a residence for the manager. The entertainment of visitors at the Government Model Farm could not be avoided. Every farmer in the country was noted for his hospitality. Meals for visitors and feed for their horses were always expected without payment. To offer payment would have been considered an insult. The government could not afford to do otherwise, and Manager Barker was expected to provide the best for the many visitors who were publicly invited to inspect this new Model Farm. This, of course, meant additional expense. Prohibition was unknown and the entertainment provided was made pleasanter for many by the liberality of liquid refreshments.

***

The popularity of the Model Farm was soon evident. There were days when the auction sales of young cattle were held that were anticipated with real pleasure. But it was not so easy to explain to the more sober minded representatives of the Legislature why the deficit was increasing. There were several counties in the Province jealous of Kings because it had the Model Farm. There were good farms in Sunbury and Carleton and York which were considered better adapted for the purpose than the Otty farm. As Honourable Daniel Hanington explained the Board of Agriculture first tried to get the Beer farm; then the Harrison farm, and voted by a majority of one against the Otty Farm.

But there were objections to all of these on many counts, and finally the Otty Farm was accepted because it was accessible to the Intercolonial railway, which really ran through the highland portion of the holding. A new railway station was built and called "Model Farm." There was no doubt of its convenience. The farm buildings were at least a mile distant, but they were adjacent to the inter-vale portion of the large farm where most of the cultivation was done.

It was in 1885, when the Blair administration had been in power two years that the removal of the farm from Kings County was debated in the Legislature at much length. Provincial Secretary, David McLellan, asked the House to approve of a resolution that it "was not expedient for the Otty Farm to be continued as a provincial stock farm if the same can be disposed of upon terms which should be deemed reasonable by the Government." The reasons he gave seemed to be based upon the judgment of the Board of Agriculture that the farm was unsuitable, but the fact that the Murray farm in York county, which Honourable Mr. Blair represented, had been chosen to take the place of the Kings county farm made the opposition to the proposal more intense. The majority of the Government was not large. There had been no general election since the defeat of the Hanington-

Landry Government in the House in 1883 by very small margin, and to invite a vote upon the location of the stock farm or its abolition as a government measure was not the intention of such astute politicians as Messrs Blair, and McLellan. So the latter was careful to make it clear that the members were free to speak and vote as they pleased.

The free-for-all debate that followed lasted several days. E.L. Wetmore, who was one of the opposition leaders, twitted the Government with lack of courage in not facing the problem as an administration. "To save their offices," he said, "they are not prepared to stand by their policy. They have imperiled that by making the question an open one." The vote upon the resolution was taken three days later and carried nineteen to eighteen. Honourable Dr. Vail, one member for Kings, was absent, or it was thought the vote would have been a tie; and as the Speaker vote was recorded in the negative, and Mr. Barbarie was in the chair, it is really doubtful what the result might have been. But, as it was, such sturdy supporters of the new administration as A. A. Stockton, who had been elected to succeed Hon. Mr. Elder, deceased, John V. Ellis, C. H. LaBillois, Honourable R. J. Ritchie, Killam and LeBlanc were upon Mr. Hanington's side and against the removal from Otty's Farm.

***

The next resolution was that public opinion would favor the continuance of a stock farm, and this passed with out much discussion thirty to eight. Many of those opposed to the Otty Farm were in favor of a stock farm elsewhere. Then Premier Blair made his bid for assent to the purchase of the Murray farm in York county at $20,000. He explained why the farm was suitable for the purpose. Hibbard of Charlotte county moved in amendment, seconded by Honourable James Mitchell, the Surveyor General, that the farm be located…county. John V. Ellis …the county upon having so....farms and moved another....that the farm be located in the section of the Province, as convenient as possible to the Intercolonial railway. That amendment carried by twenty four to fifteen. Mr. Ellis had the support of all the Saint John, K...Westmorland, Albert, Kent, Northumberland, and North Shore members, and nothing more was heard of a Provincial Stock Farm.

Due to the fact that the excerpt was taken from a torn newspaper, the last paragraph is missing sections. This newspaper clipping can be viewed in the Ward Scrapbook Collection at the Provincial Archives of New Brunswick, Fredericton Archival No. F111 33 RS184 C.3.a on microfilm.

The above picture is of Murray and Ruth Crowley when they lived on the Stock Farm, long after it had been used as a Provincial Stock Farm.

The Stock Farm Homestead; the children in the photo are Ruth Crowley and Murray Crowley. The women are Edith (Saunders) Porter and Ethel (Saunders) Crowley. The man is currently unidentified. The picture was taken in the early 1920's.

    Originally the Ottys owned all the land from the Buckley Homestead down to the Stock Farm Road before they rented the land to the government. In the 1851 Census for Kings County there is an Allan Otty of age 62 listed. Allan Otty was an English man who was employed as a ½ Pay Commander. It is recorded that his date of entry into the colony was in 1818. Before the Ottys, the Palmers owned the property, but then there was a marriage between the Ottys and the Palmers. Phoebe Otty, married Allan Coville Otty, (1827-1884), a descendant of his English ancestor, Allan Otty. Phoebe Otty was born in August 1829 to John Palmer and Allida Ford of Hampton.

The name of the lady between Miss Augusta Otty and Miss Emma Otty is unknown.

Three of the Otty sisters - from left to right, Miss Augusta Otty, Miss Emma Otty (center) and the last sister is unidentified. The exact date of the picture is unknown, but is believed to be around the late nineteenth or early twentieth century.

Names within Quispamsis that have Changed, or Vanished over the Years

For numerous reasons names of streets, roads, hills, or places have changed over the years. For example the Old Coach Road was originally called the Station Road, (named after the railway station), and later became the Quispamsis Road. The Quispamsis Road was dead-ended on either side of the railroad, when the former CNR Overhead bridge known as the 'hump bridge' was removed for safety reasons and replaced with the current day pedestrian bridge. The portion between the Hampton Road and the railroad was renamed Old Coach Road, and the portion from the railroad to the Gondola Point Road continued to be known as the Quispamsis Road. (See more information under Street Names section.)

Another example is the Quispamsis Lake, which was renamed Ritchie Lake after Sir William J. Ritchie, who owned property around the lake before being appointed as the Chief Justice of Canada in 1879. Refer to the section entitled Distinguished Residents for more information on Sir William Ritchie.

Other examples of how names have changed over the years include:

1) Fairvale (not to be mistaken for Fairville, which is now a part of Saint John West), was at one time called Fairleigh.

2) Rothesay was called Kennebecasis or Kennebecasis Bay until 1860.

3) Stoneycroft was not given its name until the 1870's. Prior to that it may have been referred to as Wetmore's, the Eleven Mile House, the Twelve Mile House, and Lakefield Inn. Refer to the section entitled Stoneycroft for more information.

4) At the corner of the Model Farm Road and Meenan's Cove Road there is a steep hill, formerly known as the Sandpit Hill. (Named after the gravel pit that was in existence in this area until the early 1980's.) This name seems to have vanished since the closure of the gravel pit.

5) Montgomery Hill is another name that has gradually ceased to exist. A hill between the Buckley Homestead and the Model Farm Train Station was referred to as the Montgomery Hill, named after the Montgomery family who lived on the Hampton Road.

6) The Pettingill Road, at one time, was called the Ritchie Lake Road. The name "Pettingill" comes from the surname of one of the first families that resided on that road, (later became the Hicks' homestead), located near Kensington Avenue.

7) Before the construction of the Gondola Point Arterial, both Diggle Drive and McEachern Road were a continuation of the Chamberlain Road. The new highway bisected the Chamberlain Road thus making a name change necessary.

8) The Colton Brook Road at one time connected the Hampton Road to the Mackay Highway. When the railway bridge was removed for safety reasons, the road was deadended on either side; with the portion off the Hampton Road being renamed Shadetree Lane. (See "Other Settlers" section for more information on the Colton Brook Road.)

9) What we know today as the Rothesay Road and the Hampton Road were once part of the Great Post Road that lead from Saint John to Hampton. This road came into existence in the 1820's. The building of this road played a very important part in the history of Quispamsis. The Great Post Road is also referred to as "the road from Hennigar's to Ketchum's", or "the road past Wetmore's". The reference to Wetmore's is connected to Caleb Wetmore Jr. who built a house we know as Stoneycroft, which he appears to have used as an inn. From 1830 - 1839, the Post Road became a very important road of travel as it replaced the Westmorland Road as the primary route between Saint John and Hampton.

Acadians

As early as 1719 the British government gave instructions to their representatives in Nova Scotia to expel the Acadians, (French settlers in the Maritimes), who refused to sign an unconditional oath of allegiance to Great Britain. The 1755 Expulsion of the Acadians from Nova Scotia forced many to seek homes in other areas of the world. The Acadians overtook one of the ships carrying exiled Acadians to South Carolina and changed directions, sailing north to the Saint John River. By 1756 approximately 1000 Acadians had settled along the Saint John River. Some of these individuals were later recaptured by the British and shipped out while others moved on to settle in Quebec.

Hammond River Park contains man-made rock emplacements, which are believed to be the remnants of one of these early Acadian settlements. It was also rumored that the Acadians who had settled in this region had planned to dig a canal for defensive purposes between the Kennebecasis River and the Hammond River through Meenan's Cove, most likely parallel to today's railroad tracks.

The Tibideau's or Thibadeau's were one of the principal Acadian families found in New Brunswick. They resided for a time along the present day Stock Farm Road, adjacent to the Acadian cemetery. The Tibideau's eventually resettled in the Madawaska region like many other Acadians upon the arrival of the Loyalists and the establishment of the Province of New Brunswick. Before moving, Mr. Tibideau sold his property to the Loyalist Christopher Sower. Mr. Sower built a two-story log building on the land to be used as both his residence and a printing office. For more information on Christopher Sower refer to the sections entitled Loyalists and Businesses, Hotels, & Stores.

Loyalists

Early settlers of Quispamsis often used the water routes first traveled by the First Nations people who originally occupied the area. One such water route was the Kennebecasis River, originally spelled "Canabecasius" in grants given to British Officers in 1765. Records from a census done in 1767 show that 15 French families lived in the area known then as French Village between the British Conquest of North America and the arrival of the Loyalists in 1783. From examining a map prepared and published in 1788 by Robert Campbell, it has become clear that the area known as French Village when the census was taken encompassed the future Village of Quispamsis.

In 1783, the population dramatically grew with the arrival of British Loyalists from the United States of America. The Loyalists settled in a number of areas including the Hammond River. The following excerpt is from a history text that describes the Hammond River area during the eighteenth century. The history also discusses Smithtown, Upham, Nauwigewauk, and the Valley of the Salt Springs Brook. This article, "A Rambling History of The Hammond River Valley" by H. L. Smith, gives the reader a sense of the Loyalists' lifestyles. This document was found at the Provincial Archives of New Brunswick and was dated November 24, 1949.

"A Rambling History of The Hammond River Valley"
By H. L. Smith

"Previous to the coming of the Loyalists in 1783 little is known of the river now called the "Hammond". It is known that it was called "Nauwigewauk" by the Maliseet Indians who, with a few French settlers, inhabited the hilly country along its winding course. The name, "Nauwigewauk", means "a river among the hills". "wauk" being the Maliseet word for "river".

In those far off days the valley and surrounding country were forested with a heavy growth of pine, spruce and hemlock, with beech, maple, and ash on the higher ridges.

With the coming of the U.E. Loyalists the whole length of the valley soon changed its appearance. Even the name of the river was changed and became known as the "Hammond", named after a certain Major Hammond who had been granted a large section of land on its right bank. It was said that an ordinary settler received a grant of 250 acres, if he was married. A single man got half a lot.

These industrious and enterprising folk were not long in establishing themselves in their new country. They cleared the level sections-called by them intervals; then gradually enlarged their clearings until, some years later, more land was under cultivation than is now in evidence.

In those days they had to dispense with many formalities, which in our modern life seem quite necessary. The McLeod-Fenwick wedding was an instance of this: The McLeod and Fenwick families lived on adjoining farms some miles northeast of where Hampton now stands.

A young McLeod and a Miss Fenwick became engaged to be married when the next traveling missionary, with legal rights, should come their way. This happy event occurred on one fine Spring day when every one was busy, as usual. The young man was ploughing in a field across the line, and the bride-to-be was working butter. When the news was told them he left his horses standing and she left her tray of butter. They stood up before the minister and were married. Soon after, the groom returned to his ploughing and the bride to her butter making.

Not many years later, solidly constructed framed houses were built, some of which still stand and are occupied by descendants of these sturdy settlers."

The French Acadians and the English Loyalists did not always live in harmony. In 1783, three gentlemen, Captain Ford, Mr. Sherwood, and Mr. Golding, bought land owned by the French settlers in French Village. The French, not wishing to live among the English, took their property and set out for the Cocagne River in Kent County to live among people of their own nationality. Many also relocated to Madawaska. There has been some historical evidence to suggest that when the Loyalists settled in the Hammond River area, they were granted land already lived on by French Acadians, without having to pay for it.

From 1820 to 1829, the Quispamsis we live in today was primarily unsettled consisting mainly of wilderness. However, some of the people who owned land in the area were: Joseph Bailey, James Kierstead, Nathaniel Warren, and John Harris Wright. The majority of these people were Loyalists.

James Kierstead was born September 24, 1756 in Jamaica, New York. He married Elizabeth Shaw in New York on January 5, 1774. By a deed dated January 29, 1785, James Kierstead was awarded land in Kennebecasis. In another deed, dated March 6, 1824, Mr. Kierstead was described as the schoolmaster for the Kennebecasis River. At this time, there were no school buildings in the area suggesting that Mr. Kierstead would have moved from area to area living with the residents of the children he taught. James Kierstead died Oct 3, 1846 at the age of 90; his wife had died earlier, February 3, 1845, also at the age of 90. They were both buried in a graveyard in Gondola Point.

Not all of the grants of land issued by the government were immediately settled. Grants were issued to worthy subjects like General Benedict Arnold, one of the leading commanders in the American Revolutionary Army who transferred his allegiance to the British when Congress would not recognize his claims. After the war, which the British lost, Benedict Arnold lived in London for four years before settling on land granted to him in Saint John. Many of the original land grants and subdivisions in this area were not settled until the mid nineteenth century when Irish immigrants sought refugee in Canada from the potato famine in Ireland. Refer to the section entitled Other Settlers for more information on the Irish Settlers.

Addison Smith, a Loyalist who settled in the Gondola Point area, is credited with starting the ferry service in Gondola Point in 1787.

This ferry operated out of the same general area as the ferry does presently.

One of the earliest industries recorded in New Brunswick history was the Printing Office operated by Christopher Sower. Mr. Sower purchased approximately 300 acres of land along the Hammond River from Mr. Tibideau in 1790. Refer to the section entitled Businesses, Hotels, & Stores for more information on Mr. Sower and his printing press.

Other Settlers

Pre-Loyalists:

In addition to the Acadians of French Village, there were also British pre-Loyalist settlers in the area that is now known as Nauwigewauk. Benjamin Darling's family was among these pre-Loyalist settlers. Darlings Island derives its name from the Darling family, which was the first English-speaking group of settlers on the banks of the Kennebecasis River. Benjamin Darling was born in 1730 in Massachusetts, and came to the area before the American Revolution. Through trades with First Nations people, he obtained possession of an island from the Chief at Nauwigewauk in exchange for two barrels of corn, one barrel of flour, a grindstone, powder and shot, knives, hatchets, and other tools. This island would later become known as Darlings Island.

An interesting point to consider is that during pre-Loyalist times, settlers did not build on the river shore, but traveled a mile or so inland to protect themselves from attacks by New England privateers.

Irish:

Several Irish immigrants, who moved to Canada to escape the potato famine, made their home in Quispamsis. Mr. George Saunders' great grandfather emigrated from Ireland, in the early nineteenth century and settled in the Chamberlain-Meenan's Cove area of Quispamsis. Neil McLaughlin came to Canada in 1831 and settled on the land where the Sobeys store is currently located on the Hampton Road. Neil McLaughlin Jr. was only five when his family came to Canada. Later he built his house on the Colton Brook Road, formerly called Hell Street. One of his sons, William McLaughlin (born in 1857), bought a house located near Blair Siding on Route 100. William McLaughlin's Homestead was within walking distance to the Buckley Homestead, another family with strong roots in the community who originally lived on the Colton Brook Road. This road, much like the former Quispamsis Road, became divided when the former railway overpass bridge was removed due to its deteriorating condition. The two sections now have different names; one section is still referred to as Colton Brook Road, while the section that connects to the Hampton Road is referred to as Shadetree Lane.

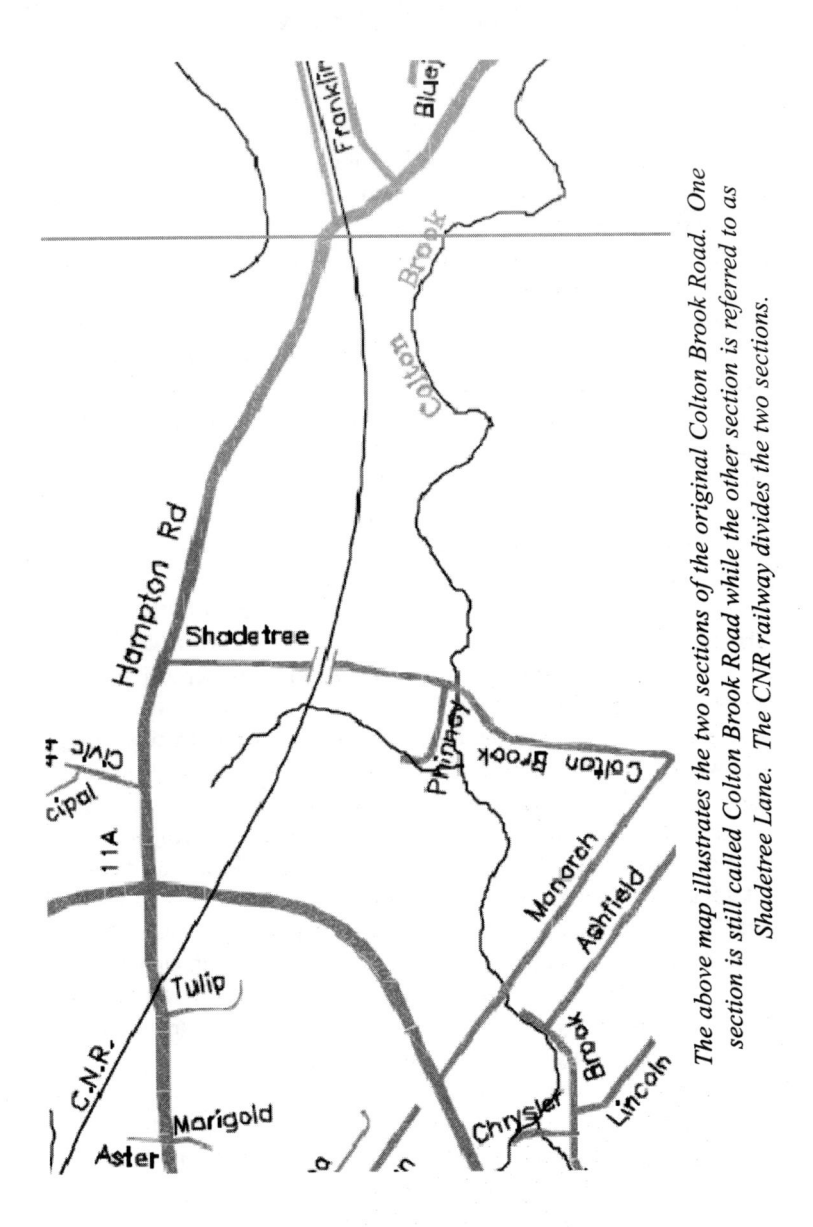

The above map illustrates the two sections of the original Colton Brook Road. One section is still called Colton Brook Road while the other section is referred to as Shadetree Lane. The CNR railway divides the two sections.

First Nations

The local residents of Quispamsis often relied heavily upon the axe handles carved by the First Nations people who frequented the area. After a long and harsh winter of splitting and chopping wood, many male residents required new axe handles. The First Nations people preferred to create their products out of wood from the ash trees that could be found. This type of wood made a stronger product. Often the First Nations people would trade the axe handles for a bag of potatoes, or a warm meal. Residents would often employ First Nations people to perform odd jobs around their property, such as chopping wood. In return the First Nations person would be paid or invited in for a meal.

Laughing Louie:

Many of the older residents of Quispamsis either have a story or have heard a story about Louie Morris, better known as Laughing Louie. He has been described as a friendly character of Maliseet or Mi'kmaq descent. It was thought that he and other First Nations people who frequented the area would spend the winter in Nova Scotia and then return to New Brunswick when spring and summer arrived. The Kennebecasis was a common destination for fishing, trapping, and cutting lumber. Many of the First Nations people who frequented this area were well known for their craftsmanship.

Laughing Louie was well known by the residents of Quispamsis for making axe handles that he sold all over Kings County. He made his bed wherever his work took him. Maliseet and Mi'kmaq Vital Statistics from New Brunswick Church Records claim that he had a cabin near the Black Settlement Road. There have also been accounts of him going to mass at St. Anthony's Catholic Church in Upham, New Brunswick. Even within the Quispamsis area, there were several different locations where he may have hung his hat and knap sack full of axe handles for a good night's sleep.

Possible locations where Laughing Louie may have lived in the Quispamsis area include a cabin on the top of Maple Mountain, a culvert underneath the train tracks by the Model Farm Train Station on the Hampton Road, or a camp located off the Pettingill Road. Other sources claim he lived in a camp in the woods along the tracks before the Higgins Farm on the Model Farm Road. It was also said that he and his friends would go into the Ritchie Lake Railway Station to stay warm at night, as there was a small wood stove in the station. Around this time period, there was an established Indian Camp located near today's Oakville Acres Subdivision, across from Sobeys in Rothesay. One key point that many residents of Quispamsis can recall is that Laughing Louie did not stay in one permanent place.

Laughing Louie was called "Laughing Louie" due to his well-known boisterous laugh that could be heard down the road. Once Laughing Louie started laughing he would not stop. People can recall him laughing so hard that he would actually fall down and roll around laughing. Many believed that his surname may have been Laugherty but, in actual fact, it was Morris. He was a tall man, over six feet, and on some occasions, to a very small child, he may have seemed a little scary. However the majority of people liked Laughing Louie.

It has been said that Laughing Louie was a friend to almost the entire community. He was often found joking with the young children of the area. Catherine Crowley can remember her father asking Laughing Louie which one of his daughters he wanted. He said he wanted her because she was dark haired so she looked more Indian than her sisters who were all blonde.

Laughing Louie loved his tea. Many people would give him packets of tea just because they liked him so much. Tobacco and salt were two other favorite commodities of Louie's. In more than one household, Laughing Louie was known to take the saltshaker off the back of the stove and pour salt into his mouth. Several residents believed he thought it was medicine, or perhaps he may have just liked the taste of salt.

Laughing Louie was a man of the woods, and therefore had limited funds. Truman Copp, made an old age pension available for Laughing Louie. In 1962 Louie Morris died and was buried on the Shubenacadie Reserve.

A local resident donated the following two articles about Laughing Louie to the Town. The articles were written by Warren Searle and presented by the Kings County Record.

Legend of Laughing Louie

I sat in Silence overlooking Walton Lake on the Kingston Peninsula just as I had done more than 40 years ago. The log beneath me was hardly the one that I rested on while supervising a group of neighborhood boys on a weekend camping trip, but it was very near the same spot. The ghost was there all right; I could feel him in a way that only those who have experienced the same phenomenon could understand. In death he was laughing at us mortals in the same way that he laughed at us in life. Allow me to introduce you to an old acquaintance, "Laughing Louie," the Indian.

To all the residents of Kings County and beyond who are 40 years or more, no introduction is necessary because everybody knew him or knew of him. At times he would show up in Saint John, but if ever there was "a man of no stated address," it was Laughing Louie. He roamed the countryside from Long Reach to Upham and over to Grand Lake. He had shelters in the woods all over the county, some that he had constructed himself or had simply taken possession. The most sophisticated of his dwellings would be referred to as shacks, but some were simply borrowed rolls of tarpaper slung between the trunks of trees and over the branches.

When Louie laughed, he did so from the pit of his stomach, and many people I have spoken to swear that his laugh could be heard a mile away. One man told me how as a kid, he left school one day to walk to a country store on his way home. In the distance he thought he heard a roar that could only come from the throat of a lion. Cautiously following it up, he arrived at the store and there tumbling in the dust was Louie reacting to the joke the locals were feeding him.

Young children were nearly frightened to death when Louie roared, and if in the house when

Louie was being fed by their mothers, they would head for the attic or crawl under a chair, but when they got older they went out of their way to get Louie laughing.

One question that intrigued me was "what was Louie's last name?" Many including myself, had no idea, but I was offered six different ones to choose from, but the one that surfaced the most frequently was "Morris." This indeed was his last name as confirmed by Chief Maloney of the First Nation Reserve at Shubenacadie, N.S. Other questions that arose were "Where was Louie born and when?" and "Where and when did he die?" Well, apparently he came from somewhere in the Annapolis Valley, but even the Nova Scotia natives are not sure just where or when. It has been established, however, that he died and was buried on the Shubenacadie Reserve in 1962.

Wherever he came from, and whoever has the missing pieces to this man who became a legend in his own day, I am sure that Laughing Louie is having the last laugh on us mortals left behind attempting to put his life back together.

- *Warren Searle*

Louie's baskets were romantic symbols

Years before the Second World War, a group of natives squatted on land adjacent to the CN Railway at Fairvale Station not far from Louie's cabin. They lived in an assortment of shacks and managed to live off proceeds from baskets they made and sold in Saint John. Louie made baskets too, but usually traded them for favors, like food.

Scores of Kings County women fed Louie when he arrived on their doorsteps, and in exchange he would give them a basket or a promise of one. Apart from the fine food that Louie was offered at Ada Copp's in Quispamsis, he was also attracted to that spot by a large whetstone behind the house. Louie knew where all the grindstones in Kings County were located, because he was forever fashioning draw knives or crooked knives, as they were referred to by some.

These knives were used to shave strips of ash for making baskets, and were made from old worn out files, which he got from garages and machine shops in the county. If a forge was handy, he would use it to take the temper out of the steel before grinding it down to the shape he wanted. Mostly, he built a red-hot fire in which he would place the files until they turned cherry red. After grinding, he would reheat them and put the crook in them and dump them in a pot of potato water. Louie claimed that nothing put the right temper in the blades like potato water. He would then proceed to carve a handle for them out of ash, and presto, a "Laughing Louie special draw knife" was produced.

Louie knew where all the stands of ash in the county were located: black ash for baskets, and white ash for axe handles. There was one stand of black ash that Louie wouldn't go near, however. It was located somewhere around Ward's Creek, and he claimed that many natives were killed there in a battle with the white man, and out of respect for his fallen ancestors, or perhaps out of fear, he left these tree stands where they were.

Louie had the appetite of a horse, he also had the strength of one. He would tie poles of ash together with vines, hoist them onto his shoulder and walk back through the woods to his camp with them. No ordinary man could have lifted them off the ground let alone carry them through the woods. In Upham a man told me that Louie once made a baby basket for his mother and when Louie returned to see the newborn sleeping in his creation, he bent over the basket and exclaimed, "Isn't he cute? He looks just like a little white rabbit!"

I was surprised to learn how many people still have baskets made by Laughing Louie stashed away in closets or attics. They simply don't want to part with these romantic symbols of the past.

- Presented by Kings County Record

"Laughing Louie"
CIRCA 1930

Chair believed to have been made by Laughing Louie from ashwood for the Roxborough family in Sussex, N.B., in exchange for a hot meal. Chair now owned by Muriel Delong of Hampton, N.B.

Nelly Francis:

Nelly Francis was a First Nations woman who made a living in the 1940's selling her woven baskets. Every Friday morning she would walk from the Indian Camp located in the current Oakville Acres Subdivision, down to the Fairvale station to catch the train going to Saint John. While in Saint John she would sell her baskets at the head of the Saint John City Market. Additional items sold at the market by other First Nations people included Mayflowers and other handcrafted goods. It has been said that Nelly Francis was Laughing Louie's significant other. Whether this is true or not is unknown. A local resident recollected a "story" about the heroism of Nelly Francis. According to this story Nelly Francis was walking along the train tracks one day, and discovered a broken rail. She heard the train coming so she took off her petticoat and flagged the train, the old Jitney, down. According to the tale, she was given a free life long pass to travel on the CNR for her actions. The pass was later revoked due to misuse on Nelly's behalf.

This basket was made by Nellie Francis for Frances (Burger) Saunders

Other First Nations People in Quispamsis:
    Laughing Louie and Nelly Francis were not the only prominent First Nations people in the community. There were many others. One such family lived behind the Model Farm School during the late 1940's and 1950's. Also, as stated, there was a small Indian Camp located in the present day Oakville Acres Subdivision where several First Nations people resided.
    Other items bought from First Nations people included baskets, lawn furniture, and clothes hampers. The baskets sold by the First Nations people were often hand woven and dyed various colours. The dye that was used on these baskets was obtained from the roots of shrubs and plants.

The above picture is of the First Nations crafted table that was given to Bertha Horgan's father.

In the above picture, Mr. Walter Fearing Leonard and possibly his daughter are enjoying some summer sun on wooden lawn furniture made by a local First Nations person.

The above picture is of a doll's basket that was donated by Henry A. McLeod and his wife, Grace (Harrison) McLeod of Gondola Point. Underneath the front wooden rocker, written in pencil, is the date March 22, 1889. It is on display at the Kings County Museum.

Mr. Charles Crowley purchased a basket as a crib from a First Nations person when his grandson Douglas Crowley was born in April 1942. The basket served as a crib for Mrs. Catherine Crowley's son, (Doug), and has been passed down to several other infants in the family.

Distinguished Residents

William Johnstone Ritchie:

William Johnstone Ritchie was born on October 28, 1813 in Annapolis, Nova Scotia. He came from a family with a long history of involvement in the judicial system. William's mother was Elizabeth W. Johnstone. His father, The Honourable Thomas Ritchie, was called to the bar in 1798 and became the Judge of the Supreme Court of Nova Scotia. Five sons, eleven grandsons, five great-grandsons, and three great-great grandsons followed in Thomas Ritchie's footsteps and entered into the legal profession. At least six of these family members went to the bench in Canada, including three of Thomas Ritchie's sons. William achieved the highest position of all the Ritchie lawyers.

As a young man William Ritchie was educated at the Pictou Academy, and studied law at the office of his brother, John W. Ritchie, Esq., who afterwards became Justice in Equity of Nova Scotia (The abbreviation Esq., which is short for Esquire, is a title of respect for a member of the English gentry ranking just below a knight. The title is placed after the person's name). William eventually left Nova Scotia and moved to Saint John, New Brunswick to practice law. William Johnstone Ritchie was called to the bar in New Brunswick in 1838 and was later made a Knight Bachelor (The Knight Bachelor is a part of the British honour system. A Knight Bachelor is a title granted to a gentleman who has been made a knight by the British Monarch, but is not a member of the organized Order of Chivalry). On August 17, 1855, William Ritchie was given the appointment of Justice of the Supreme Court of N.B. Ritchie was the Chief Justice of N.B. from December 6, 1865 until October 8, 1875 when he was named one of the Puisne Judges of the Supreme Court of Canada (A Puisne Judge is a French name for a judge of a court who is not the Chief Justice or Associate Chief Justice of that court). Sir William. J. Ritchie was appointed as the Chief Justice of Canada on January 11, 1879. He held this office until he died in Ottawa on September 25, 1892 at age 79. He was survived by his second wife and 14 children. He was an advocate of responsible government and supported economic progress and development.

William Ritchie was first married in 1843 to Martha Strang, the daughter of a Mr. John Strang of St Andrews. They had a son, William Pollok, on August 12, 1844, followed by a daughter, Martha

Margaret, who was born on December 4, 1846. Sir Ritchie's beloved wife died one year later in 1847. A widower at the young age of thirty-three he and his two young children moved in with relatives who lived on Prince William Street in Saint John, New Brunswick. Prior to his second marriage, he purchased a large tract of land adjacent to a little lake, approximately 18 km (11 miles) from Saint John in present day Quispamsis for 1,000 pounds. In 1858 Sir Ritchie married his second wife, Grace Vernon Nicholson, the daughter of Thomas L. Nicholson, of Saint John and stepdaughter of Vice-Admiral William Fitz William Owen.

The entrance to his estate, which he called Kawatcoose, was located on the Quispamsis Road 69 meters (75 yards) away from the Hampton Road. At the entrance to the estate there was a gate made of two stone pillars with a chain between them, and a gatehouse. Down a lane about half a kilometre surrounded by woods was the Ritchie residence. William Ritchie owned a stately two-storey home that over looked the Quispamsis Lake, which would later be known as Ritchie Lake. There was a coach house located on the property and the estate had a large veranda. The lawns and gardens were landscaped down to the water where Ritchie had a number of boats. Rose bushes and lilac trees decorated the property and grapevines covered the buildings. Around the lake there was a bridle path.

When the European and North American Railway was completed in the nineteenth century, it ran within 91 meters (100 yards) of the Ritchie estate. The railway station was also in very close proximity to the lake. Soon after the completion of the railway the Ritchie family decided to move to Ottawa. Sir Ritchie died September 25, 1892. When he died, Sir Ritchie was the father of eight sons and six daughters. Lady Ritchie died May 7, 1911.

William Ritchie's former estate of Kawatcoose was later named in honour of him and is now called Ritchie Lake. It is believed that the estate was converted into a summer hotel after the Ritchie family moved to Ottawa. The building eventually burned, leaving only the stone foundation, which was still visible up until the 1940's.

For more information on Sir William Ritchie refer to Gordon Bale's book entitled "Chief Justice William Johnstone Ritchie: Responsible Government and Judicial Review." Ottawa: Carleton University Press, 1991.

The above picture is of William Ritchie (National Archives of Canada, Neg. No. PA27038)

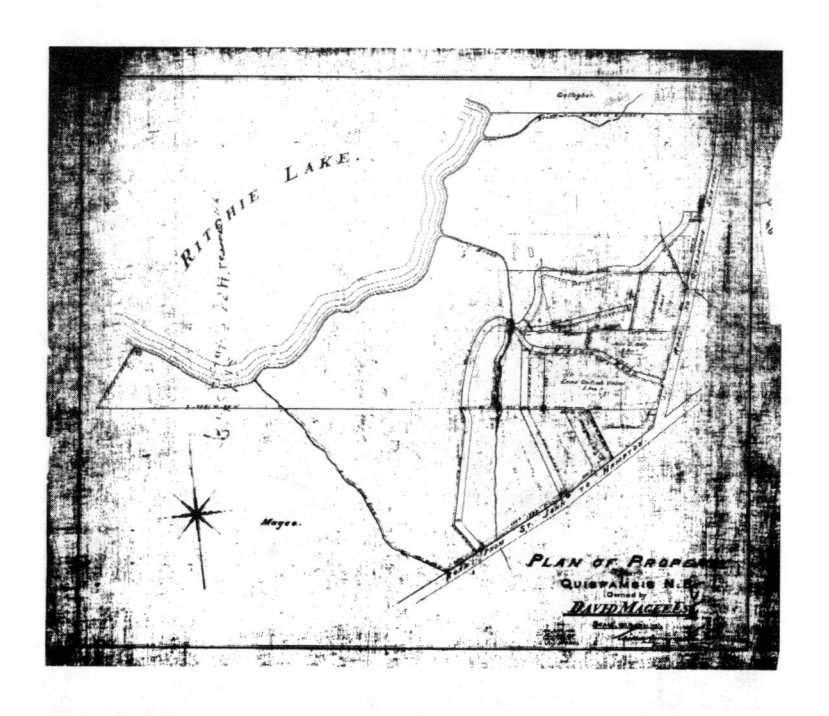

Ned Sowery:

Ned Sowery was the Provincial Police Constable who lived on the Hampton Road, next door to the present day KV Food Bank (Dates are unknown). Ned Sowery operated in this area, and around the rest of New Brunswick sometime before Harry Miller began his duties in the 1950's. Mr. Sowery was responsible for upholding the law and duties such as conducting driver's tests. He was also an active member of the community with one of his major accomplishments being the construction of Memorial Field. (For more information on this refer to the section entitled Recreation.) In 1984, as per the following article that appeared in The Kings County Record on March 7, 1984, Ned Sowery was awarded the town's Citizen of the Year Award by the Mayor of the day, Emil T. Olsen.

CITIZEN OF THE YEAR: Mayor Emil Olsen of Quispamsis presented Ned Sowry with that town's Citizen of the Year Award during special bicentennial activities in February. Mr. Sowry, 84, shown in the centre above with Mrs. Sowry. (Photo by Alice O'Neill).

Ned Sowery honored

By ALICE O'NEILL

"Where is he? I hope he hasn't gone home. Maybe we should have told him earlier."

"He's still here. He's over in the stands watching all the kids skating."

These were last minute worries of some Quispamsis councillors as they prepared to tell Edward "Ned" Sowery he was receiving the Citizen-of-the-Year Award at a special ceremony during the bicenttennial costume skating party held Feb. 25 at the Quispamsis Arena.

They didn't have to worry because where there are kids enjoying recreation... Ned Sowery isn't far away.

Sowery, 84, was surprised and said he thought there were a lot of other people in the town who deserved the award more than him," I am very happy with being chosen though," he said.

In 1946, Sowery, who helped with the annual Rothesay Fair, received $1,100 as Quispamsis' share of the fair proceeds. Each village received a share.

He brought the land where the Quispamsis arena and ballfield now stand." I had to fight with some of the other people in the town. They wanted to erect a stone cross to the war dead. But I thought a ballfield for the kids would be much more helpful for the community," Sowery said. His whole family picked rocks and helped him level and groom the field.

Sowery, who lives next to the field, used to flood the rink from his own house well." When he flooded the rink our house would freeze because the door was open for hours as the water was pumped from our well through a 300 foot hose," recalls Mrs. Sowery.

Ned Sowery continued to run the rink and ballfield for 13 years. Although the site changed in buildings and fields over the years the name Quispamsis Memorial Field has remained in honor of those from Quispamsis who served during the war.

Sowery is a member of Kennebecasis Legion No. 58. He served in First World War.

Quispamsis councillors didn't have to worry about finding Ned Sowery .. he is always out enjoying hockey games, summer games and just being around the young people of the town.

Harry Miller:

Harry Miller and his car – a familiar sight in Rothesay

Photo taken October 5, 1974

    Harry Miller (May 19, 1919 to March 5, 1975) was the first police officer to operate in the Town of Rothesay and began his service in 1951. He operated the police station around the clock out of his home in Rothesay with the assistance of his wife, Yonnie Miller, and their three daughters. Even though he was a Rothesay resident, he was well known by everyone in Quispamsis.

    When Harry Miller first became a police officer he did not own a police car. But it was said that he caught speeders regardless. Chief

Miller would reportedly run after cars exceeding the speed limit on foot or hide behind telephone polls and jump out in front of the speeders. Imagine a Rothesay Regional Police Officer using this tactic today! Some of his other methods of prohibiting unlawful behaviour also consisted of some seemingly unorthodox police practices; however, Chief Miller was certainly unique in the way he enforced the Motor Vehicle Legislation.

A resident of Quispamsis remembers Harry Miller pulling him over and issuing him a ticket for speeding. The interesting point was that this speeding resident was a young lad who was riding his bicycle. Regardless, bicycle or automobile, Chief Miller believed it was important to enforce the 30 miles per hour speed limit.

As part of his duties as Police Chief, Harry Miller also conducted driver's tests. One Gondola Point resident can recall when taking her driver's test, Chief Miller telling her to "keep it between the ditches".

Harry Miller eventually received help in his duties of policing the area. Melvin Saunders is well known as being the individual who helped Mr. Miller prior to arrival of the first police recruits with college training. Harry Miller Middle School in Rothesay is named in honour of Chief Miller.

The following is an excerpt from an article on Harry Miller that appeared in the Evening Times Globe on Monday April 9, 2001 and was written by Mia Urquhart.

The Little Police Force That Could

When Harry Miller was hired 50 years ago by the Rothesay Police Force, he was the Rothesay Police Force.

For 18 years, he was its chief and only member. The police station was his house and his wife, Yonnie, answered the calls and acted as the dispatcher.

It was April 1951 and the Village of Rothesay couldn't afford much. There was no police car and the only equipment was an old hat, badge, and whistle donated by the Saint John Police Department.

Chief Miller also got a stopwatch.

Ironically, the boy who set provincial and Maritime speed records for long-distance running grew up to become the nemesis of speeders in Rothesay. He measured off sections of the main road through Rothesay and used the stopwatch to time drivers as they passed. If they were speeding, he'd wave them over to the side of the road.

Today's law enforcer in the Kennebecasis Valley, the Rothesay Regional Police Force, honours Chief Miller on its Web site.

"By necessity, his methods of enforcing the Motor Vehicle Act were unorthodox but effective. His manner of catching speeders was an example of his ingenuity. Chief Miller would stick out his thumb to hitch a ride and after being picked up he would watch the speedometer. If the driver exceeded the speed limit, Chief Miller would issue a speeding ticket to the unsuspecting motorist."

Eventually the Village of Rothesay was able to afford a police car for the chief.

Geoffrey Sayre, Rothesay's Mayor at the time and the man who hired Harry Miller, remembers that first car. It was a second-hand Dodge that cost the village $325.

Mr. Sayre, who was also Rothesay's fire chief, said he immediately recognized potential in the young man he hired.

"He was young and agile and fast, and it just seemed like a good bet."

In those days, explained Mr. Sayre, "if you didn't live in Rothesay, you weren't allowed there past midnight." And if Chief Miller caught you in his town, he'd stop you to see what your business there was. Then he'd make sure you left town.

"I don't know when he slept," said Mr. Sayre, "because he was awake all night."

Mrs. Miller remembers those early days, when the police force was run out of her house. She said her husband was on duty 24 hours a day, seven days a week. There was no such thing as time off to spend with his family.

"Anyone who called and needed him, he would go out," said Mrs. Miller. "We understood. Suppertime was a little difficult, I suppose. We had to keep his dinner warm quite often. But we understood. It wasn't easy being a policeman, and he was the only one, at first."

In 1969, two policemen were added and the force's coverage extended to nearby communities. By 1974 when Chief Miller was given a recliner chair for his 23 years of service, there were six officers, three cars, and the police headquarters was moved to Town Hall.

Henry MacEachern:

Henry MacEachern was a well-liked citizen who, for many years, jokingly proclaimed himself the 'Mayor of Quispamsis'. Mr. MacEachern died December 14, 1978. While he was alive he devoted his time and energy to improving Quispamsis. The following article appeared in The Telegraph-Journal on Saturday, February 19, 1983.

'Mayor Henry' Would Have Been Proud

Mayor Henry would be proud. And why not? Henry MacEachern, the man known to many as the unofficial mayor of Quispamsis, could have looked about his beloved community and watched a new arena built, seen a large senior citizens complex take shape, walked through the new civic building, and have been able to boast that his once-little village is now a town.

"It's too bad he passed away," reflects Edgar MacEachern, on his father who died December 14, 1978 at the age of 86. "He would have been really pleased to see all this happen. If he were around now to have seen the advances...well, it would have been something else."

Henry MacEachern gave his time and ample energies toward the betterment of Quispamsis and its residents.

He was a prime mover in the spirited Quispamsis Community Club; he helped in the Telegraph-Times Christmas Charity Empty Stocking Fund; he spearheaded the purchase of a Quispamsis field to be used to honour Second World War veterans; he was the founder of the traveling Newspaper Boys Harmonica Band which lists among its alumni well-known entertainers Ned Landry and Normie Hamilton; and he was a participant and president of both a hockey and a softball league.

Then there were his eagerly awaited Christmas visits when, dressed as Santa Claus, he would go home-to-home in Quispamsis giving candy to youngsters and spreading the community good will.

Recalls long-time Quispamsis resident Eleanor Jones: "He was one of the leaders in the village there was no question about it. There was a group of men that would go to work on a train and they would meet there in the morning and talk and settle their problems..."

But Henry MacEachern is best remembered for his endless public relations efforts on behalf of the many causes he championed-not the least of which was the enhancement of Quispamsis. Although Henry did not possess the honorary mayoralty, Edgar claims it was friends and acquaintances who gave Henry the title.

The elder MacEachern worked for 57 years in the Telegraph-Journal and Evening Times-Globe composing room. This meant he was only a flight of stairs away from the newsroom where reporters waited to tell the Province and the world about the latest happenings in Quispamsis.

"There were so many stories about Quispamsis in the paper then," laughs Edgar. "And Dad's name always seemed to be in the stories. It got to be a bit embarrassing after a while..."

Adds Edgar: "He always seemed to know what was going on. No matter what it was, he always seemed to be heading up something in the community... I think that is why they called him the mayor of Quispamsis."

Telegraph-Journal

Eleanor Jones:

Eleanor Jones was a local unofficial historian and resident of Quispamsis for over forty years. She moved to Quispamsis in 1940 from her home in Saint John. While living in Quispamsis, Mrs. Jones worked part-time at Rothesay Senior High School's library, while her husband was a retired commercial traveler. Mrs. Jones retired as librarian from Rothesay Senior High School, now Harry Miller Junior

Eleanor Jones

High, in 1975. It was during her employment at Rothesay Senior High School that sparked her interest in the community's history. As a librarian, students at the school would question her about the local history of the area. That repeated request from the high school students led Eleanor Jones to research and write down the history of the Town of Quispamsis. Mrs. Jones performed hours of research along with conducting numerous interviews with the older residents of the area. When she was finished she delivered a paper, containing the information she obtained to the Kings County Historical Society.

In the 1970's, Mrs. Jones took an active interest in the present day affairs of the community. Her two main interests were UNICEF and her work with the Quispamsis United Church group. She was the provincial youth convener for UNICEF. Percy and Eleanor Jones helped create the first Quiz-pamsis, a quiz based on the research she had done on Quispamsis. Mrs. Jones's research has contributed to our current understanding of the Town's past, and the creation of this document.

M. Caroline (Carrie) Prince, (1895 - 1980):
    Miss Prince was an organist at Holy Trinity Church in Hammond River and the first lady vestrywoman in the Province of New Brunswick. One of her brothers, Gilbert Prince, was the Provincial Minister of Forestry. Miss Prince sold property to Mr. David Allan Buckland to allow him to construct Buckland Meadows Campground. Even though she was an older woman at the time, Miss Prince helped construct the road that was built leading into Buckland Meadows Campground.
    Miss Prince was the type of woman who was known to help out in any way she could during a crisis. In 1972, when Buckland Meadows Campground burnt to the ground, Mrs. Prince provided fresh water to all the campers who stayed at the campsite for the week it was open following the fire.

HONORED — Miss Mary Carolyn Prince, 82, was honored by Holy Trinity Church and community for her contribution to Hammond River community life over many years. Shown above presenting her with a bouquet of flowers, are, from left: Tricia Wilson, daughter of Mr. and Mrs. James Wilson, and Tammy Deasington, daughter of Mr. and Mrs. Brian Deasington. [Photo by Bill Hart].

Miss M. Caroline Prince Honored

Members of Holy Trinity Church, Hammond River, and the community, were at Nauwigewauk Community Centre Sunday Dec. 4, to honor a churchwoman and organist for many years and Sunday was Miss Mary Carolyn Mary Prince night and a perfect evening to pay tribute to a perfectly lovely and grand lady.

Dressed in a red outfit Miss Prince, 83, was accompanied by her niece and nephew Mr. and Mrs. Allan Fulchur.

Born in Hammond River, she is the daughter of the late Samuel and Mary Prince. The only living member of her family Miss Prince had three brothers Gilbert, George and Dr. Samuel Prince.

One of the oldest members of the Hammond River community Miss Prince is still very active in the church and is the oldest active member of Holy Trinity Church. She is als an active member of the A.C.W. and is a past president of that organization.

She has had 67 years of service to the church and has played the organ since the age of 16 years old. The first was a pipe organ and she had to have someone work the pump while she played. She has been playing the organ off and on for some 60 years at Holy Trinity Church, St. Augustine, Quispamsis, and St. Luke's Church Gondola Point.

She is also a life member of The Alexandra Society of King's College, Halifax, a Dominion Life member of the WA and honorary life president of the Kingston deanery of the ACW.

Rev. Stuart Allan introduced Miss Prince. Rev. Gilbert Edsforth said he was there to pay tribute to a great lady whom he has known and respected for many years; a woman who was alway there when needed and a superb organist who still plays when needed.

A presentation of a cheque was made to Miss Prince by wardens John Hart and William McKay. There also was a presentation by the Hammond River Church Choir and a gift of flowers on behalf of her friends by five-year-old Tricia Wilson, daughter of Mr. and Mrs. James Wilson and five-year-old Tammy Deasington, daughter of Mr. and Mrs. Brian Deasington.

Greetings and best wishes on her retirement were received from many friends and a letter was sent to Miss Prince from Right Rev. Harold L. Nutter, bishop of Fredericton and Canon and Mrs. W. E. Hart of Bloomfield Station.

Thanking everyone Miss Prince said "I'm sure you all agree with me that this is a wonderful neighborhood to be brought up in and with Father Allan to look after my spiritual needs, Dr. Snow of Hampton to look after my medical needs, I thank you one and all."

Miss M. Caroline Prince

The community of Hammond River and area will honor Miss M. Caroline Prince on Sunday at 8 p.m. at Nauwigewauk Community Hall. Everyone in the area is welcome to come and help make it a day to remember. Miss Prince is 83 and has made an outstanding contribution to the life of the community for many years.

Visitors

King and Queen of Great Britain:

The King and Queen of Great Britain, King George VI and Queen Elizabeth stopped at the Rothesay Train Station, and traveled through Quispamsis while on their trip across Canada. School children of all ages were allowed out of school to wave flags as the procession passed by. Mrs. Irene Flower can recall placing coins on the railway track, along with some of her other classmates, to have the train press them as a souvenir of the special occasion. The coins were kept for a long time as a memento of the day the King and Queen of Great Britain traveled through their small community. This particular royal visit occurred in June of 1939.

Prime Minister Paul Martin Comes to Town:

On April 14, 2004, Prime Minister Paul Martin, along with Fundy Royal M.P., John Herron, attended a roundtable meeting with mayors and municipal leaders in Mr. Herron's riding at the Quispamsis Town Hall. Among the items discussed was the Fundy Trail, which has opened up previously unreachable coastal areas while preserving the ecological balance of the area. Upon completion, it is hoped the Trail will increase tourism to the Province and greatly contribute to the Bay of Fundy Experience. The other item for discussion was funding for rural municipalities.

Prime Minister, Paul Martin, with Quispamsis Mayor, Ron Maloney, prior to the round-table discussion.

Prime Minister Paul Martin leading a roundtable discussion in the Council Chambers at the Quispamsis Town Hall. From left to right: Mayor Oscar Boyd, Mayor Ron Maloney, Prime Minister Martin, M.P. John Herron, Mayor Bill Bishop

Senator Joseph Day & Premier Bernard Lord Visit Quispamsis:

March 12, 2004, Senator Joseph Day; the Honourable Bernard Lord, Premier of New Brunswick; Quispamsis Mayor, Ron Maloney and Hampton Mayor, James Hovey attended a Canada-New Brunswick Infrastructure Program Investments announcement at the Quispamsis Town Hall. The two Towns combined received more than $7.3 million to upgrade their wastewater systems.

The $6.2 million Quispamsis project involved decommissioning of Matthews Cove Wastewater Treatment Facility, construction of two sewage lift stations, 1600 metres of forcemain and 2680 metres of gravity sewer lines, and the expansion of the Longwood Wastewater Treatment Facility.

Left to Right: Quispamsis Mayor, Ron Maloney, MLA & Minister of the Environment, Brenda Fowlie, Premier Bernard Lord, Senator Joseph Day and Hampton Mayor, James Hovey.

Left to Right: Councillor Gordon Friars, Councillor Mary Schryer, MLA Brenda Fowlie, Mayor Ron Maloney, Premier Bernard Lord, MP John Herron, Deputy Mayor Murray Driscoll, Senator Joseph Day, Councillor Daryl Bishop and Councillor Gerry Garnett
March 12, 2004.

Cottages

In the early days, the communities of Quispamsis and Gondola Point were primarily composed of forested land. As time went on, the areas gradually developed into farmlands. Further developments over time, lead to the areas becoming known as 'cottage country'. Quispamsis and Gondola Point became very popular locations for summerhouses or cottages. People from Saint John would travel by horse and buggy, and later by train and automobile, to the communities of Quispamsis and Gondola Point to enjoy the relaxed atmosphere and the country air for the summer months.

Almost everyone had a garden of some size in the early to mid 1900's. It was a challenge not to have a garden in those days, with so few stores around. One difficulty faced by the individuals who were planting these gardens, which is still faced by many residents of Quispamsis today, was the matter of keeping deer out of vegetable and flower gardens. However, in the past, there was also the additional difficulty of chasing moose away when the large animals tried to nibble on cottager's produce. Many of the individuals summering in cottages also kept chickens as a source of fresh eggs and poultry throughout the summer.

Anyone who summered or lived in the Quispamsis area seventy or eighty years ago will testify to the abundance of wild berries that grew in the fields, along the banks of brooks, in the woods, and in backyards. Children would often be sent to pick berries from the marvelous crops of wild strawberries, raspberries, blueberries, and blackberries that could be found in the area.

Two of the more prominent families that owned summer cottages in this area were the Leonards and the Johnstons. Both of these families summered in Quispamsis for a number of years and became highly involved in the activities that took place in the community.

The Leonards:

The Leonard family summerhouse

Walter Leonard at age 90

The Leonard family was a prominent family who summered in the Quispamsis area in the early to mid 1900's. Their summer home, which they referred to as Quispam, was located at the end of the Pettingill Road, near where St. Augustine's Church is presently found. Their grand summerhouse was situated between the church and the train station. Walter Fearing Leonard (1854 - 1946), who founded Leonard's Brothers Fisheries in Port Hawkesbury, initially owned the summerhouse. The summerhouse burned down in the late 1940's.

The Leonard summerhouse and barn from a distance.

The Johnstons:
Mr. Cecil Johnston helped construct Hovey Road, which is now connected to the Old Coach Road, so that his father and grandfather could get their vehicle down to their cottage. The Hovey Road was built using anything they could find to use as bedding. Mr. Johnston explained that if one was "to take up the road, you would find old bed springs, and God knows what else in there as bedding for the road." The Johnston cottage was located at the intersection of the Hovey Road and the Station Road, (present day Old Coach Road). The Johnstons purchased the property in the late 1920's and sold it in 1968. Mr.

Johnston remembers as a child summering at the cottage, a very special place in the Johnston family's life, and often fondly referred to the cottage as "The Farm."

The following are pictures of "The Farm."

"The Farm" 1944

Johnston Farm 1923

Churches & Cemeteries

There are numerous churches and some cemeteries in the Quispamsis area. The map and legend below identify 16 churches in the Quispamsis area of various denominations. However, not all of these churches were present one hundred years ago, nor are all the churches that were built in the past still standing today. The following map depicts the beginnings of a brief survey of the churches from the Quispamsis area over time.

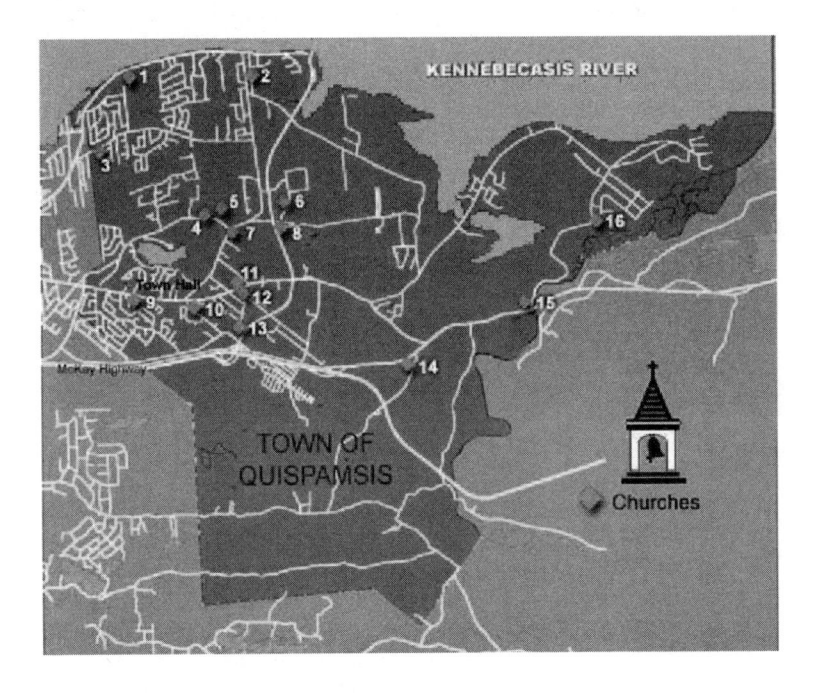

Church Denomination	Number on Map
Apostolic Pentecostal	1
Christian Fellowship	8
First Bible Baptist	9
Holy Trinity Anglican	15
Jehovah's Witness	14
Kennebecasis Baptist	11

Kings Valley Wesleyan 10
Kingsway Assembly..6
Quispamsis United..12
Rothesay Baptist 3
Saint Andrew's Kirk United 16
St. Augustine's Anglican 7
St. Lukes Anglican 2
St. Marks Catholic 4
Trinity Baptist Reform...5
Vineyard Christian Fellowship..13

Quispamsis Roman Catholic Church:
      According to a 1905 newspaper report from the Kings County Historical and Archival Society, a Roman Catholic Church and a "shantytown" were constructed in Quispamsis in 1854 to serve the Irish who were working on the railway.

Holy Trinity Anglican Church:

Holy Trinity was constructed in 1862. The location chosen for the church was on the main road, south of the Hammond River Bridge across from the Stock Farm Road intersection with the Hampton Road. The church was built by Allan Otty, Captain John Ford, John Palmer, and other devoted residents of the community. The first service was held on January 1, 1863. When the Church first opened, the Hampton Rector supervised the services held at the church. However, when the Parish of Rothesay was created, the services at the church came under the direction of the Rothesay Rector.

On May 16, 1915 a formal letter from the Lord Bishop was read out loud in Holy Trinity Church, Hammond River. The notice explained His Lordship's intention of creating a new parish forthwith. In 1915, Holy Trinity was taken from the Parish of Rothesay, and with two other churches in the area, became the Parish of Hammond River. The following excerpt was extracted from A History of The Parish of Hammond River 1915-1955 written by Rev. J.H.A. Holmes:

> "In June 1914, arrangements were made by the Lord Bishop of Fredericton, (Rev. John A. Richardson), by which districts of Hammond River, French Village, and Smithtown should become a separate Missionary District for ecclesiastical purposes. The parish of Rothesay should relinquish that part of the parish known as Hammond River with the Church of Holy Trinity, while the Parish of Hampton should be relieved of French Village, with the Church of St. Andrew, and Smithtown, with the Church of the Holy Trinity, and also the village of Nauwigewauk, and Darling's Island..."

The Parish Rectory was housed in the lower flat of Red House, which was owned by the Otty's. This house was located on the corner of the Hampton Road and the Model Farm Road. The exact time that the lower flat of Red House served as the rectory is unknown, but it is known that it was before 1920.

On May 18, 1920 the original Holy Trinity burnt down. The church caught fire due to a nearby forest fire that was started from sparks created from a passing train. The railway was responsible for the fire as Mr. John Darling of Hammond River recalls. It is postulated that the railway may have given the Parish money for the construction of a new church, as no one can recall any fundraising being done for the construction of a new Church. Some parts of the original Holy Trinity Church were salvaged. The pews from inside the church were saved and stored in the Crowley barn at their home on the Stock Farm. Among other salvaged items were the Prayer Desk, Altar, and Lectern. The concrete steps of the church are still there today.

First Anglican Church in Hammond River Burned in 1920.

The above picture of Holy Trinity Anglican Church was during the horse and buggy days. Notice behind the church the locations where the horses were hitched.

Before the original Holy Trinity burnt, Sunday School was held at the Preacher's house. It was a Rothesay Priest who would come to the Church and teach Sunday School. The Rothesay Priest's time was precious though because he had to cover such a large Parish. The former Parish of Rothesay consisted of five Churches: St. Luke's in Gondola Point, Holy Trinity in Hammond River, St. James the Less in

Renforth, the little Mission Church in Quispamsis, and a Church in Nauwigewauk.

The graveyard for the old Trinity Church is still located on the Stock Farm Road. In the archives at the Kings County Museum are records of the names of the people buried in the Holy Trinity Anglican Cemetery in Hammond River.

HOLY TRINITY ANGLICAN

Mr. Beverly Paddock was commissioned to build the new church, and he did so based on plans used in the construction of St. Barnabas Church located on the Sandy Point Road. Mr. Paddock also built the pulpit for the Church.

On January 31, 1923 the Right Reverend John A. Richardson, the 3rd Bishop of Fredericton, consecrated the new church a little less than three years after the first one burned down. This church, located at the intersection of the Hammond River Road and Route 100, directly before the Hammond River bridge, still operates today.

The first couple to be married at the new church, the Anglican Church of Holy Trinity, was Mr. Clarence Henderson and Miss Jean Dickson. Their daughter was also the first child to be christened in the new church.

Saint Andrew's Kirk (United Church):

Saint Andrew's Kirk held its first service in 1842. The Church was built after the Scottish people in the area decided, in a meeting held October 6, 1841 in the Methodist meeting hall, to build a Presbyterian Church. The first minister of the new Church was the Reverend Andrew Donald, whose Parish consisted of Churches found in Norton, Salt Springs, and the Hammond River area. The church was built as a Presbyterian church, but is now a United Church. The church cemetery is located on the church property, near the west bank of the Hammond River, along the Hammond River Road, north of the Mackay Highway.

John MacDonald and Bertha Porter were the first couple to be married in the Saint Andrew's Kirk United. The MacDonald wedding party is pictured above. The two flower girls are (left to right) Louis (Humphrey) Gamble and Ruth Crowley (year currently unknown).

The following are Sunday School pictures that were taken at Saint Andrew's Kirk (appear to be in the 1960's).

Among those pictured in the above photo are Bill Woods, {back row}, Richard Floyd, {third row, 2nd from left}, Donnie McQuinn, {third row, 3rd from left}, George Floyd, second row, 1st from left}, Wayne McQuinn, {front row, 4th from left}, and Beth Floyd (Thompson), {front row, 3rd from left}

St. Luke's Anglican Church:

    St. Luke's Anglican Church is located in Gondola Point, on the Quispamsis Road, or what has commonly been referred to as Church Hill. The church cemetery is located in the churchyard, across the road from the Baptist cemetery. The church was built in 1832 through the efforts of Bishop Inglis, but the design of the Church is attributed to Edwin Fairweather.

St. Augustine's Anglican Church:

St. Augustine's Anglican Church has been remodeled over the years; it is located at the bottom of the Pettingill Road where it intersects with the Quispamsis Road.

The picture above was taken August 11, 1958. Mrs. Grace Saunders (Hawkins) can be seen in the front on the right.

St Augustines Anglican

Little Baptist Church:
Residents of Gondola Point commonly refer to this Church as the Little Baptist Church. It is unclear at this time if that was the actual name of the Church. This Church was located on the Gondola Point Road. The cemetery located on this property contains stones dating back to the year 1846. Just prior to the cemetery was a meetinghouse, a building that was used for meeting and religious services. The meetinghouse was used prior to the establishment of the Baptist Church. Currently standing in this location is the Apostolic Pentecostal Church.

Quispamsis United Church:

In the early 1920's a small group of people who had previously been meeting together in halls, living rooms, and on verandahs were inspired by Agnes and Harry Allingham to build a small hall. Until recent years the hall was located on the Hampton Road near the corner of the Quispamsis Road. The hall was used regularly for the teaching of Sunday School until the outbreak of the Second World War. At this time the hall fell into disuse. However in the late 1940's as the community of Quispamsis began to grow, the hall was reopened and used regularly.

In 1958 this interdenominational group bought a piece of Miss Florence Phillips' property located adjacent to the Hampton Road. A basement was then constructed and roofed over. For a number of years, until 1965, this basement served as a place of worship under the direction of the minister from St. David's United Church in Rothesay. In 1965, the present sanctuary was built through the dedication of fifteen families. On Oct 17, 1965 the Saint John Presbytery dedicated the new church as Quispamsis United Church.

On July 1, 1979 the Quispamsis congregation separated from the Rothesay congregation of St. David's and formed a new congregation. Reverend James MacDonald was the first minister of this new congregation.

On April 16, 1983, the Saint John Presbytery dedicated the construction of a new Christian Education extension to the church to meet the demands of the growing congregation. At this time only the lower portion of the extension was completed. The upper portion was completed September 23, 1984.

St. Mark's Roman Catholic Church:

The three Crosses in the courtyard are reminders of the death of Christ. They also symbolize the three original communities encompassed by the Parish.

Because of the rapid growth of the Rothesay Parish, particularly to the northeast, Bishop A. J. Gilbert erected the Parish of St. Mark's on March 31, 1978. It embraces the territory from the railway underpass in Rothesay, (formerly Fairvale), to Hammond River. St. Mark's serves Quispamsis, and the former Gondola Point and much of the former Fairvale.

Prior to construction of the church building in 1979, Mass was celebrated at the Fairvale Community Center and the Quispamsis Elementary School. Christmas, 1979, was the occasion for the first Mass in the new edifice.

In recent years the territory served by St. Mark's has been the fastest growing area in the Province. At its inception, the Parish comprised 420 families. Presently, there are over 5,000 individuals from close to 1,700 households.

Reverend Kevin Barry was the first Pastor, with Sister Doreen McGuire, S.C.I.C. as Pastoral Assistant. Reverend Brian Hansen was appointed in August 1989. Two years later Sister Constance Foley, S.C.I.C. was assigned as Pastoral Assistant. In August of 1999, Sister Anne Somers was assigned Pastoral Associate. Reverend Donald Breen was appointed Pastor July 1, 2000.

Pictures of other churches in the area taken by Eleanor Jones:

First Bible Baptist, Hampton Road

Trinity Baptist Reform, Pettingill Road

Businesses, Hotels, and Stores

Printing Press:

Christopher Sower III was born on January 27, 1754 at Germantown, in Philadelphia, Pennsylvania. His parents were Christopher Sower II, and Catharine Sharpnach. His father was born on September 26, 1721 at Iaasphe, in Witgenstein, Germany. He came to the United States with his father, Christopher Sower I, in 1724, (Sower can also be spelled as Saueror or Saur). Christopher Sower I was a Doctor and a Printer. Christopher II was also a Printer, like his father.

Christopher Sower III, keeping with the family tradition, was a Printer by occupation. He sought Royal protection, and retired from the United States with the British troops after they lost the American Revolutionary War. Following the conclusion of the war, and the confiscation of his Pennsylvania Estate in 1779, Christopher Sower III lived in New York and London for a period of time with his wife and children before settling in Saint John, New Brunswick in 1784. In the early 1790's, the Sowers moved to the 300-acre Brookville Farm, in the Hammond River area.

One of the earliest businesses recorded in the Town's history is the printing office owned by Christopher Sower III where he published the "Royal Gazette". Records of the "Royal Gazette" date back as far as 1785, so it can be assumed that Mr. Sower published issues of the Gazette in Saint John prior to relocating to Hammond River. The printing press Mr. Sower used was located in a two-storey building on the Brookville Farm that served as both a residence and an office.

Over the years Christopher Sower III played a number of roles in the community including Postmaster-General of the Province in 1792. Mr. Sower's involvement in the community ended in 1799 when he left New Brunswick to visit his ailing brother in Baltimore. Sower later died in Baltimore, Maryland of apoplexy in July 1799. Apoplexy is an old medical term that can be used interchangeably with cerebrovascular accident, (CVA or stroke), however this term can also have other meanings. His wife, Hannah Knorr, died March 21, 1837. Sower had six children, five girls and one boy. In 1806 Brookville, the property initially purchased by Mr. Sower in the Hammond River, was sold when the remainder of the family who lived on the estate moved to Baltimore.

Perfume Production:

The Great Regal Skunk Works was located near the top of current day Regal Drive, which was originally named after the establishment. This facility specialized in the extraction of oils from skunks. These oils were then processed for use in the production of perfume.

Studio:

It is rumored that there was an establishment at the end of the Stock Farm Road that took people's "likenesses". This business would have existed prior to 1916, and is said to have been a place of beauty, with a variety of cultivated plants surrounding the studio. Perhaps, this tin plate picture was taken at that studio. A local resident had the picture among her possessions; however, the date and name of the lady in this picture is unknown.

Haworth Farm:

Dave Haworth at one time operated a farm where the Kings Valley Wesleyan Church is currently located on the Hampton Road. On his farm Mr. Haworth raised jersey cows. Using the milk he got from his cows he operated a small milk route. The farm was in existence in the 1940's and probably earlier. (Exact dates are unknown.) Mr. Haworth also cut hay on his farm from a little island in the Hammond River.

The above picture was taken of Joan Tonge, Jean Tonge, and Harold Tonge, from the front yard of their home on the Hampton Road. Harold is actually sitting on the road. In the background are the Deamer and Haworth Farms. This picture was taken sometime in the 1950's.

Pettingill Road Farms:

There were a number of farms located on the Pettingill Road - the Carvel Farm, the MacAfee Farm, the Hall Farm, and the Pettingill Farm. The Pettingill Road was named after the Pettingills, one of the first families on the road. Their farm was located where Kensington Avenue intersects the Pettingill Road. The original farmhouse has long since been renovated, and still serves as a residence today.

Hillhurst Farm:

Frank Roberts operated Hillhurst Farm in Gondola Point, a

dairy farm, and by 1920 standards it was considered to be a fairly large operation with about 40 cows to milk by hand. The farm consisted of two houses, a dairy building, a large cattle and horse barn, an ice shed, and several out buildings including a large hen house. The milk from this farm was delivered to customers in Rothesay and to areas as far away as Renforth. Milk was transported in cans and then poured into the customers' containers at their homes. Later quart milk bottles with paper stoppers were used for the delivery of milk with cream being delivered in smaller bottles. The dairy farm separated some milk for cream, while the skim milk was reserved for the calves and pigs. Most of the milk was bottled, placed in water with ice in wooden tanks that had wire compartments to hold the bottles upright.

The original farm consisted of two hundred acres. Half of the farm was hay meadows, while the other half held a large spring and dam where the cows were watered. Some of the land was also used to grow turnips. Hillhurst Farm eventually closed after the introduction of pasteurized milk to the province, as it was not profitable to transport the milk into Saint John to be pasteurized. Part of the land that Hillhurst Farm occupied has been turned into a housing development.

(Source of Information, notes contributed by Guildford Roberts, of Gondola Point, 2005).

Hammond River Farm:

The above painting of the Hammond River Farm was done by L.J. Hickie Bartlett whose mother, Annie Hickie, use to live on the property.

Keith Dickson originally established this farm and farmhouse in the 1700's along what is known today as the Old Neck Road. Dr. Jack Thompson currently owns the property and operated his dental practice out of the building for a number of years. The home has undergone a number of modifications over the years. Some portions were replaced due to fire damage.

Hillhurst House:

The building that currently (2006) houses Gondola Point Grocery, (previously housed Scholten's, Wilson's and Jimmy's), on the Gondola Point Road was at one time a hotel called Hillhurst House. The hotel was built and run by Thomas Burlington Roberts, brother to Hillhurst Farm owner, Frank Roberts. Hillhurst House was built around the turn of the century. Originally, Thomas Roberts had operated a hotel in Boston for retired wealthy individuals. The building in Gondola Point was used as a summer resort to get away from the heat. Behind the hotel was a wharf where the riverboats would bring passengers from as far away as the United States to summer at the hotel. Other guests to Hillhurst House would come to Saint John by boat, then by rail to the Fairvale Station, and finally by carriage to the hotel. The hotel was also used in the summer for serving meals to people from Saint John who drove out on weekends in carriages. Their horses would be rested and fed while they enjoyed a first class meal in the dining room, before returning to Saint John. The hotel had a park, and benches located under a grove of large cedar trees on the beach.

The original building had a large kitchen, pantry, china room, two double parlors, and a formal dining room. On the first floor there were two flush toilets, and two small bedrooms for the hired help. The second floor had six bedrooms and two linen closets.

Guilford Roberts's mother, Mary Ann McAleer, was a cook at Hillhurst House prior to meeting and marrying his father, Walter Roberts. Walter was Thomas Roberts's son, and had operated a blacksmith shop in the Hammond River, before moving to Gondola Point. Guilford, born on January 7, 1917, was Thomas Roberts's grandson, and later owned Hillhurst House until 1961 or 1962.

In 1946 a service station was built in front of the hotel. When this was done, the lower floor of the hotel was converted into a store and the upper floor of the building was converted into an apartment. When the service station was built, the barn and carriage shed were torn down.

In the early 1960's, Guilford Roberts sold the property to Ray MacKean who in turn sold it to Doug Templeton. Doug Templeton sold the property to Scholten's. The service station was eventually moved to Harry Arnold's property on Shipyard Road.

Hillhurst House

Walter Roberts Blacksmith Shop:

As a young man Walter Roberts, father of Guilford Roberts, worked for a time in Saint John as a Blacksmith. Eventually Mr. Roberts decided to open up his own Blacksmith Shop in the Hammond River area. He eventually moved his shop to the Gondola Point Road near his father's business, Hillhurst House. The construction of the Blacksmith Shop in Hammond River and the relocation of the shop to the Gondola Point area all occurred before 1917.

The Three Bear Cottage:

The Three Bear Cottage was a tearoom owned and operated by Kristina Matthews in the early to mid-1900's. This cottage was located just above the Mullet property on the Gondola Point Road, near Saunders Drive, on the riverside. Besides operating the tearoom, Ms. Matthews was well known for being a world traveler who could speak five or six languages. Ms. Matthews was also the organist for St. Luke's Church. The cottage also served as the headquarters for the Boy Scout group she lead. Ms. Matthews was known to teach her Scouts how to canoe.

Flewelling's Store:

Mr. Flewelling owned the first general store in the Village of Gondola Point, Flewelling's store. Every Saturday night, several locals would gather there, around the old pot bellied stove for stories and card games. Before opening the store, Mr. Flewelling had been a teacher and was later appointed to be the Justice of the Peace. The wharf located below the store was appropriately named the Flewelling Wharf. Perry Saunders later took over management of the store and added a post office (dates unknown) to the operation.

McIntosh Store:

The building in the background is the McIntosh Store. The back of the photo was labeled "Pal and Rover playing in front of Andy McIntosh's store". The picture was taken by a member of the Tonge family who lived on the opposite side of the road. The entrance of the store was through a door found on the side of the building. The building acted as both a house and store. In front of the store is a sign for Robin Hood Flour.

Andy McIntosh operated McIntosh's store in the 1930's and 1940's on the Hampton Road in the building that currently houses the K.V. Food Bank. This store sold a variety of items including chocolate bars for a nickel, a bottle of pop also a nickel, and penny candy. Cecil Johnston recalls that the store sold, "a marvelous ginger beer", that was bottled in stone bottles. The exact date when the store opened and when it closed is still being researched. It is known that once the store ceased operation, the building was used as a residence. In the 1970's, the building became the first Municipal Office in Quispamsis, and served this purpose until 1984, when the Municipal Office, or Town Hall was relocated to Municipal Drive in the front area of the Works Garage.

The building currently houses the KV Food Bank

Whittaker's Canteen:

Mr. Whittaker owned a canteen where he sold hot dogs, drinks, and a variety of other items. The canteen was located on the Hampton Road, where the Old Time Diner is currently situated. Mr. Whittaker eventually sold the property to John Haslett who opened Haslett Store or commonly known as John's General Store. Mr. Whittaker eventually became a Reverend of the Anglican Church.

1950's General Stores:

In the 1950's there were several stores located in the Quispamsis and Rothesay areas. Some of these were Buchan's Community Store, Kelly's store, Haslett's store and O'Blenis' store. Buchan's and O'Blenis' were located near the Quispamsis and Fairvale boundary on the Hampton Road. Many would also remember Ottie Marr's White Rose service station located beside Buchan's Community Store.

Kelly's Store:

The Kelly's store was owned by the Kelly's and was located across from the Kings Valley Wesleyan Church, on the Hampton Road. The Kelly's sold groceries, and often provided delivery of groceries directly to their customers' homes.

Haslett's Store (formerly Whittaker's Canteen):

The Haslett's store was located at 315 Hampton Road where the Old Time Diner currently operates. John and Evelyn Haslett owned and operated John's General Store, also referred to as Haslett's store. Originally Mr. Haslett was from the Kingston Peninsula. While living on the Peninsula, John Haslett supported himself by selling groceries out of his van. His dream, however, was to start a business of his own so he moved to Quispamsis. Mr. Haslett's parents and their other children followed him to Quispamsis in search of a better school for his siblings to attend.

John and Evelyn Haslett married in 1952. They purchased the property where the former one room Quispamsis schoolhouse was located from Mr. Whittaker and opened Haslett's store. The old schoolhouse acted as John and Evelyn's home for a number of years. They eventually connected the old one room schoolhouse to Haslett's store by building a passageway between the two. They used the passageway for storing supplies, such as tires and presto logs.

John's General Store sold a variety of items including bread for 19 cents a loaf, and milk from Dave Haworth's farm. One interesting fact about the property is that some of the old fashion rose bushes that were planted around the store by Evelyn Haslett still exist today, located at the back of the diner. The store was located on the corner lot at the intersection of what was then called the Quispamsis Road, (Old Coach Road today), and the Hampton Road.

1952, John's General Store and the Haslett home, the former Quispamsis Schoolhouse

Mrs. Haslett can recall trading groceries for axes and baskets made by Laughing Louie and his friends. She can also remember Laughing Louie filling up her doorway when he visited; he was a tall big man. Refer to the section entitled First Nations for more information on Laughing Louie.

Evelyn Haslett and her sister-in-law, Irene Haslett, holding the old Quispamsis Road sign.

John's General Store was later sold to Earle and Laura Meade, who operated Meade's Grocery Store from approximately 1963 to 1982. The youngest of the three Meade children, Bob, recalls living in the old schoolhouse for a couple of years while the family rented out their Chamberlain Road home. The passageway between the house and the store survived well into the 60's, although somewhat dilapidated. Bob remembers, as a child, being terrified of the odd rodent while running from the house to the store through this passage that his mother used as a store room. Although he never did actually see any mice, the thought was always there in the mind of a child. His father eventually built an expansion on the rear of the new store and it became the store room.

Bob Meade recalls every weekday morning the whole family would load into the car and drive up to the store to open at 7:00 a.m. *'Dad would drop us at the store and I would walk over to the school later on. Dad was always the first one at his work in the morning, at Acme Construction, then Lounsburys. The family always looked forward to going 'up to the camp', (pronounced as one word, upthecamp), in Gagetown every Saturday evening after the store closed at 6:00 p.m. Mother and Dad kept this ritual up for 18 years while raising the three of us.'*

Mr. Meade passed away in the summer of 2002 and his wife after Christmas that same year.

Clark's Store:

Clark's store was located just after the train overpass when heading toward the Hampton Road from the Model Farm Road area. Harold Clark originally owned the store but his children, Ernie and Minnie, later took charge of its operation. The store was a popular place for young children to buy candy on their way home from the Model Farm School. Across from Clark's store was a building where the Clarks stored feed and flour.

Robinson's Store:

Quispamsis residents also frequented Robinson's store in Rothesay, located at the corner of the Gondola Point Road. Owned by Mr. Robinson, and subsequently run by his son-in-law, Lou Merritt. It was then renamed Merritt's store.

Diggle's Store:
Across the road from Robinson's store was Diggle's store, owned and operated by Mr. Diggle. Also, there was a service station in the same general area as Robinson's and Diggle's. This service station was operated by Lee Sherwood and was located across from the Rothesay Consolidated School. Clarence Brown later owned the service station.

Daly's Store:
Gordon Lindsay originally established the store at present day Daly's at 525 Hampton Road in the early 1950's. Richard and Annie Gates bought it in the late 1960's and it passed on to the Andersons in the early 1970's. From there it was acquired by present day owners, the Daly Family.

Hammond River Country Café:
The present day Hammond River Country Café, (formerly the Mandarin House), at 954 Hampton Road, was established by Albert Coates in the 1960's and even for one season had a motorcycle racetrack on the interval below the restaurant. It has had many owners and transformations since that time.

Hammond River Irving:
Bev Fowler was one of the last owners of a convenience store and dairy bar beside what was Hammond River Irving, on the property adjacent to the Hammond River Country Café. Before becoming a store, it was a bakery, run by a family from the Kingston Penninsula.

Hammond River Raceway:
The Hammond River Raceway was located on Murray Crowley's Farm off the Stock Farm Road, and was operated by the Hatfield family. Joe Thompson recalls it was a popular activity on Sunday afternoons for many years during the 1970's and 1980's

A general note on stores extracted from Tales of The Kennebecasis, the unknown author captures what life was like in the early community.

"The Village Store"

"At the village store much farm produce was "traded in" for goods. Some took their pork to the Saint John market, and occasionally their butter and poultry, and fat cattle. Butchers came from the city to buy calves, steers, sheep and lambs. Feed for cattle, horses, hogs and poultry was all home grown. Beyond tea, sugar, molasses, oil and the like, the average family bought little.

The Kings County village in those days was a friendly and neighborly community-as it still is-but very different, though happy enough, were the farmers who knew no bicycles, no motor cars, no phonographs, no telephones, no radio. Pianos were rare, but there were organs for Sunday, and the fiddles for the dances that horrified the more straight laced but that had a growing attraction for the younger generation. The temperance society bred orators and gave a fine opportunity for a bit of courting going and coming."

Blue Ridge Cabins:
At the foot of Stoneycroft Hill, Mr. Kelly, (father of Alan Kelly first Mayor of Quispamsis 1966 - 1968), owned and rented ten tourist cabins. These buildings were called the Blue Ridge Cabins due to the bluish hills of Long Island that could be seen off in the distance. The cabins were eventually sold and moved to Nauwigewauk where they became part of the Green Dolphin Motel and Cottages. In 2000, the motel sold the cabins and many were relocated and are in use today as hunting camps.

Blue Ridge Cabins, above, around 1947.
The road behind the cabins is the Hampton Road.

Buckland Meadows Campground:

David Allan Buckland owned and operated a campground on the Model Farm Road. Mr. Buckland built the campground in 1964 after purchasing the 100 acres of waterfront property from Carrie Prince in 1963. Miss Prince originally had another buyer for the land but favoured what Mr. Buckland wanted to do with the land.

Buckland Meadows Campground operated from 1963 to 1976, generally opening the last week of June and closing the first week of September. When it first opened, the camping rates were two dollars for regular sites or two dollars and fifty cents for sites with electricity. The rates increased over the years. Visitors to Buckland Meadows Campground came from all around the world including, but not limited to, Europe, the United States, and other parts of Canada.

Picture of the Buckland Meadows Campground.

A picture of the beach at Buckland Meadows Campground

    The old Prince barn, constructed in the 1800's, served as the campground's main centre. David Buckland used the barn as a store, canteen, and a place to show movies. The store sold firewood and general grocery items such as milk, bread, and ice. A local bakery supplied the store with homemade bread, cookies, and donuts.

    The recreation room contained a television, piano, and ping-pong table. The walls were decorated with posters and old wagon wheels were converted into light fixtures. Campers could play cards, ping-pong, and checkers, read magazines, or watch television. Travel films were shown three nights a week.

The above picture shows the recreation room at Buckland Meadows Campground. Note the wagon wheel light fixtures.

Wagon rides were held in the evenings for the children. Mr. Buckland's car pulled the wagon. Other activities that took place at the campground included swimming at the beach, boating around the Kennebecasis River, hiking wooded trails, participating in games such as horseshoes, playing at the playground, and fishing for the catch of the day. Some campers would pay the ferry operator between two and five dollars to stop the ferry in the middle of the river, or to cross the river slowly, so that they could fish. This was only done as long as no other passengers would be inconvenienced.

The above picture shows Mr. Buckland's car pulling the wagon full of children.

The campground's facilities included flush toilets, dumping stations, picnic tables, a sun deck, a scenic outlook, and hot showers. The showers cost twenty-five cents, but payment was based on the honour system.

On August 8, 1972, at five in the morning, Mr. Cunningham, a fisherman from Gondola Point, noticed flames leaping from the chicken coop at Buckland Meadows Campground. He quickly alerted the individuals staying at the campground. It is believed that the fire started from a grass fire. Four fire trucks from Hampton and Nauwigewauk responded to the blaze. Everything from the campground was lost except two pianos and some photos. At this time Carrie Prince still lived in her home, even though Mr. Buckland owned the land. In this time of need, Miss Prince provided fresh drinking water to the campground for the one week it was open after the fire.

Barn on fire at Buckland Meadows, on August 8, 1972.

Mr. Buckland rebuilt the campground after the fire and the campground was open for business in the spring of 1973. Before reopening the campground he made some improvements that included the construction of some roads. The campground closed for the last time in 1976.

Fox Farms

There were a number of fox farms in the Quispamsis area in the early to mid 1900s. Three of the more prominent fox farmers were Archie, Vinton, and Trueman Copp. Archie Copp also operated some tourist cabins on the land that is currently occupied by the Kennebecasis Public Library. Trueman Copp's fox raising operation was located near the present day First Bible Baptist Church on the Hampton Road. All three fox farms were in close proximity to each other.

Any of the young boys, such as Gilford Roberts who is perhaps one of the longest living residents of Gondola Point, can recall catching rabbits and selling them to Trueman Copp as feed for his foxes. Trueman Copp would pay any boy who snared him a rabbit 10 cents. He would pay the local boys a dollar for a one hundred pound bag of hake fished from the Kennebecasis River. Farmers would also be given money for any old horses they may have wanted to sell. Mr. Copp would come by with his money and a rifle to shoot the old horse to use as feed for his foxes. Trueman Copp was also the school superintendent.

There were other individuals who operated fox farms in this region. One such individual, Mr. Squidd, owned a fox farm at the intersection of the Hampton Road and Marr Road, where Kennebecasis Drugs is currently located.

Peddlers:

There were a number of peddlers who would go door-to-door selling homemade remedies, pots, frying pans, gadgets, ointments, vanilla extract, and food. Peddlers also performed useful tasks such as sharpening scissors and knives. Two of the peddlers who serviced the Quispamsis area were Hamilton Cochrane, and Ernie Marr. Years ago, peddlers would travel by wagon, selling their wares out of the back. In later years, automobiles were used to carry goods from house-to-house.

Delivery Services:
Residents who lived far from any local stores often relied on vendors of fish, vegetables, meat, and bread to deliver these items to their homes by truck. Mr. Dixon, who lived and operated a store in Rothesay, sold meat from the back of his vehicle up until the late 1950's. Another gentleman who sold meat to residents of the Quispamsis area was Alden Saunders.

Business in Quispamsis in the 1980's:
Three of the largest employers in the Town of Quispamsis in 1983 were the Co-op (eighty employees), the Kennebecasis Home Hardware Store (twenty employees), and the Town of Quispamsis (ten employees). As the years progressed more and more businesses developed in Quispamsis. In 1987, the Town Council of the day rezoned a large track of land for the Village Place Shopping Mall in the area of the Hampton Road/Pettingill Road intersection. This development helped shape what has become known as the downtown area of Quispamsis today. It was one of the Town's most controversial rezonings of all time.

Business development in the 21st century will continue to grow in the Millennium Drive Business Park District.

Post Offices

More than 2000 post offices were in operation in New Brunswick from 1783, when the first post office was established in Saint John, until 1930. Postmasters maintained early post offices in the Province. The position of Postmaster was sometimes a political appointment. It was not uncommon for a postmaster to be discharged from his duties because he supported the wrong political party.

In other cases, often the wife of the postmaster would assume his responsibilities after he was forced to leave his position due to advanced age, illness, or death. Many post offices were run from private homes. In this case, both the husband and wife would act as postmaster, even though the Post Office Department would only appoint the husband as the postmaster. The title of postmaster often remained in a family for many generations and it was not uncommon for some terms of office to last up to forty years. By 1930, the majority of the small post offices were closed with the postal service being provided by a rural mail delivery system.

In the Quispamsis area there were three post offices, the Quispamsis Post Office, the Hammond River Post Office, and the Gondola Point Post Office. The Quispamsis Post Office, located five kilometers northeast of Rothesay, opened its doors on August 1, 1883. The postmaster was W. Darling who held the position until the close of the office on May 15, 1930.

The Hammond River Post Office, located 11 kilometers northeast of Rothesay, was at one point known as the Jubilee Post Office. The post office opened on June 1, 1900 and closed on October 18, 1939. The postmasters included S. Dickson (June 1900 - January 1911), J. Porter (April 1911 - September 1920), and H. Dodge (January 1921 - October 1939).

Located six kilometers north of Rothesay was the Gondola Point Post Office. It was in operation from July 1, 1883 to November 22, 1947. The first postmaster was J. Flewelling (July 1883 - October 1919), owner of Flewelling's store, where the Post Office was initially located. Upon the closure of Flewelling's store, the Post Office moved across the road to Perry Saunders' home. Perry Saunders was postmaster from December 1, 1919 until 1947 when the post office was closed.

Older Homes

Peat Homestead:

Dr. Gilbert B. Peat had a big yellow house located on what later became the Peat Drive Park at the corner of the Hampton Road and Peat Drive, both named in the doctor's honour. Gilbert Peat was a doctor who practiced in the City of Saint John, but resided in Quispamsis until1956 when he became the Mayor of Saint John. A local resident of Quispamsis found one of his patient logbooks. The logbook contained entries dating from October 1931 to February 1932. The entries in this book noted the patient's name and address, how much he charged the patient, and the patient's illness. Some of the ailments Dr. Peat treated patients for included anemia, the common cold, coughs, indigestion, rheumatism, neurosis, headaches, liver problems, and scabies.

Meenan Homestead:

Mr. Meenan owned a farmhouse on the property located at the intersection of the Chamberlain Road and the Meenan's Cove Road. Meenan's Cove Beach was originally located off Mr. Meenan's property. For more information about Meenan's Cove Beach refer to the section entitled Beaches.

Saunders Homestead:

The land across the road from Mr. Meenan's farm on the big hill going up the Chamberlain Road was originally part of the Saunders' homestead property. In later years, Ted Walsh owned a section of this land. Prior to Mr. Walsh's ownership of the land, there was a house located on the property that would have been the original farmhouse owned by the family of George Saunders. Harvey and Betty fleet eventually purchased the old Saunders' property from Mr. Walsh in 1968 or 1969. The Fleets converted the 150 acres of land they purchased into the current Colonial Drive and Regal Drive subdivisions. Since the Fleet's purchase of the property, the property has changed ownership a few more times.

Otty/Crowley Homesteads:

The original Otty land grant ranged from the Buckley land all the way to the Stock Farm. Colonel Allen Otty, father of Augusta Otty

(Miss Gus for short) and Emma Otty, owned the Red House on the corner of the Hampton Road and Model Farm Road after renting their home on the Stock Farm Road to the Government.

Members of the Crowley family have long since owned both the Red House and the Stock Farm.

OTTY   RUTH CROWLEY

Red House

MURRAY CROWLEY

Stock Farm Road Homestead

The Otty Family also marked off land on the Hammond River intervals and sold them in an auction to farmers who needed land to hay. Some of the local farmers also stored hay at the Otty's barn on the Stock Farm.

Other Older Homes:
The following are pictures Eleanor Jones took of old homes that were once, or are still currently found in Quispamsis.

CARVEL   JOHN HUGHS

The above house is on the Pettingill Road, and currently owned by the Stuart Family.

D. BETTLE

On the Hampton Road, near Kennebecasis Valley High School.

GEORGE HIGGINS

Model Farm Road

GEO. McAFEE

Pettingill Road (near Quispamsis Middle School)

Harold Bishop

Chamberlain Road

Harding

Hammond River Road

GEORGE THOMAS SAUNDERS
Chamberlain Road

A. DILL
CAPT. MILLER

DR. "KIRKWOOD"   K SALLOWS
Kirkland.

Hampton Road, (across from Stoneycroft House)

Keirstead Homestead - Pettingill Road (near Ritchie Lake)

Keirstead Homestead (Ritchie Property - Old Coach Road)

JOHNSTONE
Hampton Road

Johnston Homestead, current site of Wesleyan Church.

Johnston Homestead, 1940

McEachern Drive

NORTHRUP   R. KIPPERS

Hampton Road

WELLINGTON   SAUNDERS

Quispamsis Road, no longer standing.

Prince Farm, (M. Caroline Prince), Model Farm Road.

PRINCE

Model Farm Road

Darling Homestead (Old Neck Road)

George Gerald Buckley and Margaret Rachel Saunders were married in 1877. They resided all of their married life in what became known as the Buckley homestead. The house no longer stands.

*Mr. Truman Copp's house on Ranch Avenue,
(across from The Landing).*

*Saunders Home on Chamberlain, owned by William Elias and
Grace J. Saunders.*

Jennie and Keltie Tonge at Angie Allingham's house, Hampton Road, just before KVHS. Currently Milligans

Tonge/Lovegrove Property, 349 Hampton Road in 1952.

Home of Manton Harrison, Lower Beech Hill, Gondola Point.

The house in the upper right corner, was the Mullett home, Gondola Point Road. Jean (Mullett) Wilson's home in Gondola Point burned down in 1920, when she was just three years old.

Early 1920's Gondola Point Home.

"Gondola Point Home" was all that was marked on the above photo.

House was bought unfinished by Oscar W. Saunders when he married Elizabeth Belyea. House was located in Gondola Point.

Saunders Homestead in Gondola Point, lived in by Horton Saunders in 1983.

Mr. Tuffs' house on Chamberlain Road, January 1941

"Aunt Kitty's Place" on the Stock Farm Road. In the picture are: Mark Jones, Ruth Crowley, and Murray Crowley

House on Chamberlain Road

Harmon & Mable Saunders Homestead, the original home was moved from Hammond River to Gondola Point and, over the years, added on to several times over.

Stoneycroft (11 Mile House)

Stoneycroft is located at 255 Hampton Road. In August 2005, Stoneycroft had its 185th birthday. The Historical Resources Administration declared Stoneycroft a historical site in 1979.

Above is a picture of Stoneycroft in the spring. Note that, at present, (2006) Stoneycroft does not have a veranda on the front like it did in this photo. Below is a picture of Stoneycroft as it is seen today.

This area was entirely wooded until five men were issued land grants on August 23, 1820. Caleb Wetmore Sr. received 500 acres; Ezrahiah Wetmore, James Wetmore, Caleb Wetmore Jr., and Joseph Bailey were granted 200 acres apiece.

Caleb Wetmore Sr. was from New York originally but eventually settled in Saint John, New Brunswick. In 1805 he became an Alderman, (a member of a municipal legislative body in a town or city), for the City of Saint John. Later Caleb Wetmore Sr. moved to the King's County area where he died in 1853.

Picture drawn by David Taylor, 1989.

Caleb Wetmore Jr. built Stoneycroft for his new bride, Ann Whelpley, in 1820. Mr. Wetmore (1799 - 1884) was a joiner, a woodworker whose work involved making items by joining pieces of wood, by trade. It has been assumed that he would have participated in the construction of his home, perhaps in the decorative carvings that can be found on the building. Caleb Wetmore was also the Commissioner of Roads for a period of time in the 1830's.

Picture drawn by Annette Michaud and Jocelyn Tonge, 1989.

Prior to the 1820's, the main route used for traveling to Hampton from Saint John was along the Westmorland Road. In the 1820's, work began on the Post Road to create a more direct route to Hampton from Saint John. When the Post Road eventually opened, the land surrounding it became more valuable. Caleb Wetmore had a tavern license in the 1820's. His land had developed into an inn, tavern, and tearoom for community gatherings. Caleb Wetmore sold his house and property in 1836 due to the increase in its land value. The following advertisement appeared in the New Brunswick Courier on the 18th of June 1836.

> "Two hundred and fifty acres of good land, well situated, being eleven miles from St. John, and on the post road leading to Halifax, with a good dwelling house (two stories high) and two good barns. About thirty acres of land is cleared, and the remainder well timbered. The situation is well adapted for a House of Entertainment, it being half

way between St. John and Hampton Ferry."

-New Brunswick Courier,
18 June 1836.

Picture drawn by Andrew Kilpatrick, 1989.

  A place of entertainment is exactly what the house built by Caleb Wetmore Jr. became over the years that followed. John E. Stuart purchased the 70 acres of Caleb Wetmore's property in 1837, and turned the house into an inn. The inn was used for auctions and other events, acting as a place of entertainment for the community.

  A prominent Saint John businessman by the name of Robert Keltie owned the property from 1839 to 1855. In 1855, Mr. Keltie sold the property to Andrew Thompson. When Robert Keltie owned the property, he rented it to at least two gentlemen; first to John King Campbell, then later to John Harris Wright. During this time, the inn was known as the Lakefield Inn, which was the name this area had been called at that particular time. The rest of the Wetmore property was advertised for sale at a Sheriff's auction in 1839.

Sharon Munn drew the above artwork, 1989.

Drawing by Doug Little, 1989.

Mr. John King Campbell posted the following description of the Inn in the New Brunswick Courier on the 12th of October 1839:

"The subscriber having leased that excellent stand for business in Kings County, known as Lakefield Inn, about twelve miles from the city of Saint John on the great Post Road to Halifax, hopes by strict attention to business to merit a share of public favour..."
-New Brunswick Courier, 12 October 1839.

On February 20, 1841 John K. Campbell's son of eleven months died at Lakefield Inn. Ten years later the 1851 census shows John K. Campbell as a hotel keeper in Saint John (probably the New Brunswick Hotel at 11 Charlotte Street). Twenty-two year old Charles Campbell, another son of John K. Campbell, was listed as an innkeeper in the Parish of Hampton. Quispamsis would have been a part of the Parish of Hampton at this time.

Another person who leased Stoneycroft was John Harris Wright. He owned property in Quispamsis, but his home was near what is now the corner of the Quispamsis and Pettingill Roads. On June 9, 1819, Mr. Wright married Jane Warren. The 1851 census lists his name as an innkeeper in the Parish of Hampton.

Side note: On December 2, 1849, Charles Campbell son of John K. Campbell married Eliza Ann Wright, daughter of John H. Wright. Perhaps there was a business partnership between the two families.

Kings County records show that tavern licenses were held by John K. Campbell from 1840 to 1850; John H. Wright for the years 1848 to 1854, and Charles Campbell was licensed from 1851 to 1854 and 1856 to 1861.

At one time Stoneycroft was known as the Eleven Mile House. It was used as a popular resting place for farmers on their travels to and from Saint John. Coachmen on the Post Road between Saint John and Halifax also used the Eleven Mile House as a changing place for horses. The Nine Mile House was in Rothesay and the Three Mile House and Tavern was in Saint John where the current Three Mile Steakhouse & Pub is today.

The name "Stoneycroft" came into existence when David

Magee and Matthew Manks bought the property from William Kennedy in 1870. Four years later, Mr. David Magee, a prominent businessman from Saint John, solely owned the property. He named the former coach stop "Stoneycroft" after his former family home in Coleraine, Ireland. Prior to the 1870's, Stoneycroft was referred to as Wetmore's, the Eleven Mile House, possibly the Twelve Mile House, and Lakefield Inn. The Magee family farmed the land associated with the building.

The following quote is from a Magee Family Memoir-

"I adored the barn. One door opened onto the horse stalls, and it was hard to remember that the Bantam rooster and hen always roosted at the top of the nearest stall. There would be a great flapping and cackling and cowing when the door was opened suddenly. Very unsettling for the young!"

Drawing by Mona Chase, 1989.

Stoneycroft is majestically located on a hill, referred to as Magee Hill, named after the Magee Family. The house is located 152 metres, (500 feet), above sea level, and from the second storey windows, one can see for 32 kilometres (20 miles).

Two ladies of the Magee family announced in 1913 the opening of a tearoom at Stoneycroft. They also referred to it as the old Eleven Mile House.

The following excerpt was found in The Standard, Friday, 23, May, 1913:

"Very unique cards have been issued by the Misses Magee announcing that they will be prepared to serve afternoon tea on and after tomorrow at 'Stoneycroft' (the old Eleven Mile House). Many have already begun to make plans for a run out to Quispamsis during the summer months, it being a delightful drive from the city."

Picture drawn by Alison Ross, 1989.

When the Magee family owned Stoneycroft, they would host a picnic in the summer for all the children who attended the local Sunday Schools. During the picnic, games and races were set up for the children to play, and prizes were handed out to the various winners. Cecil Johnston can recall being awarded a lined exercise book for schoolwork, but upon not showing much enthusiasm for the workbook, he was given a kaleidoscope.

The John Morris Robinson family purchased Stoneycroft from the Magee family in 1937. The Robinson family brought several of their family heirlooms to the house. One possession was a silver tea urn, which had been given to Colonel Beverly Robinson as a present from Prince William, (later King William IV). Prince William had been entertained at the Robinson family home. This historic tea urn is very valuable and of magnificent craftsmanship.

Drawing by Jennifer Ellis, 1989.

Another heirloom of the Robinson family is a clock showing the time, season, and weather. The clock belonged to ancestors of John

Morris Robinson and originated from the First Chartered Bank in Saint John.

In its time, Stoneycroft was known for its fine dining. It had become a popular establishment for dinner on special occasions by the 1950's. The Gourmet's Guide to Good Eating rated Stoneycroft as "Excellent" and the following was written in the guide:

> "Stoneycroft-Route 2, 11 miles from Saint John. Open daily by appointment. A la carte and table d'hote. Luncheon about $2.50. Dinner about $3.50. No liquor."

Stoneycroft was also frequently used for wedding receptions. It was one of only four locations in New Brunswick listed in the guide for fine dining. Two of the four New Brunswick restaurants identified in the guide were owned and operated by the Robinsons; - Stoneycroft and the Trading Post at Reversing Falls.

The current owners of Stoneycroft, Judy and Stephen Delaney, bought the house from the Robinson's in 1989. Upon buying the house the Delaneys began renovations. Pictured below are some of the artifacts that the Delaneys found in the walls and under the floorboards.

It has been rumored that there is a ghost that haunts Stoneycroft. Legend has it that a man's portrait seems to turn up in various places in the house. The question of whether he is responsible for the mysterious noises and strange lights reported by numerous other residents remains unanswered.

Owners of Stoneycroft:

1820 - 1837	Caleb Wetmore, Jr.
November 24, 1837 - 1839	John E. Stuart
October 16, 1839 - 1855	Robert Keltie:
1842 - 1844	Rented to John Campbell
	Rented to Charles Campbell
1849 - 1854	Rented to John Harris Wright
September 29, 1855 - 1861	Andrew Thompson
August 21, 1861 - 1870	William Kennedy
August 20, 1870 - 1874	David Magee and Matthew Manks
January 12, 1874 - 1937	The David Magee Family

1937 - 1989 John Morris Robinson
1989 - Present Judy and Stephen Delaney

Stephen Delaney holding some of the artifacts he and his wife found in the house. Picture donated by Paula White of KV Style.

Sources of information and images for this section were obtained from a number of sources. One such source was the 1989 Kennebecasis Valley High School art students' calendar, artwork displayed throughout this section, based on the story of Stoneycroft. KVHS English teacher, Vivian Wright, led the students in their research of Stoneycroft. Another vital source of information was the Summer Historical Research Project the Town of Quispamsis conducted in the

1980's by researchers Wendy Field and Paula White. Information was also obtained from interviews conducted by Petra Kalverboer for the town of Quispamsis in the summer of 2005.

Drawing by Suella Dupuis, 1989.

River Scenes

View of Kennebecasis River from Gondola Point.

Water Mill at Waddell's Mill at Reed's Point on the Kingston Peninsula across from Gondola Point Beach. Taken in 1909 or 1910.

Waddell Mill at Reed's Point, New Brunswick, on Monday June 19, 1950. The Mill burnt to the ground.

Photo of the Waddell Mill, taken in 1938.

*Roy Waddell's barn on fire as a result of the fire
spreading from the Waddell Mill.
Photo taken from Gondola Point on June 19, 1950.*

Reed's Point
N.B.

Log Boom in the Kennebecasis River. Photo of Nita Driscoll taken during the mid-1960's s in front of her family, the MacMurray's, summer home on the upper side of where the Perry Point Bridge once existed

Moss Glen, N.B.

Bridges

Perry's Point Bridge:
When the Perry's Point bridge existed, it connected Flewelling's Mill in Perry's Point to the Prince Farm in Jubilee, (now the Model Farm Road). The construction date of the first Perry's Point bridge is unknown, but church records from the area suggest it was in use as early as 1810. The second bridge was constructed around the late 1870's by A. E. Killam of Moncton. The Perry's Point bridge was about three-quarters of a mile in length and the largest in the Province. Telephone wires were strung across the bridge. The bridge was constructed approximately two kilometres down river from the Presbyterian Church, now St. Andrews Kirk United Church, at Hammond River for the convenience of Parishioners crossing the river to attend Church service.

Pictured above is Mr. Hedley, the driver of the single horse and wagon. The caption under the picture read: "The long bridge at Perry's is on the highway from St. John to Kingston, the Belleisle and midlands of Kings County. The road from Jubilee Station to it has in view the picturesque Hammond River outlet."

Department records show a contract, dated November 17, 1887, for extensive repairs done to the bridge. The contractors were George and B. H. Appleby Carleton of Saint John who agreed to fix the bridge for $5,000. In December of 1887, the first payment of $1,200 was paid to them. The following article, which appeared in the news on May 1, 1887, details the state of the Bridge before repairs were made.

> "The bridge at Perry's Point, Kings County was rendered unfit for traffic a few days ago by a large flow of ice, estimated at about 200 acres that started from Meenan's Cove with a heavy south wind carrying with it three of the 50 foot spans and two abutments from above the center of the bridge. This is the first time in the memory of Perry's Point's oldest inhabitants' memory that such a fell of ice was seen floating about the river at this place.
>
> The Government has put on a free ferry for foot passengers and will repair the bridge at once.
>
> The mail route between Kingston and Rothesay will be changed on the first of May and will run between Kingston and Saunders Crossing, ICR via Perry's Point. It will be very convenient for the mail driver until the bridge is ready for traffic again. Levert Cosman who has the mail contract, carries it 26 miles daily for $194.00 per year."

Perry's Point Bridge washed out on January 6, 1909 by a freshet. A freshet is an overflow of a waterway caused by the thawing of snow or ice or a heavy rainfall. Only a small section of the old bridge was destroyed so it could have been repaired. Unfortunately, local farmers acquired the lumber from the bridge to use on their farms. In 1910 the steel draw, which allowed busy steamer traffic on the river to go up and down the river without hindrance, was removed from the bridge. The turnstyle portion of the bridge was located near the mill, (Kingston Peninsula), side of the bridge. The remainder of the bridge was dismantled in 1913. The wooden cribwork filled with rocks are still in the Kennebecasis River where the bridge once stood. In recent years, there have been occasions of boats hitting these abutments when the water is extremely low. When the bridge was in operation it carried a heavy flow of traffic. After the bridge was dismantled a ferry replaced it. Refer to the section entitled Transportation by Water for more information on the ferry service.

Above: Photo of Perry's Point Bridge from Kingston Peninsula.

Plans for the construction of the Perry's Point Bridge:

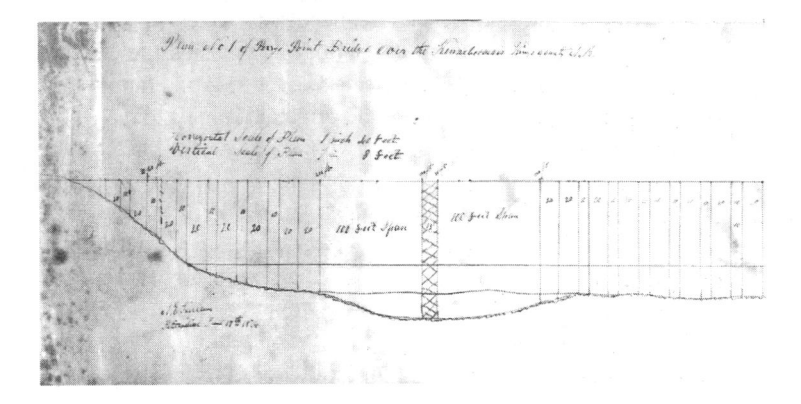

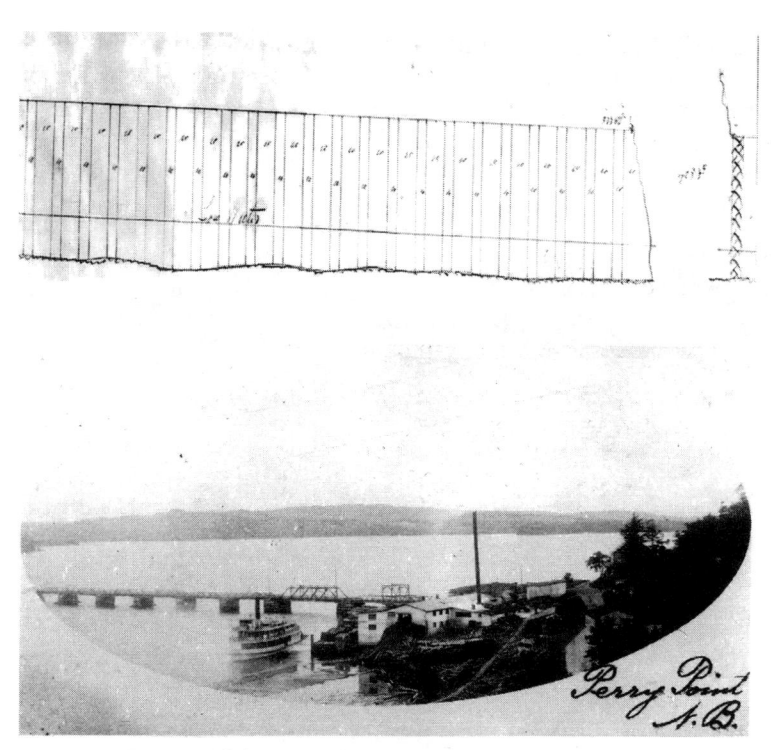

Picture of the Perry's Point Bridge, date unknown.

Model Farm Road Covered Bridge:
    The 147 foot Model Farm Road covered bridge was built in 1925, and spanned an inlet of the Kennebecasis River near today's Meenan's Cove Park. An old wooden bridge pre-existed the covered bridge, but was washed out with the spring freshet in 1925. In the short time span between the washing out of the original bridge and the building of the new covered bridge, the Sherwood family who lived on the Model Farm Road near the bridge, according to Mr. John Higgins, brought pedestrians across the water in their small boat.
    The Model Farm Road covered bridge was eventually dismantled in the spring of 1980 after it was determined to be unsafe for fire trucks. It was replaced with the current concrete bridge. A replica of the Model Farm Road covered bridge was built in 1994 at the entrance of the Meenan's Cove walking trail.

Above is the Old Model Farm Road Covered Bridge.

The replica, which is found at the entrance of the Meenan's Cove Walking Trail, is pictured above.

Nancy Hart painted this inspiring representation of the Model Farm Covered Bridge.

Covered Bridge Is Coming Down

- - But Some Quispamsis Residents Don't Like It

By KHALID MALIK
Staff Writer

Some Quispamsis residents are making a last ditch effort to save the Meehan's Cove covered bridge on Model Farm Road but as things stand now they might be too late to do it.

One of the residents, Joseph McNamara, yesterday managed to make a last minute addition to the village council's agenda for the meeting Tuesday 7 p.m. And at least four more people have indicated that they will attend the meeting in an attempt to press the council to urge the province to retain the bridge.

But as it is now a three-member crew of the provincial highways department is working on the tearing-down process for the last two days.

Robert Bonnell, district engineer for the department in Sussex, said the roof and side-boards of the bridge will be taken down now and in August the remaining bridge will be replaced by a pipe culvert at a cost of around $70,000.

Though there's another access to the area through the Neck Road, Mr. Bonnell said efforts to restrict the bridge use have failed.

Quispamsis Mayor Sterling E. Gilmore himself is not very enthusiastic about saving the bridge and says "I can't understand why people want to retain it."

Mr. Gilmore says the bridge is unsafe and he doesn't think of it as a tourist attraction.

He said he doesn't know what he and his five-member council can do to save the bridge because it's under provincial jurisdiction. "They (provincial authorities) are good to tell us what they're doing with it. They don't have to," he said.

The council "might or might not" decide to support the residents in their effort to save the bridge, he said.

In an interview Friday, Mr. Gilmore had said the village tried to find people who were interested in preserving covered bridges to do something about it but didn't receive any response.

Many people in the area have expressed strong feelings against the demolition of the bridge. They say the bridge lends "color and beauty" to the area and is a tourist attraction.

Miss Caroline Prince, one of the oldest residents in the area, said "they say there're about 14 more covered bridges in Kings County but they're not around here."

She also couldn't understand how a culvert would work "in a river like this which rises and falls so sharply. Sometimes the water touches the road level," she said.

Miss Prince has two pictures of the bridge and she intends to keep them now "as souvenirs."

Mrs Paul Kelbaugh thinks tearing down of the bridge is a "terrible thing to do." She said the authorities are tearing it down now but "a time will come when they'll have to spend a fortune building them again."

Mrs. Winnie Steer, who came from England 11 years ago and has been living in Quispamsis for the last four years, said "when you come from a place where you can't find such things, you value them more."

Mrs. Steer likes the rustic quality of the covered bridge and says "so far as I'm concerned they should just leave it there as it is.

"It's just too beautiful. It's one of the most delightful spots our here. I really do feel that the tourists who pass this way do appreciate it. It's beyond me how these things (demolition) can happen.

"Much to my dismay when I found the crew pulling down the bridge this morning I said to myself there's nothing one can do about it. That's it," she said.

Mrs. Steer said the authorities could do a number of things with the bridge. They could leave it as such; they could reinforce it (it's well worth spending money on it"), and if they want to widen the road they can use it as one way of a two-way bridge.

Mrs Helen Ellis says "there's no reason to tear down the bridge because it's reasonably structurally sound.

"I'm not an expert on bridges but if it is not sound why can't they repair it. It's cheaper to buy wood and repair it than tearing it down and building another one from scratch," she said.

Mrs. Ellis said the bridge "adds to the scenery around here" and gives access to the people taking their boats to the Kennebecasis River which a culvert won't do.

Mr. McNamara is particularly worried about the culvert because he says it would not be able to cope with spring water in the river.

THE MEEHAN'S COVE covered bridge, shown above, long a tourist attraction in the Quispamsis area, is being torn down by provincial government work crews. But a number of area residents don't like the idea and are digging in for a last-ditch battle to save the bridge. They will air their concern during Tuesday's Quispamsis Village Council meeting. Below, at left, a workman is shown carrying a sheet of metal which has been removed from the roof of the structure.

July, 1976

STAND OR FALL? — The fate of the Meehan's Cove Bridge is still up in the air after the Quispamsis Village Council told concerned residents last night they would ask the province to reconsider repairing it. Demolition of the bridge, shown in this picture taken a few days ago, has since halted.

Will Ask Province To Consider Repairs

The Quispamsis Village Council promised last night to re-examine the possibility of repairing the Meehans Cove covered bridge in conjunction with the provincial transportation department.

But Mayor Sterling Gilmore told local residents opposing the demolition of the old bridge: "We're not trying to extend any hopes to you. You fellows can go back to the provincial government on your own behalf." He suggested the residents contact Transportation Minister Wilfred G. Bishop and deputy-minister E. G. Allen.

Demolition of the bridge was not going on this morning, and A. Robert Bonnell of Sussex, district engineer for the department of transport said last week that the covered bridge would not be torn down until some time in August.

There were 30 to 40 people at last night's council meeting, and most seemed more concerned with the condition of the Model Farm Road than with preservation of the covered bridge.

Murray Driscoll presented an oral brief calling for hard surfacing of the road on behalf of its residents. "You can't do much with the bridge, but you can do something about the road." He said the Model Farm Road serviced 73 homes and had been on council's list of "top priority" problems for years.

Council told Mr. Driscoll that $102,000 earmarked for the surfacing of the road wouldn't be forthcoming from the province, but said it would "re-assess moneys" in its road fund and would "put our best foot forward to work on your road."

Mr. Driscoll told council that a private contractor had surfacing the road from the covered bridge to the Neck Road would run from $50,000 to $60,000, while provincial estimates for the same stretch of road were much higher. Council agreed to listen to the private contractor's proposal in a meeting of the road committee this evening.

The principle spokesman for

the residents trying to preserve the covered bridge was Joseph McNamara, who said his main concern was the reduced space beneath a culvert. He said that tide-driven ice would not have room to pass through in the spring, which could cause flooding.

"If metal pipes are put in, my home could flood in an instant," he said. "A culvert plugged with ice could flood me up to the second storey. At least replace it with another bridge."

Mr. McNamara said another bridge would be "a heck of a lot better than looking out at a tin can. Retain it or repair it until it can be replaced with another bridge," he said.

Mayor Gilmore said when council had spoken with transportation department officials "safety was a key thing."

"There was no mention of safety in Joe's remarks," he said. "There is no way we want school buses falling through that bridge because of our neglect."

Council told the citizens the cost of repairing the bridge was estimated at $100,000 by provincial engineers and the bridge would have to be replaced with a culvert for economic reasons.

Mr. McNamara maintained the old bridge could be made safe for much less.

There were no representatives of the provincial transportation department at the meeting. The provincial government is responsible for the bridge, and was approached by council to do something about it because it felt the present bridge was unsafe.

The bridge, located on the Model Farm Road between the main Quispamsis road and the Neck Road, can be replaced by a pipe culvert at a cost of $70,000 according to Mr. Bonnell.

He said last week the bridge could not be restored well enough to carry heavy vehicles, and that an attempt to limit traffic by placing signs restricting the weigh of vehicles was unsuccessful.

Mayor Gilmore said last night council had approached Milton Gregg who has been active in saving covered bridges in other areas of the province. He said Mr. Gregg gave them "his moral support," but could produce no money to help preserve the bridge or move it to another location.

"We considered putting another crossing in an leav the old bridge there, as but that's uneconomica day and age," the ma

July 1976

Hump Back Bridge:
    The bridge that spanned the railway tracks at the Quispamsis Train Station on the Quispamsis Road was often referred to as the Hump Back Bridge. The one-lane bridge had a hump in it to allow clearance for train traffic to flow freely under the bridge. It was risky to cross in a vehicle as oncoming traffic was not visible until motorists reached the top of the hump. Motorists often blew their horns when approaching the bridge to warn oncoming motorists of their presence. In later years, traffic lights were installed to permit only one lane of traffic to cross at a time.
    Due to the bridge's deteriorating condition, and the number of accidents that occurred on the bridge, coupled with the high costs of replacing it with a safer structure, the Hump Back Bridge was dismantled in the early 1980's. The Quispamsis Road was dead-ended on both sides of the bridge, and the shorter portion was renamed the Old Coach Road. This coincided with the opening of the Gondola Point Arterial, which provided motorists with an alternate route. Subsequently, in 1993, a pedestrian bridge was installed at this railway crossing.

This gentleman and Vera (Leonard) Emery (who came to Quispamsis to summer from Eastport, Maine) are pictured on the Hump Back Bridge.

This bridge on the Quispamsis road is considered by many to be dangerous. Residents would like the Province to build a new one.

The Kennebecasis Valley Post

This article was taken from the Kennebecasis Valley Post and details the dangers that motorists faced when attempting to cross the bridge:

Hazardous Hump Bridge on the Quispamsis Road

The bridge over the railroad tracks on the Quispamsis Road must be seen to be believed. It is not until you are half way across and starting down that you can see if there's traffic approaching you.

Nearby residents have considered this a hazardous bridge for many years. Now the increased traffic on the road makes it even more hazardous. On Sundays, eight or nine cars on each side of the bridge can be waiting to cross after St. Mark's, St. Augustine, Quispamsis United, and Rothesay Baptist let out.

Mrs. Fred Rafferty wrote to the Quispamsis Village Council expressing her concern. She states "that there is even more hazard since the sign 'One Lane' was placed at each end of the bridge" She states "two cars can meet on this bridge without colliding if both keep well to their own side, but with the sign saying 'One Lane' more people keep to the middle of the bridge."

She goes on to say that she doubts if a large truck and a large car could meet without side-swiping"

When a collision does occur, both parties consider that they had the right of way.

The majority of the accidents are minor ones; many go unreported. But three years ago there was a bad head on collision. A car was "backed over the bank by the approaching vehicle." Luckily they survived the accident without even broken bones, recalls Mrs. Rafferty.

The Quispamsis Council discussed her letter at their last Council Meeting Feb. 4th. They recall exchanges after the serious accident in 1977. Councillor Roger Nesbitt suggested that it is time to reactivate the concern.

Mayor John Robinson explained that bridges are the responsibility of the Department of Transportation or the C.N.R. The only authority the village has is to close the bridge or make it one way."
T   The Raffertys explained to me that the bridge was not always a bridge over the crossing. It was built around 1907 according to Mr. Rafferty. The road went down and up and around on the other bank, "The approaches are just fill,".

Mrs. Rafferty suggested several possible solutions - one, is to install a traffic light that turns "red at one approach when it is green at the other," another solution is a wider two lane bridge, that would be C.N.R.'s responsibility.

Her last solution is to make it truly a one way abridge. That would be inconvenient for residents like Mrs. Rafferty, but she explains "there would be more inconvenient for residents like Mrs. Rafferty, but she explains "there would be more inconvenience to me and my family if iT were to be involved in a bad accident on the bridge."

The Quismasis Council directed Village Manager Don Scott to investigate the traffic flow and bring back a proposal to their March 4th meeting. Residents can express their concern by writing the Council, CNR and Deputy Minister of Transportation.

Hammond River Covered Bridge (French Village Road):
    This bridge was constructed in 1912 on the French Village Road, between Quispamsis and the Hampton Parish, spanning the Hammond River. This bridge is still standing and in use today. Below are two pictures of the bridge. The first picture is a photo of the bridge that was taken in 1994, while the second picture was taken in 2006.

Photo by Jo-Anne Hooper - 1994

Transportation

The Quispamsis area has seen a number of forms of transportation over the years. In the 1800's and the early 1900's one of the major means of transportation in Quispamsis was the riverboat; however, with the rapid changes in technology in the twentieth century, this method of travel became obsolete. The riverboat era ended in 1946 when the D.J. Purdy was beached in Gondola Point. Railway, automobile, and bus transportation eventually replaced the riverboats in the area. With the exception of two ferries, the rivers that border alongside Quispamsis today are primarily used for pleasure.

Transportation by Water

Transportation by water was one of the first forms of transportation available to both the First Nations and early Europeans. In this region, water transportation occurred on both the Kennebecasis River and the Hammond River during the summer and winter months. Water transportation was one of the essential systems used to export and import goods to the Kennebecasis Valley.

Riverboats:
Numerous riverboats traveled up and down the rivers bordering Quispamsis. Some of the more famous riverboats were the General Smyth (1816 - ?), the Hampton (1906 - 1920), the Champlain (1904 - 1922), the Victoria (1897 - 1916), the Olivette (1893 - 1898), the Clifton, the Majestic (1899 - 1942), the Premier (1907 - ?), and the D.J. Purdy (? - 1946). Several riverboats journeyed up and down the river every day and made stops at all of the wharfs along the Kennebecasis River. When traveling from Saint John, one of the first stops would have been the Rothesay wharf. The riverboat would then continue on its route and travel between Long Island and Mather's Island. The riverboat would then stop at a wharf between Long Island and Gondola Point, possibly Roberts Wharf before continuing to Moss Glen, then Flewelling Wharf in Gondola Point where the riverboats would have off-loaded supplies. The riverboats would travel along the river as far as Hampton.

The two best known wood burning steam engine vessels in New Brunswick were the Clifton and the Hampton. These vessels, along with many others, were responsible for carrying both passengers and freight along the river. These vessels also played an important role in the economy and development of the region. The steamers were responsible for bringing supplies from Saint John to residents and storeowners located in the outlying regions. On their return trip to the City of Saint John, the ships would bring back items such as fruit, vegetables, and berries they had collected from the remote areas.

When the riverboats first began running they were fuelled with wood that was purchased from local residents. Later the vessels were propelled by coal. On the weekends, when the riverboats were not in operation, dances would be held onboard and were attended by members of the surrounding communities.

Traveling on these riverboats was not always safe. The rivers posed numerous hazards including floating debris, sand bars, and collisions, especially at night. Not only were the rivers hazardous but the riverboats were as well. Until the late 1800's, the riverboats were composed primarily of wood and also burned wood for fuel. Understandably, this led to a constant risk of fires erupting throughout the vessels. Even so, most individuals who traveled on these boats will testify that it was an enjoyable experience.

"Above is a picture of a riverboat at a wharf on the north end of Long Island. Pictured in the background is Mather's Island."

Flewelling Wharf at Gondola Point - a common stop for riverboats travelling the Kennebecasis River.

Era of the River Steamers, Beginning 1816 -Author Unknown

"Nothing in local history can match the fond memory of the little steamers that once sailed on the Saint John River. Long before Fredericton and Saint John were linked with good highways, or the railway, the river ferries provided passenger and freight service between the two cities. They filled both business and social needs.

At the height of the period, they sailed on regular runs up the Saint John, even beyond Fredericton and Woodstock, up the Kennebecasis to Hampton, through Jemseg Creek to Chipman, while others plied the Miramichi. Summer trips and special excursions provided pleasure and relaxation because the courses led through the lovely heartland of New Brunswick."

The General Smyth:
    The first riverboat to travel the waters of the Kennebecasis was the General Smyth. The General Smyth was built in 1816 and was one of four steamships in all of British America. As author Dorothy Dearborn, wrote "The General Smyth was the pride of New Brunswick and would have been the pride of Canada had Canada existed in 1816!"

The Hampton:
    The Hampton was built in 1906 in Hampton, New Brunswick, and was first operated on the Kennebecasis River. The Hampton was the last stern wheeled steamer to sail on the Kennebecasis River.

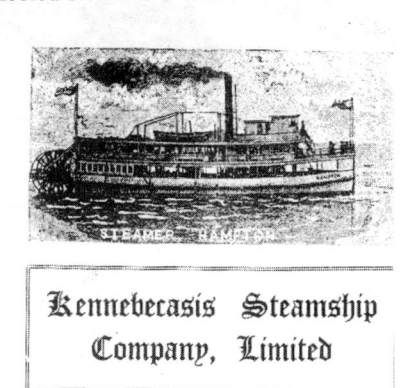

Kennebecasis Steamship Company, Limited

ROUTE:
SAINT JOHN TO HAMPTON,
Kings County, New Brunswick.

E. A. FLEWWELLING,	PRESIDENT.
S. H. FLEWWELLING,	SEC.-TREAS.
CAPT. A. T. MABEE,	MANAGER.

Steamer "Hampton" Time Table
Until July 1st.
MONDAY, WEDNESDAY, SATURDAY.

Leave Hampton,	6 a. m.
Leave St. John,	3 p. m.

This Time Table in effect before and after Excursion Season.

Return Tickets, 60 cents

Arranged and Published by
C. H. FLEWWELLING,
for the K. S. S. Co.

Above: An advertisement for the Hampton Riverboat.

HAMPTON 1906-20
On Kennebacasis River

Early photo of the steamer called the Hampton taken at the Hampton Wharf in NB. Unknown date for the photo, but taken in horse and buggy days, possibly early 1900's.

Picture of the Hampton before the sides were closed in.

The above photo is of the steamer called the Hampton stopping in Gondola Point, NB. The back of the original photo was designed as a postcard.

165

The Champlain:

The Champlain (1904-22). The caption reads: Sign on Wharf advertises Saint John Clothing Store owned by Walter Pidgeon's Father.

Picture of the Champlain (1904-22).

The Victoria:

The Victoria was built in 1897 in Saint John, New Brunswick. She was designed, like all riverboats, to carry cargo.

Picture of the Victoria (1897-1916)

Above is a picture of the Victoria on the Saint John River near Sheffield

The Olivette:

The above picture is of the Olivette (1893-1898)

The Majestic:

The Majestic (1899-1942). The Majestic was beached at Nauwigewauk.

The Majestic was built in Toronto in 1899 and began servicing the Saint John area in 1902 when a shipping company in Saint John purchased the vessel. T. A. Jarvis of Nauwigewauk was the last owner of the Majestic and had her beached in May of 1946 between Darling's Island and Nauwigewauk. He had hoped to turn the boat into a nightclub but no permits or licenses were issued due to the dangers of her location. The Majestic eventually caught fire and was destroyed.

The caption states that the Majestic "Began St. John Service 1902"

The Premier:
The "Premier", was launched for the first time in June 1907. The following passage appeared on June 8, 1907 in the Saint John, New Brunswick Semi-Weekly Telegraph:

"The Ceremony at Clifton Tuesday Largely Attended."

"To the sound of loud cheering and with a number of people on her trip decks, the new Kennebecasis ferry boat, the Premier, took the water gracefully at Clifton Tuesday afternoon, and the occasion was one of great merry making and

rejoicing.
Large crowds gathered at the Clifton grounds early in the afternoon, and proceeded to enjoy themselves. At 5 o'clock the launch took place. Standing on the deck, the Honourable Wm. Pugsley spoke words of congratulations and said that as representative of Kings County he had done all he could to help along the project.

Mrs. Harry Gilbert stepped to the rail with a bottle of champagne in her hand, and with one blow shattered the glass. The new steamer slid down gracefully and settled in the waters as the crowd cheered lustily.

Those in attendance proceeded to enjoy the evening in royal good style. A concert was given at 8 o'clock and dancing was indulged in."

A picture of the Premier docking at Gondola Point Beach.

The D.J. Purdy:

The D.J. Purdy was another well known riverboat, and the last to be built in New Brunswick, and sail the waters of this area. The picture below is of the Purdy's crew. Captain Fred S. Mabee is the gentleman on the top deck, second from left.

Above pictures the D.J. Purdy (1924-46) passing the Premier on the Saint John River.

Picture of the D.J. Purdy

The D.J. Purdy

Captain Fred S. Mabee and John Barton on the D.J. Purdy.

    The D.J. Purdy ended up being permanently located at the Gondola Point Beach in 1946. The D.J. Purdy made her final trip from Fredericton on September 30, 1946. It was beached there in an area referred to as the Frog Pond. The hull of the old riverboat was filled with sand.
    Jack Jones tried to make the D.J. Purdy into an entertainment centre that contained a dance hall, a casino with slot machines, and a bar. However, this casino type of entertainment may have been a little too early at the time for the country atmosphere of this area. In the early 1950's a fire mysteriously destroyed the old riverboat.

Prior to being beached, the D.J. Purdy made several trips up and down the Kennebecasis River transporting passengers. Many Quispamsis community members can recall Sunday School outings aboard the Purdy. Each summer they would travel up the Saint John River with their Sunday School instructors to wonderful places such as Crystal Beach. Just imagine sitting aboard the D.J. Purdy and watching the scenery and hills roll by. The picture below shows the type of benches that were originally on the D.J. Purdy. The benches' seats flipped over allowing passengers to change the direction they were facing.

The bench in the above photo was originally aboard the D.J. Purdy. This bench from the Purdy was found at Mr. Dave Buckland's campground on the Model Farm Road. The campground however did burn down and the bench was lost forever in the fire. Refer to the section entitled Businesses, Hotels & Stores for more details about Buckland Meadows Campground.

D. J. Purdy beached at Gondola Point.

Ferries:

The Gondola Point Ferry was in operation as early as the 1860's. In October of 1865 the following regulations respecting the ferry at Gondola Point were published. These regulations ordered that the following rates and fares would be charged for crossing:

For a Foot Passenger	05 cents
For a Passenger with a horse	16 cents
For a single horse carriage with horse and driver	25 cents
For a double horse carriage, with two horses and driver	25 cents
For children under the age of 12, except those at the breast	04 cents
For horses and neat cattle, each	10 cents
For hogs, young cattle, and sheep	04 cents

Pitt Ferry:

The William Pitt Ferry currently operates between Quispamsis off the Gondola Point Arterial and the Kingston Penisula and was named after Captain William Abraham Pitt (1841-1909) of Reed's Point on the Kingston Peninsula, who invented the first underwater cable ferry at this location.

William Pitt, also referred to as Billy Pitt, was always doing his best to serve the public. Captain Pitt originally sailed and sculled a ferry back and forth along the one-mile stretch of water between Reed's Point and Gondola Point. In 1901, before setting his sights on creating an underwater cable ferry, he built a steamboat to run from Reed's Point to Rothesay, Moss Glen, Long Island and back to Gondola Point again. The steamer was called the Adino Paddock. The steamboat was only in operation for one year before it was sold at a public auction, due to the fact that it was not a profitable acquisition according to Dr. Paddock, who was perhaps Pitt's father in-law.

Even at the age of sixty, Mr. Pitt did not slow down in his need to improve the river transportation between Reeds Point and Gondola Point. While in New England he witnessed a ferryboat that was being guided by an overhead cable. He took the idea home and informed his wife, Mary Eliza Paddock, of his plan for a new ferry. His wife, who initially thought this idea would be the end of him, was later a source of inspiration. While sewing late one evening she accidentally stuck her finger with a needle. Mr. Pitt's idea for the underwater cable ferry came as he watched her spool of thread drop to the ground and unravel.

Picture of Mr. and Mrs. Pitt

In the winter of 1903 William Pitt received his shipment of a huge reel of cable to be used in the creation of his underwater cable ferry. This cable was put in place over the ice that formed in the Kennebecasis River between Reeds Point and Gondola Point. When the spring came the ice would melt and his underwater cable would be in place. His new ferry was introduced to the Kennebecasis River in 1903 and later became the model for all other ferries built in New Brunswick.

Mr. Pitt owned and operated the ferry for a number of years before selling it in the 1920's to the provincial government. Even after selling the ferry to the government he continued to oversee its operation. Mr. Pitt was well known for telling his ferry passengers jokes and stories during the river crossing.

Today the ferry is a free service but, at one time, there was a 25 cent charge for cars, 10 cents per adult passenger, and 5 cents per child. "So, as you got older you sank down the seat a little farther so you would not have to pay 10 cents" according to Mr. George Teed who summered over on the Kingston Peninsula as a child. Young people were employed to park cars on the ferry.

Several people who lived in and around the Gondola Point area can recall the tragic day when Mr. Pitt caught his arm in a belt he was attempting to push back onto the flywheel and was seriously injured. He died very shortly after the accident from his injuries.

The above picture is of Gondola Point Ferry/Pitt Ferry, 1920's.

Harold Wright's *Historic Saint John*
Gondola Point ferry, 1930

Above: The Gondola Point Ferry (The Pitt Ferry), 1930.

Gondola Point Ferry Trip -Summer Excursion

*Gondola Point Ferry Landing, Ferry in the background.
Picture taken May 24, 1949.*

Above: Picture of the Gondola Point Ferry, early 1920's

Perry Point Ferry:

The Perry Point ferry replaced the Perry Point bridge after it was swept away with the freshet of January 6, 1909. In the 1930's, it was common for people to take their horses aboard the ferry in the summer and spring. The Perry Point Ferry was still in use in the late 1960's. Often campers from Buckland Meadows Campground would slip the Perry Point Ferry operator two to five dollars to slowly cross the river or to stop in the middle so they could fish.

In 1958, there were numerous comments in the newspaper discussing the Perry Point ferry. The ferry had been built approximately 12 years earlier in Upper Gagetown, (around 1946), and had been in service until 1957 at McNally's on the St. John River, about 12 miles north of Fredericton. In the summer of 1957, it was brought down river to Perry Point to replace one of the ferries that needed repairs but sank in the fall of that same year. One correspondent who stressed his concern about the ferry wrote that the 81 year-old operator, Roy Wetmore, wore a life jacket while operating the ferry the two weeks prior to its sinking. He also is said to have commented, "It's rounded all out of shape and is an awful looking sight." It remained submerged for the entire winter. In the spring, it was hauled out and the regular ferry was returned to service after repairs were complete.

Transportation on the rivers in the winter:

Mr. Otty Sherwood.

Otty Sherwood, the first Mayor of Gondola Point, (Born on February 17, 1921), can still remember many of the stories his father once told him about his grandfather, Robert Sherwood. Otty Sherwood can also remember summering in a cottage just before the old covered bridge on the Model Farm Road. His grandfather also owned a small farm near the old covered bridge down the road from the Higgins' Farms. In the winter, the road would not be plowed so his grandfather would travel from place to place along the frozen river. His grandfather would pull a hand held sled and walk up the river to Indian Town, (now Milledgeville). If no snow was on the ice, Mr. Sherwood would skate. He would pull a sled that contained his chickens' eggs and the like to sell at the Saint John City Market. After he sold the eggs and made any purchases, he would return home again by way of the river. Otty Sherwood remembers one occasion when his grandfather skated into a 'burst' in the ice, and returned home looking like a 'jarred icicle'! (A burst occurs when the tide comes up and places pressure on the ice and cracks develop.)

In the winter, ferries did not operate, but people still had to cross the river for survival. Local farmers would often take their horses across the river on the ice. On several occasions the horses would have to be pulled out of the river after the ice had broken beneath them while hauling wood across the ice. In the following picture little pine trees are placed in the ice to act as a roadway across from Moss Glen to Gondola Point.

Posing in the picture are Hatty Smith and her son, Thomas Smith. This picture would have been taken between 1939 and 1945 when her husband, Thomas Smith, was overseas fighting. Unfortunately he did not return from the Second World War.

After the Second World War, the government became responsible for ploughing the ice in the wintertime, where the Pitt ferry normally operated, to provide a roadway for the Kingston Peninsula residents.

There are numerous historical diary entries regarding the ice breaking and the ability to travel on the Kennebecasis River.

Excerpts from the Diary of D. P. Wetmore:

April 20, 1872: "Justin went to St. John today, crossed on the ice, got his horse in the ice near the shipyard coming home this evening."

April 26, 1872: "Very dull this morning. Rained a little. They began to ferry here yesterday. David put out some current and gooseberry plants last evening."

Excerpts from the Diary of Amelia Holder:

April 9, 1874: "Oh dear, the river is between ice and water and there is no way of getting either up or down. I am in hopes the ice will go out soon and then I will go to town and buy some things."

Excerpts from the Diary of H.D. Wetmore:

April 7, 1884: "Mail wagon crossed ice this morning- last time."

April 10, 1884: "Ice looking bad-no crossing for two days. Another hen set this evening."

April 14, 1884: "First team crossed at ferry today."

April 14, 1885: "Fine-cutting wood all day-Ice wasting fast, last crossing with horse here yesterday."

April 18, 1885: "Fine and warm. Ice and snow wasting fast. Gondola Point ferry running today."

April 14, 1886: "Fine. Mail wagon crossed ice here today for last time-looking very weak in places."

April 17, 1886: "Gondola Point ferry opened today."

April 14, 1887: "Horse got in the ice near shore here today."

April 19, 1887: "Repairing boots and shoes today. Ice wasting slowly at Gondola Point. No crossing the ice on foot since Saturday."

April 19, 1888: "Gondola Point Ferry running today."

March 30, 1889: "Ice getting very poor. Last crossing with a horse here on Saturday. Crossing on foot until Wednesday. Gondola Point ferry opens today but no crossing except to mail."

Excerpts from the Diary of Rea S. Giggey of Whitehead:

April 20, 1908: "The ice went out on April 20, 1908."

April 20, 1909: "The last team crossed here April 6; the ice went out April 20, 1909."

March 21, 1910: "Last team crossed here March 21."

March 25, 1910: "Steamer Majestic made her first trip up the river on Good Friday, March 25."

April 2, 1910: "Maggie Miller made her first trip."

These diary entries reflect the importance these residents placed on the river. Daily life relied on being able to travel on the river.

The ice of the surrounding rivers was used for a variety of purposes, in the wintertime. It was not uncommon for residents to have an icehouse in their backyard. Icehouses would be covered with packed sawdust to help prevent the ice from melting in the summer months. Ice would be hauled away from the river using a team of horses and a sled, or later, by a waiting truck. Many people purchased their ice from icemen. Gordon Scribner of Rothesay may have been the last man to deliver ice in this region. People who lived near a river or a pond would often harvest their own ice rather than buying ice from an iceman.

The above picture was taken from an original at the Kings County Museum in Hampton. The description on this photo labelled 70.9, "An ice saw made by the local blacksmith." Donor: Miss Caroline Prince of Hammond River. This ice saw was probably used on the Hammond River and the Kennebecasis River.
(Dates and names unknown.)

*Unknown man hauling ice,
photograph also compliments of Kings County Museum.*

Prior to 1917, the Boston Ice Company would have purchased ice from Gondola Point and shipped it back to Boston for refrigeration usage. Guilford Roberts can remember skating under these old icehouses along the Kennebecasis River in Gondola Point. These icehouses were built on stilts and in the wintertime they would be packed with ice and sawdust. The schooners from Boston would come up in the summer, when the river was open, and take the ice from the icehouses back to Boston with them.

Transportation by Coach:

Before the arrival of the train in the late 1800's, horses were one of the main methods of long distance transportation. There were many coach stops along the road between Quispamsis and Saint John, for the comfort of travelers and to allow the drivers to change horses. There were at least four coach stops between Saint John and Quispamsis. The two coach stops in Saint John were the One Mile House, which was located at the corner of Russell Street and Rothesay Avenue, and the Three Mile House, which was located at the intersection of McAllister Drive and Rothesay Avenue. The old Three Mile House is now a part of the Three Mile Steakhouse and Pub. In Rothesay there was the Nine Mile House, which was located at Rothesay corner and was for many years known as the Kennedy House, and later became an Irving Service Station, which was recently decommissioned. The fourth coach stop was in Quispamsis at the Eleven Mile House, at the residence now referred to as Stoneycroft on the Hampton Road. For more information on Stoneycroft refer to the section entitled Stoneycroft.

Transportation by Railway:

The main railway in this area in the late 1800's was the Intercolonial Railway, (ICR). The Railway, which was also referred to as the European and North American Railway, connected Saint John with Shediac. The first sod was turned for the Intercolonial Railway on September 14, 1853. Today the railway is named the Canadian National Railway (CNR).

The section of the railway, which ran from Nine Mile House in Rothesay to Groom's Cove, (now called Lakeside), was scheduled to be finished July 30, 1859. In 1857, the European and North American Railway decided not to name their railway station in Lakefield after the community as they had traditionally done. Instead the railway company named their train station the Maliseet name, 'Quispamsis'. The name Quispamsis later became the name of the community. The railway line was completed and in service by July 30, 1860.

A man named Edward Lahey, a laborer on the Railroad, was killed on Friday at the 11 mile house, by falling off a derrick, while in the act of hoisting stones. He was about 25 years of age; from Cork, Ireland, where he left a wife and five children, some two years ago.

Morning News, 14 February 1859

Robert Stafford drew the above picture.

The following excerpt was extracted from the Morning News, 14 February 1859:

"A man named Edward Lahey, a laborer on the Railroad, was killed on Friday at the 11 mile house*, by falling off a derrick, while in the act of hoisting stones. He was about 25 years of age; from Cork, Ireland, where he left a wife and five children, some two years ago."

*The 11 mile house is in reference to the Stoneycroft House.

There were numerous little train stations along the route from Hampton to Saint John. In Quispamsis, there was a total of five different railway stations or stops - the Hammond River Train Station, the Model Farm Train Station, the Blair's Siding Train Station, the Quispamsis Train Station, and the Ritchie Lake Train Station. There were also the Fairvale and Rothesay train stations.

This is a photo of the Saint John morning train taken in Sussex just before departing for its journey to all the little train stations between Sussex and Saint John.

Two trains left for Saint John on a daily basis. One left Hampton at 7 a.m., while the other left Sussex at 8 am. Return trips to Hampton and Sussex were made from Saint John in the early evening at 5 pm and 6 p.m..

The Saint John Station was called Union Station and was located where Harbour Station stands today. The Union Station was a beautiful building with a marble interior. A monthly ticket for the Saint John trains cost approximately $2.98 in 1928. In the 1930's the cost of a train ticket had increased to $5.98.

The grade from Rothesay to Quispamsis was one of the steepest grades in the province for freight trains to climb. Some freight trains, in order to have enough momentum to climb this grade, would be split into two sections. Some of the freight cars would be taken up the grade and placed on the siding, while the rest of the freight cars were brought up the steep incline. Once all the freight cars were at the top of the grade the train would be put back together and would continue on to its final destination.

The Quispamsis Train Station:

The Quispamsis Train Station, or the 'shelter' as local residents sometimes called it, stood on the east side of a steel bridge on the Station Road, (present day Old Coach Road).

Jack Leonard, a summer resident of Quispamsis, standing by the tracks at the Quispamsis Station.

Incidentally, the Quispamsis railway bridge played a significant role in determining a young boy's manliness. In those days it was said boys who could climb up on the bridge guardrail and walk from one side to the other had achieved manhood. Perhaps that is what the gentleman in the following picture was trying to prove.

The Quispamsis Train Station's Station Master was Mr. Darling. He owned a house on Rafferty Court, a road located off Station Road. Sources indicate that one of the Train Station operators used Morse code to tell when trains would be approaching the station. This very well could have been Mr. Darling. After Mr. Darling's tenure as Station Master, a family named Gould assumed the operation. Unlike Mr. Darling, the Goulds used a section of the train station as their home. A door off the passenger's waiting room separated the family's living quarters from the rest of the station. The Gould family was still living in the train station in 1949.

The Fairvale Train Station:

The Fairvale Train Station was located near the intersection of Gondola Point Road and Maliseet Drive. One unique feature about this train station was the little stove it housed. This stove was used to warm the passengers waiting for the train. Skaters who were skating on the nearby pond also made use of the stove to warm up on frigid winter days.

The Fairvale Station is in the far right in the above picture. The picture was taken looking up the hill towards Gondola Point.

The Ritchie Lake Train Station:

The Ritchie Lake Station also contained a small wood stove so that passengers could be warm while waiting for the train. Irene Flower can recall her father, Frank Cameron, snowshoeing down the middle of the Pettingill Road in the winter on his way to the station to catch the train to work. He would leave his snowshoes at the station until he returned on the train from his day's work at Barnes Hopkins Printing Co. in Saint John.

The above picture is dated May 1939. It is taken at the Ritchie Lake Train Station in Quispamsis. The train station is decorated with banners and small Union Jack flags, probably for the beginning of World War II, as many troop trains would have passed through this area. The four children in the photo are Don, Betty, Doug, and Irene Cameron who were all residents of the Pettingill Road and Ritchie Lake area.

Eleanor Jones and her son Doug Jones took the above picture in the late 1980's.

The Ritchie Lake station is no longer used as a train station, but the building continues to stand on a property along the Old Coach Road. John Hughes initially bought the train station from the railway company but he later sold it to Mr. Phil Withers.

The Model Farm Station:

The Model Farm Train Station was located behind the dwelling known as Red House, which is located at the intersection of the Model Farm Road and the Hampton Road. Ruth Crowley currently occupies the Red House. The road to the site of the old station is still present on the right hand side of the Hampton Road, just before the train bridge.

Mr. and Mrs. William Meenan were the stationmasters at the Model Farm Train Station. It is speculated that they are related to Jack Meenan and his sister who lived on the Meenan's Cove Road and were the owners of the original Meenan's Cove Beach property. One feature that made the Model Farm Train Station unique from the other train stations in Quispamsis was that it also housed the Otty Glen Post Office. Mrs. Meenan also operated the Post Office, which remained in operation until the early 1930's. The exact dates of operation of the Post Office and the Train Station are unknown.

The train ride from the Saint John Train Station to the Model Farm Train Station would have taken approximately forty-five minutes According to Eleanor Jones, many of the railway workers settled on the land between the Blair Siding Train Station and the Model Farm Train Station. The railway companies and government generously awarded the workers parcels of land along this road for their labors.

The Hammond River Train Station:

In 1901 the Hammond River Train Station was built. In that same year, the area known as Hammond River was renamed Jubilee. In this time period the Hammond River Train Station was referred to as The Jubilee Train Station. However, after 1916 the area reverted back to its former name.

The Hammond River Station burnt down in 1954 but had been converted into a house long before the fire occurred. At the time of the fire Ralph and May Moore, who had a son named Kenny, owned the house. The exact date that this train station was converted into a house is unknown.

The above picture is of the Hammond River Train Station.

Trains:

    The morning train was also commonly referred to as the milk train as milk from the farms would be loaded onto the train in big milk cans. The train would stop at all the stations along the route (Model Farm, Blair's, Quispamsis, Ritchie Lake, Fairvale and Rothesay,) to pick up milk and passengers. In the early 1920's the milk was brought to the train station in a horse drawn wagon. The milk was then sent to Baxter's Milk, the dairy processing factory in Saint John.

    The Jitney was a diesel-operated train that ran only between Hampton and Saint John. The Jitney would traverse the same tracks as the morning train but would do so approximately an hour after the other train had come through.

    The train was a major mode of transportation until it was discontinued shortly after the Second World War due to the invention of more convenient methods of travel such as the automobile. In their time the trains made several trips a day through the area, transporting residents to and from work in the city. The train also provided an opportunity for passengers to socialize with each other during the commute or while waiting in the train stations. In many ways the train brought the community together.

Transportation by Bicycle:

In the early to mid 1900's teenagers were not able to use the family car like they do today. Individuals of all ages relied heavily on their feet for walking, or for peddling their bicycles, to get from place to place. It was not uncommon to see a young couple who were courting walking down the middle of the Hampton Road or to see individuals biking to Rothesay, then Gondola Point, then back to Quispamsis.

Cecil Johnston could often be seen riding his bike when he summered in Quispamsis. Attached to the back of his bike was a parcel carrier, to which a cardboard carton was tied. He and his dog, Rex, took many trips from his cottage on the Hovey Road down to the Quispamsis Train Station in order to buy a paper from the paper carrier that traveled on the train. The price of a paper in the early 1930's was about 5 cents.

Cecil Johnston's bicycle and his dog Rex who is in the cardboard carton that is on the back of the bike.

In the summertime, young people could often be seen on their bikes cycling to the nearest swimming place. Those who lived in the centre of Quispamsis may have biked to the train station and left their bikes there while they followed the train tracks down to Ritchie Lake.

At Ritchie Lake there were designated changing areas within the bushes for both the boys and the girls. The Gondola Point Beach was another popular beach people biked to in order to take a swim.

Transportation by Automobile:

After the Second World War, the automobile became the popular mode of transportation. Many people test-drove new cars, on the hills of the Quispamsis Road and the Meenan's Cove Road to gauge their performance. The first family to own a car along the Quispamsis Road was the Loves. In 1940, Cecil John Drayden Love and Estella Bernice (Graves) Love bought a 1939 Buick. Even though they owned a car and gas was only 4.8 cents per litre (18 cents a gallon), it was still cheaper to take the train into Saint John.

Don Cameron, early 1950's.

Mr. Smith - Milkman, 1937.

Vehicle owned by Mr. Cecil Johnston, 1949.

Patricia (Boudreau) Cameron – 1950's.

Transportation by Bus:

One of the early predecessors of the bus in this area was the school van. The school van, which was pulled by a team of horses, was used to transport up to 30 children to school in Rothesay. The driver of the van would receive a payment of $5.00 per day but was responsible for supplying the horses and their feed. The children using this van left home at 7 am and were returned home at 6 p.m. or later depending on where the child lived, the condition of the roads, and the weather. Bids would be placed to decide who would become the school van driver. Harmon Saunders, Bob Marr, Herb Saunders, Harold Hayes, and Walter Saunders were all van drivers at some point. The van mainly serviced these children from the Forrester's Cove and Gondola Point areas. Refer to the section entitled Schools for more information on the school vans.

The first public bus to travel from Saint John to the Quispamsis area began in 1935. This bus was called the Saint John Motor Line and would run three or four times a day from Saint John to Gondola Point and back. Bob Mullett was assigned the task of keeping the Gondola Point Road, which was paved at this time, plowed for the bus.

The public bus service to the Kennebecasis Valley ceased operation in the 1970's due to the high cost of providing this service, not to return again until 2007 with the new Park and Ride COMEX Public Bus Service which makes several trips in and out of Saint John, Monday thru Friday.

Schools

During the early years in New Brunswick there were very few educational facilities in rural areas. In 1819, very few people could read or write. In the areas between Rothesay and Upham, then called Hampton, only a few people could write their names. By 1872, the Free Common School Act came along, improving these issues.

By 1900 there were five one-room schoolhouses in the Quispamsis area for children to attend. Which school one's child attended was primarily dependent upon where the child lived. The one-room schoolhouses were located in Gondola Point, Quispamsis, Model Farm, Forrester's Cove, and Hammond River. It has been said that schools in the area were built two miles apart so no child would have to walk more than one mile.

Gondola Point Schoolhouse:

The Gondola Point School was originally a part of School District 3, in the Parish of Rothesay. This one-room schoolhouse was located at the corner of present day Sherwood Park Subdivision near the Kennebecasis River. The schoolhouse was built primarily of wood and was in use as early as 1877. Lee Flewelling was the teacher in 1877 before he opened Flewelling's Store in Gondola Point and became a Postmaster. Refer to the section entitled Businesses, Hotels, & Stores for more information on Flewelling's Store. The Second Royal Reader was the textbook used in this school in 1890. The Reader was composed of text in both of Canada's official languages, English and French. The original globe used in the Gondola Point School for geography lessons is currently (2006) located at the Kings County Museum in Hampton. Found below is a description of the globe as presented by the King's County Archives.

The original globe can be viewed at the Kings County Museum.

Article 72.38 at the Kings County Archives, Description of the Globe at the archives:

"This world globe has a graduated latitude scale and in black print on a circular label it says: "W & A. K. Johnson Edinburgh and London." The globe nests on a frame of fulminated wood and the base is cast iron with copper plated "Paw feet." The wooden frame has the months of the year and the names of the zodiac sign, plus time zones and degrees on paper that is glued on. It was used before 1916 in the Gondola Point School. Donor: Henry A. (Grace Harrison) McLeod."

The doors of the Gondola Point Schoolhouse were closed officially in June of 1916 due to the opening of Rothesay Consolidated School in 1915. Forrester's Cove School and Renforth School were also closed at this time.

Students and Teacher at the Gondola Point School taken in the early 1900's. Back Row-Lew Merritt, Abbot Albert, Viola Saunders, Oswald (Ossie) Saunders, Mary Saunders, Flossie Saunders. Teacher Miss Fanny Whelpley. Middle Row: Dorothy Vincent, Myrtle Vincent, Clair Vincent, Robert Mullett, Mary Mullett, Christina Mullett, (Mullett sisters in dark dresses), Kneeling: Elsie Vincent, Perry Saunders.

The last teacher who had taught in the Gondola Point School was May Harrington in 1915-1916. Some of the school's past teacher's included; Margaret Brooks (1912-1914), Louise Scovil (1911), Winnifred Dixon (1910), Muriel DeMille (1906-1907), Margaret Pickle (1900), Maggie Burgess (1899), Elizabeth Wetmore (1894-1895), Alice Kierstead (1888-1891), Mary DeVoe (1886), Constance Carter (1884), Lee Flewelling (1877), Fanny Whelpley, and Dorothy Alward.

School children at the Gondola Point School taken in 1912. Back row: Florence Saunders, Annie Saunders, Mary Mullett, Ella Saunders, Stella Mullett, Pauline Saunders, Carl Vincent, Margaret Brooks (Teacher). Middle row: Grace (Harrison) McLeod, who won the Lord Beaverbrook scholarships in 1920 for her accomplishment in mathematics. Front row: Jennie Saunders, Oscar Saunders, Ray Roberts, Theodore Saunders, Guy Vincent, Sadie Mullett, (-missing a name), Clarence Harrison, Len Smith.

The below photo is of the Gondola Point School with pupils and teacher taken in the 1900's. This copy shows the one-room schoolhouse, which was on the main road at that time. It was later made into a two building house that acted as a summerhouse owned by Carrie Green. It burned down in the 1950's.

Quispamsis School:

The Quispamsis School was in School District 4. It was located on the lot that is currently occupied by the Old Time Diner, almost directly across the street from the current day Quispamsis Elementary School. The Quispamsis School was the first school in Quispamsis. Children as far as the Westmorland Road were transported to the Quispamsis School by horse-drawn van before Westmorland constructed their own school.

Kitty McLaughlin was a life-long resident of Quispamsis. She died in 1932 at age 94. Kitty McLaughlin attended school at the Quispamsis one-room schoolhouse; therefore it can be speculated that the school was in operation in the 1840's. Ms. McLaughlin would walk to school everyday from her house, which was located across the street from where the Sobeys store is currently located on the Hampton Road.

There were 22 pupils enrolled in the Quispamsis School in 1878. Eleven years later, in 1889, the number of students enrolled had increased to 49. When Rothesay Consolidated School opened in 1915, enrollment at Quispamsis School decreased to between 20 and 30 students.

Thomas A. Haworth, who was from Great Britain, built a house a few hundred yards from the Quispamsis School on the Hampton Road in 1900. Mr. Haworth had a contract with the school to provide wood and light the school's stove.

The interior of the schoolhouse was like a typical one room schoolhouse. At the front of the school there was a boys' and girls' cloakroom and a large classroom that housed a wood stove. There was limited space around the schoolhouse for children to play, as the woods that surround the school had not been cleared at this point. For exercise the pupils would be taken down to an open field near Ritchie Lake. This field was located on the Ritchie property, the residence built and landscaped by William Ritchie who eventually became the Chief Justice of Canada. Refer to the section entitled Distinguished Residents for more information on Sir William Ritchie.

The following is a compilation of the names of students who attended the Quispamsis School in 1910. Florrie Carvell, Everett Clark, Hazel Clark, Jean Clark, Kathleen Clark, Norman Clark, Walter Clark, Jack Johnston, Lilly Johnston, Robert Johnston, Walter Kelly, Prudence Mar, James McLaughlin, Katy McLaughlin, Margaret McLaughlin, Neil McLaughlin, Edna Pierce, Grace Pierce, Charlie Sherwood, Hazel Sherwood, Pearl Titus, Raymond Titus, and Clarence Vincent. These 23 names appeared on the trustee's returns.

> "We never had a day off from school" Jim McLaughlin said, "Even winter didn't stop anyone." Out of desperation one winter day, Jim and his friend, Bob Johnston, plugged the stovepipe at the school in hopes to get a day off. The teacher soon discovered the problem, but never discovered who caused the problem.
>
> *-Taken from The Kennebecasis Valley Post, Reflections.*

The Quispamsis School closed its doors shortly after the opening of Rothesay Consolidated School in 1915. After consolidation the Quispamsis School house remained empty until it was rented as a summer cottage in the early 1930's. In 1940 the old schoolhouse was turned in to a year round residence. In 1952, John Haslett purchased the property from Mr. Whittaker who had operated a small canteen just to the right of the old schoolhouse. After the Hasletts bought the old schoolhouse and the surrounding property, they opened John's General Store. John Haslett and his wife Evelyn operated the store, which was located at the site of the current Old Time Diner. The store was connected to the old one room schoolhouse by a passageway built by the Hasletts for storing supplies. The old schoolhouse acted as the Haslett's home for some time. In 1983 the schoolhouse was still standing, beside what was then Meade's Grocery Store, and was used as a private residence. The schoolhouse that had been transformed into a house by the Hasletts, was torn down after 1983. Refer to the section entitled Businesses, Hotels, and Stores for more information on John's General Store, Meade's Grocery Store, and Whittaker Canteen.

The Model Farm School:
     The Model Farm School was situated in School District 7, in the parish of Rothesay. The school was located east of the railway overpass near the intersection of the Hampton Road and the Model Farm Road. The school was originally named Otty's Crossing School.

At the turn of the twentieth century, the school was known as the Model Farm School. J.F. Humphrey built the school and reportedly provided all the building materials and physical labor for the schoolhouse in return for a payment of approximately $1,300. The secretary would not pay him until his work was completed. It is stated that the morning he obtained his payment, Humphrey took the first train to Saint John and cashed the cheque. That same afternoon he took the train back to the Model Farm area and married his fiancé at her home in Hammond River.

Model Farm School in the 1930's

In 1884, schoolteacher R. B. Wallace taught 14 students at the Model Farm School. The names of the pupils were Ford Barker, Albert Burnside, Nellie Burnside, Ernest Clark, Jennie Clark, Norman Clark, Jennie Crowley, Fred Davis, Isaac Humphrey, James Humphrey, John Humphrey, Weslie Humphrey, Arthur Kirkpatrick, and Vollie Smith.

The pupil enrollment had increased slightly by 1913, to include 19 pupils. These students were Albert Buckley, Glennie Buckley, Purdy Buckley, Robert Buckley, Bessie Burger, Hazel Leighton, Helen Leighton, Clarence Marr, Grace Meenan, Margaret Meenan, Mary Meenan, Allida Mundee, Gordon Mundee, Jean Mundee, Violet Mundee, Alex Saunders, Lena Saunders, Nora Saunders, and Kathleen Smith.

Mrs. McQuinn would usually board the Model Farm School teacher at her home near the school. Sometime between 1913 and 1923 the school was forced to close its doors due to low enrollment. However, in 1923 the school reopened after acquiring five students; the number required to operate a school. Those five students were Murray Crowley, Ruth Crowley, Theresa Higgins, William Higgins, and Gordon McMahon. The following picture was taken a few years later as there are more than five students in the photograph. Irma Webb is the teacher behind the students.

The first teacher after the school reopened in 1923 was Irma Webb. Irene Kemp taught for several years after Irma Webb. Mrs. Kemp was heavily involved with the school. She initiated a program where students would receive hot lunches in the wintertime. The meals would be heated on the wood stove in the center of the one room schoolhouse. Boys who attended the school, such as Jim Higgins, would take turns lighting the stove. Mrs. Kemp, with the help of the students and her husband, also organized a miniature minstrel play and a pie social hosted by the school. The money raised was used to buy paint for the exterior of the schoolhouse. Volunteers from the district did the painting.

A flag, which would have been a Union Jack at this point in history, was purchased to fly on the flagpole constructed by the fathers of the pupils. Lessons were given to the children instructing them how to properly raise and lower the flag. Other improvements were made to the school and school grounds. A local resident had the following three pictures, illustrating the changes that were done to the schoolhouse.

Before

After

After

Between 1924 and 1929 the Canadian Horticultural Council of Canada, the Niagara Packers Limited, and Growers and Shippers of Fresh Fruits and Vegetables began a competition among rural schools for the best-kept school grounds. The Canadian Horticultural Council donated a silver cup to be awarded to the school with the most outstanding beautification done to the school grounds. The Model Farm School won the cup for three consecutive years. The cup later became the property of the school and is currently held in the private home of a community member.

The following excerpt, which details Model Farm winning the silver cup, was taken from a newspaper. The exact date of this newspaper clipping is unknown, but it would have been close to 1929.

> "The school at Model Farm has won the silver cup which the Horticultural Council of Canada donated for competition in beautifying rural school grounds. The cup was first offered three years ago, and this year's win is the second for the Model Farm School."

The above picture is of a picnic held during school, perhaps after the students had worked on improving the school grounds. The lady with her back to the camera was identified as Irene Kemp, the teacher. The date of picture is unknown, but was found with other pictures that were taken around 1929.

On the following page is a scanned copy of the correspondence between Kenneth C. Baxter from the head office of the Niagara Packers, in Grimsby, Ontario and Theresa Higgins, the secretary of the Model Farm School. Miss Higgins was 11 when she received this letter. The letter thanks Miss Higgins for the thank you letter she sent to Kenneth Baxter's deceased father of eighteen months. This letter, dated December 24, 1929, was sent after the Model Farm School was awarded the Cup in 1929. It would have been written after the Model Farm School had won the cup for the third time and was given the privilege of keeping the cup. Based on the fact that the company who donated the cup was based out of Grimsby, Ontario, the beautification of school grounds contest was likely a national competition.

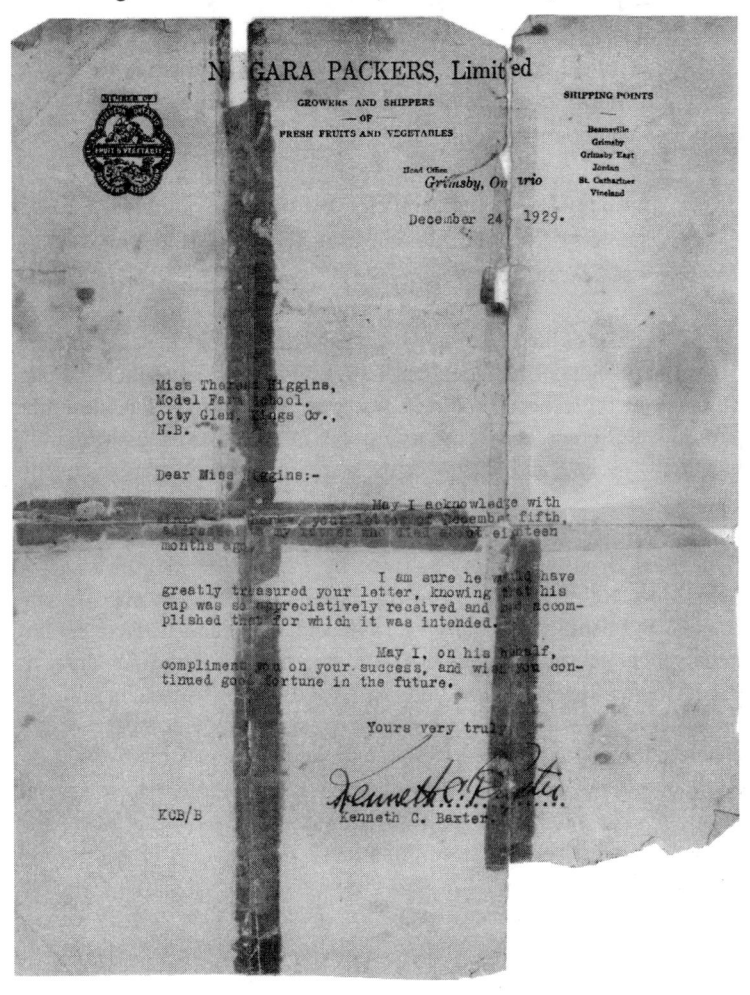

Below are some memories that were shared from individuals who had a close association with the Model Farm School.

> Mrs. Vera Stephenson was a teacher at the Model Farm School. She recalls being informed by the school secretary that due to limited funds, "once you used up your box of chalk the provision of any more is your responsibility."

> Eileen Higgins, who was a teacher at the Model Farm School from January of 1937 to June 1939, remembers traveling with her students to a music festival in Hampton. In order to participate in the music festival, they traveled by train to Hampton. The fare from the Model Farm Station to Hampton was 25 cents per person.

Some of the common games that students participated in at the Model Farm School included baseball, tag, marbles, and kick the can. Students at the other schools in the area would have played similar games. Different activities would be initiated on days when the weather was bad and the students were required to stay inside the school.

One of the textbooks used at the Model Farm School was titled "Our New Brunswick Story" written by Jessie I. Lawson, LL.D. and Jean MacCallum Sweet. This history book was published by the Canada Publishing Company in 1948 and contained text concerning items such as the coaches that ran regularly from Saint John to Fredericton, from Fredericton to Woodstock, from Chatham to Fredericton, and from Saint John to Amherst. When describing the coach that operated between Saint John and Amherst in the 1800's the textbook also describes the small communities that the coach traveled through. The pupils studying at the Model Farm would have been familiar with many of these communities.

The following excerpt was taken from a source entitled "Our New Brunswick Story."

"The Saint John-Amherst coach left Saint John at seven in the morning, and stopped at Ketchum's, Hammond River; Hayes's, Norton; Watters's at the Portage; Halstead's, Petitcodiac. The trip took three days, but the stage traveled only in the daytime; the nights were spent at comfortable inns. Anyone who wished to take this trip booked his passage the week before at John Lockhart's on the north side of King Square; and the fare to Amherst was thirty-seven shillings and sixpence."

Enrollment of pupils at the Model Farm School after the school reopened again in 1923 tended to fluctuate between 12 and 23 students until the early 1960's, when the district amalgamated with Rothesay and the school was closed. Under the Louis Robichaud Government all of the little rural schools were closed. The Model Farm school building is now a residence.

Mr. George Higgins for a time was the Secretary of the Model Farm School. As Secretary he was responsible for hiring teachers and looking after their pay. Some of the individuals who taught at the Model Farm School, and who were possibly hired by Mr. Higgins, included Theresa Glynn (Mrs. Comeau), Eileen (Stilwell) Higgins, Laura Howard, Hazel Duffy, Vera (Saunders) Stephenson, Helen Macdonald, Mrs. Beatrice H. Steeves, Dilys Loose, Jean Pickle, Mrs. Jones Baird, Maxine Richardson, Gwen Gamblin, Miss Dunn, Syliva (Wood) Clark, Irma Webb and Mrs. J. R. Kemp.

In the 1960's, sometime after the school closed, Walter McLean bought the school and converted it into a house. When he bought the house he raised it up and swung it sideways so that it was lengthwise to the road. He also supplemented the school with additions to create a bigger house.

PUBLIC SCHOOLS

CHARACTER BUILDING	Oct.	Dec.	Feb.	Apr.	June
1. COOPERATION — Works and plays well with other children. Respects rights of others.	A	A		A	A
2. RELIABILITY — Respects public and private property. Takes pride in being trusted, keeps promises, is truthful.	A	A		A	A
3. COURTESY — Polite and considerate of others.	A	A		A	A
4. INDUSTRY — Works well and steadily. Not given to idleness.	A	A		A	A
5. PROMPTNESS — Obeys promptly. Does not keep others waiting.	A	A		A	A
6. HEALTH HABITS — Sits, stands and walks correctly. Keeps clothing, hands, nails, face and teeth clean.	A	A		A	A

RATING: A - Good; B - Improvement noted; C - Improvement necessary

ATTENDANCE	Oct.	Dec.	Jan.	Feb.	Mar.	Apr.	May	Year
Days absent								
Times late								

SCHOOL WORK AND ATTENDANCE							
SCHOOL WORK	Oct.	Dec.	Jan.	Feb.	Mar.	Apr.	May
Art	80	80			B		
Language	95	81			84		
Oral Reading / Silent Reading	—				—		
Literature	80	84			89		
French	—				—		
Printing or Writing	85	80			B+		
Spelling	96	100			98		
Arithmetic	90	73			100		
Social Studies	87	79			78		
Health, Nature or General Science	67	71			78		
Music	—	89			91		
General Shop	—						
Household Arts							
Total	670	737			618		
Average	84	81.8			88.3		
Home Work	A	A			A		
General Progress	B	B			B+		

A - Excellent; B - Good; C - Fair; D - Poor

Yearly Ave — 85.6

The above is a copy of a report card issued to Ann (Thompson) Titus by her grade five teacher Maxine Richardson. Mrs. Titus attended the Model Farm School for grades one to six.

Forrester's Cove School:

Forrester's Cove school was under the jurisdiction of School District 6 in the parish of Rothesay. Forrester's Cove School was located in the area just between the junction of the Meenan's Cove Road and Rockefeller Drive. (This was the second school to operate in Gondola Point.)

The enrollment of the Forrester's Cove School averaged 23 pupils each year from 1877 until the school closed in 1915 due to consolidation. Cecelia Gallagher taught 28 pupils in 1906. The names of the students were Albert Kirkpatrick, Fred Kirkpatrick, James Kirkpatrick, Gladys Lawrence, Lillian Lawrence, Sydney Lawrence, Grace Meenan, Margaret Meenan, Grace O'Neill, Agnes Porter, Alexander Saunders, Alice Saunders, Amelia Saunders, Bessie Saunders, Edith Saunders, Flossie Saunders, Frank Saunders, Hazel Saunders, John Saunders, Lee Saunders, Myrtle Saunders, Samuel Saunders, Violet Saunders, Walter Saunders, William Saunders, Winona Saunders, Freelove Sherwood, and Florence Vail.

Hammond River School:

The Hammond River School was built in 1872 and was located in School District 5 in the parish of Rothesay. Eventually in the fall of 1904 a new school, MacDonald Consolidated School, was opened on the Kingston Peninsula and Hammond River School closed. Students who had previously attended the Hammond River School were transported by van across the Perry Point Bridge to this new school. This arrangement turned out to be problematic, especially in the winter of 1909 when the bridge washed out due to a freshet, a sudden overflow of the river resulting from heavy rainfall (or) melting snow. The school in Hammond River was reopened, as the van could no longer get to Kingston.

Anna Alley was the first teacher at Hammond River School upon its reopening in 1908. The following teachers also taught at Hammond River School before it closed: Geraldine Betts, Miss Nason, Edna Fulton, Eleanor Dickson, Irene Kemp, and Annie Darling. Annie Darling was the last teacher to teach in the school before it closed. John Darling had his Aunt Annie as a teacher when he went to the Hammond River School. At the time she lived with her brother, John Darling's father, Winfred Darling, at the Darling Homestead on the Old Neck Road.

Jean Henderson, a former student of the Hammond River School, recalls some of the procedures that were followed in the school. Jean in particular remembers the teacher reading from the Bible, reciting the Lord's Prayer, and sometimes singing a gospel hymn in the mornings. Jean can also remember saluting the Union Jack. Another recollection of Jean's was the requirement to stand up and remain standing until given permission to be seated when a visitor came to the school.

For any rural school the Christmas and June closings were special occasions for the students. The Hammond River School was no exception. Around Christmastime students would collect fir boughs and made wreaths to decorate the inside of the schoolroom. The older and taller pupils would also help decorate a Christmas tree. According to Jean Henderson the Christmas closing ceremony was always held in the evenings and speeches would be presented. The smell of the fir tree and the presents underneath the tree filled the one-room schoolhouse with an atmosphere of excitement and anticipation. Parents of the pupils brought lamps from home to light the schoolroom for the evening. In later years, the tree in the schoolhouse would be decorated with lit candles, and sparklers. The end of the year closing ceremony was just as special. As part of the activities children would put on plays. During plays the girls' cloakroom, was used as a dressing room. In June, after the last lessons were conducted, entertainment followed.

Hammond River School (1920)

Audrey Harding, Weldon Prince, Roly Darling, Dot Dodge, Mary Harding, Dot Keddy, John Darling, Winnie Darling, Ruth Prince

On Arbor Day, usually a day in the month of May, all the students of the school participated in a general cleanup of the school and its grounds. The boys were responsible for tidying up the school grounds, while the girls brought pails and cloths to clean the interior. After all the cleaning was done, there would be a picnic for all those who participated.

Like any school, the activities available to students were dependent on the weather. On days when the weather was cooperating at recess or lunchtime, the students would play baseball, hide and seek, and tag outside. On days when the weather was not cooperative at recess or lunchtime, the students would participate in activities inside the school. On those days, students would often play games that involved locating cities, rivers, mountains, and so forth, on a school map.

An inside view of the Hammond River School.

The one room schoolhouse of Hammond River School contained grades one to eight. Prizes were awarded to the students who had the highest marks upon graduation from grade eight. Upon the completion of grade eight, students could choose to continue their education at Rothesay Consolidated School or at the High School in Saint John.

In the wintertime young boys were given the chore of arriving to school early to light a fire in the wood stove. When the stove was lit the younger children, who sat closest to the fire, would be very hot while the older pupils sitting in the back would be nearly frozen.

All the furniture in the schoolhouse was handmade. The furniture primarily used by the students consisted of double desks, and benches. In those days, boys and girls sat on separate sides of the room.

Peggy Kelbaugh was born in 1915 on her father's rubber plantation in Malaya, but she grew up on a dairy farm in Hammond River. In the 1920's she attended the Hammond River School and recalls some very memorable moments.

> "Most people these days have heard of the little one room school houses that used to dot the N.B. landscape. But I wonder if people have any idea of what it was like to attend one of these schools. I went to one in the early 1920's.
>
> I grew up on a dairy farm about 18 miles from Saint John. I was an only child but lived with my 6 double first cousins. Double first cousins are the result of two sisters marrying 2 brothers. I considered these cousins my brothers and sisters. When I started school in 1921 there were 5 Hardings and five Darlings attending-You could go from grade one to grade eight. There were five Darlings in the school and their aunt, Miss Annie Darling, was the teacher.
>
> Before telling about the school I will go back to about 1919 when I was around 4 years old. Being a very small little girl I was still sleeping in a crib. We had an old grey Maltese cat as a house cat but there were about 8 male cats in the barn-kept to keep the mouse population down. The old grey cat was called "old grey". She was forever producing kittens attesting to the gang of barn suitors. One night she decided to have her kittens in my crib. I woke up to see several tiny kittens squirming around. I called

my mother who came and was horrified at the mess. She kept taking the kittens away but as soon as she took one another would appear. Being a real innocent I had no idea where they were coming from but thought it was very exciting. These kittens were of all colours, black, stripped, grey etc. Finally the 8th one was pure white. Figuring that was the last of them my mother said that we would keep the white one and it would be mine. I immediately named it "Fluffy" but at that moment it was far from fluffy. That cat grew up to follow me everywhere. Years later, one day the cousins had all gone to school and I started out on the ½ mile walk on the dusty road to the school. Soon I realized that Fluffy was following me. It seemed like the well-known nursery rhyme "Mary had a little lamb," etc. In my mind I repeated "Peggy had a little cat-it's fur was white as snow and everywhere that Peggy went that cat was sure to go."

When I got to the school I asked Miss Darling if my cat could come in the school. She said yes and maybe it would catch that "pesky" mouse that was getting in her lunch box. Now, Miss Darling always started the school day by playing on the ancient pump organ and having us sing "God Save The King" (that would be King George the fifth) and "the Maple Leaf Forever". Fluffy had been quietly sniffing around the schoolroom undoubtedly looking for that "pesky" mouse. But as soon as we started singing she was frightened and started racing around the schoolroom, even leaping over desks. Miss Darling said she must be having a fit because of our off key singing. Suddenly Fluffy gave a huge leap at the end wall of the room and her claws caught in the rough boards. She hung there and finally fell to the floor. I think her claws were nearly pulled out as I could see blood on her fur. She lay there looking dead and Miss Darling told Roly, one of her nephews, to take the cat outside. He pushed Fluffy onto the dustpan and went outside depositing her on the bank outside the school. Of course I was very upset and crying at this point. A little later there was a knock on the door and a farmer told us that there was a dead cat on the bank. He was going somewhere with a load of hay pulled by a team of horses. When he returned he informed us that the cat wasn't dead after all as it had climbed up to the top of the highest spruce tree near the schoolhouse. We all knew that cats could climb up but were afraid to come down. So I went home that day having to leave poor Fluffy in the top of the tree. It seemed that all that night I worried about how Fluffy [was] probably cold and hungry up in that tree. Next day when I got to school, Miss Darling was looking very pleased. She said that she had got roly to climb the tree and rescue the cat and it had already demolished that "pesky mouse". But she said I was to take my cat home as she didn't want a cat that was "subject to fits" in her schoolroom. I was delighted and carried Fluffy down the road and could hear strains of "The Maple Leaf Forever" wafting out of the schoolhouse. I promised Fluffy all sorts of good things to eat when we got home.

Of course there was no plumbing in the schoolroom. There was a large pot bellied wood burning stove in the center of the room. Water to drink was no problem in the winter. We filled an old scrub pail with snow and set it on the stove. In no time the snow melted and we had drinking water. In the springtime two of us were allowed to take the pail down in the nearby woods where there was a lovely spring, complete with frogs and tadpoles jumping about. I always hoped to catch a tadpole but never did. It took two of us to carry the pail of water up to the school. There was a "two hole" outhouse back of the school among some cedar trees. If you needed to go to it you raised your hand and said you had to go for #1 or # 2. Miss Darling said she had to know which because if you had to go for #2, you would be out of the schoolroom for a longer period. Of course there was no toilet paper but an old out of date Eaton's catalogue sufficed. Although it was slightly shinny it was better than the proverbial corncob.

On the large chalkboard wall at the end of the schoolroom there was a huge map of the world with all the British Empire lands in red. Also at the back there was a wooden stand holding a collection of New Brunswick stones. There was a piece of granite which we knew was used for tombstones also some quartz and mica. But the fascinating piece was white quartz containing fool's gold. There were also lots of pebbles and washed stones probably from St. Martins beach.

On another wall was a poster of all the New Brunswick birds. That has probably inspired me in later life to make a poster of the birds that we see in New Brunswick with dates of their arrival each year. Miss Darling was a great teacher and taught us a lot about nature. On a lovely spring day she would say that we would go on an "excursion." She would take us in the woods to see who would find the first violet or "Spring beauty," etc. and the first bird of the season.

Back to the use of snow. It was great for cleaning the chalk dusty floor. We would throw a shovel of snow on the floor and then sweep it up as it turned into little grey balls of snow.

As I remember the first year you were given a slate and by the second year you were allowed to have a "scribbler" far superior to the slate. The pencil used on the slate was a slim piece of stone, which made a nasty noise on the slate. The slates were just like the slates used now a days as roofing shingles. They had a red and white wooden border."

-Written by Peggy Kelbaugh

The school was eventually closed and sold. Today the old Hammond River School is a privately owned home.

Rothesay Consolidated School:
The Rothesay Consolidated School opened in 1915, and shortly thereafter all the little one-room schoolhouses in the surrounding area were closed. All of the pupils who had previously attended these one-room schoolhouses were sent to the new school in Rothesay. The Model Farm School and Wells School in the lower French Village were the last to close their doors.

Students traveled to school by foot, bike, train, horse drawn vehicles, or buses. Sometimes the pupils would take a combination of a horse drawn vehicle and then a bus to successfully reach Rothesay Consolidated. Many of the back roads were still too rough for buses to travel upon. School was never closed like it is today. Children from Four Corners, the former intersection of the Chamberlain Road and the Quispamsis Road, were driven by a horse drawn van to the Hampton Road, where they would catch the bus. The van was 7.6 meters (25 feet) long with seats on both sides and straw in the middle. The van had wheels in the summer and runners in the winter to better allow for travel through the snow-covered fields. Walter Saunders was one individual who drove the horse drawn van. Sometimes Mr. Saunders would take the children all the way to Rothesay in the van if the roads were too slippery for the bus to travel. Often the school van was cold in the winter. To pass time, children often had their own spelling bees or told stories. Occasionally, the bigger boys would try to tip the van and, when successful, all the children would be sent home.

Harmon Saunders also drove the school van from his home on the Meenan's Cove Road to Rothesay. Bricks were warmed in the oven overnight and placed on the floor of the van to help keep the childrens' feet warm. Mr. Saunders supplied buffalo blankets for the children to put on their laps.

The school van was in existence prior to the opening of Rothesay Consolidated School. Prior to driving the children to their pickup site on the Hampton Road where a bus would take the students to Rothesay Consolidated School, Walter Saunders drove students to the Quispamsis School. Walter Saunders drove the last trip made by the horse drawn van in June, 1955.

Mr. Fred F. Bishop, father of William J. Bishop, (Mayor of Rothesay, 2001 - present, 2008), and Quispamsis Councillor, Daryl Bishop, (1997 - present, 2008), drove students in the first gasoline driven school bus in Quispamsis to Rothesay Consolidated School. In the 1940's, SMT buses were used for transporting the children to and from school. The SMT buses were also employed to take the general public to and from Saint John up until the early 1970's. Fred F. Bishop drove the SMT buses in the Quispamsis and Rothesay areas for many years. Public transit has just recently come back to the Kennebecasis Valley with the new COMEX Transit System, which began in 2007. It has regular morning and late afternoon runs transporting Rothesay,

Quispamsis and Hampton residents to and from Saint John.

Rothesay Consolidated School originally only had five classrooms, plus rooms for home economics and manual training. There were separate entrances into the school for boys and girls. Some of the teachers lived as far away as Hampton and traveled back and forth to the school by train while other teachers boarded at the Kennedy House in Rothesay.

When the school first opened it housed grades one to eleven, with grade eleven being the graduation year. As time progressed grade twelve was eventually adopted. Many of the subjects taught in the school are similar to the subjects taught in school today. One subject that was taught in the early 1900's, but has since been removed from the curriculum in New Brunswick, was Latin. In those days Latin was instructed beginning in grade seven.

A typical morning at Rothesay Consolidated School consisted of roll call, the teacher reading from the Bible, reciting the Lord's Prayer, and then lessons would begin. Once a week there would be an assembly held that the whole school would attend. The teachers would sit up on a special platform in the room, and during the assembly songs would be sung.

Guilford Roberts can recall a big garden being located along one side the school. As part of the pupils' education, they had to learn how to maintain a garden. When school closed for the summer, students were responsible for having gardens or raising chickens. A school inspector or teacher would inspect how the gardens or chickens were progressing. The students would receive marks based on how well their garden or chickens were kept. In the fall when the school reopened, there would be a fair where the children would display the products of their summer projects; their vegetables or their chickens and eggs. Mr. Roberts recalls that one of the chickens he took to school in a cage laid the biggest egg so he received extra marks.

Also located on the school property was a cenotaph dedicated to the War Veterans. It was always decorated quite impressively on Remembrance Day when a public ceremony would be held at the cenotaph. As a young student at Rothesay Consolidated, Murray J. H. Carpenter can recall that it was a very somber occasion. The cenotaph was later relocated to the Rothesay Common.

Rothesay Consolidated School, date unknown

Barb Maybee and Joan Saunders (Wheaton) on the steps of Rothesay Consolidated, year unknown.

Students in grade ten or eleven at Rothesay Consolidated School.

*Margaret Poley, Phyllis Saunders (Bettle) and
June Buckley at Rothesay Consolidated,
Grade 11.*

Bon Harriet, the boy in the white jacket standing in front of Rothesay Consolidated School. He was sent to Canada from England during the Second World War as a War Child. Refer to the section entitled Involvement in the Wars for more information on Bon Harriet.

Vera Stephenson's grade one class, 1923 or 1924. Vera Stephenson is third from the left in the back row. Hope Hunter is first from the left in the back row. Audrey Stanley was absent from photo. Helen Salivan is in the middle row third from the right. Grace Dobbins is first from left middle row.

Picture taken on the steps of Rothesay Consolidated School. Date unknown.

Jean Wilson is the third student from the right in the back row. This is her grade five picture taken in 1927.

Jean Wilson's grade one picture, taken in 1923.

Students on the steps of Rothesay Consolidated School. Norman Saunders is the boy in the stripped shirt in front row, and Phyllis (Saunders) is the girl next to him. Joan Buckley, Joan Wheaton, and Betty Gilliland are also in this photograph.

Betty and Ruth Chamberlain on the steps of Rothesay Consolidated School.

Graduation photo of Jean (Tonge) Lovegrove in 1947.

Rothesay Graduation or Reunion, photo dated September 24, 1956. This picture was found among Mrs. E. Jones' notes and photos. Mr. S. D. Patterson, Principal, is in the front row.

Public Schools Today:
There are four public schools for students to attend in Quispamsis. Two of these schools, Quispamsis Elementary, (Hampton Road), and Lakefield Elementary, (Kensington Avenue) are elementary schools that serve students attending kindergarten through grade five. Quispamsis Middle School, (Pettingill Road), houses students in grades six through eight. Kennebecasis Valley High School, (Hampton Road), is the largest school in Quispamsis, and one of the largest in the Province, and offers public education to grades nine through twelve.

General School Information:
Below are three report cards, the first two are from the Model Farm School and the third is from Rothesay Consolidated School. By comparing these report cards with present day report cards, you will notice the similarities in the subjects taught.

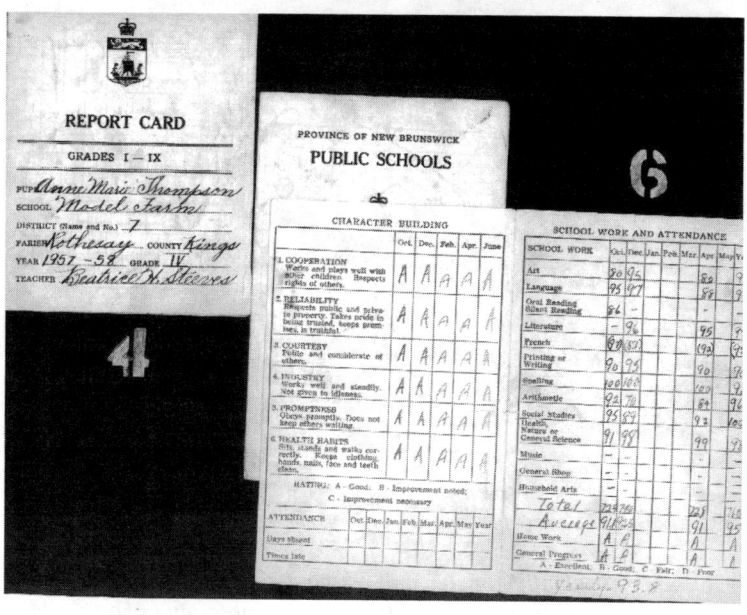

REPORT CARD

GRADES I – IX

PUPIL *Anna Marie Thompson*
SCHOOL *Model Farm*
DISTRICT (Name and No.) *7*
PARISH *Rothesay* COUNTY *Kings*
YEAR *1957 – 58* GRADE *IV*
TEACHER *Beatrice N. Steeves*

PROVINCE OF NEW BRUNSWICK
PUBLIC SCHOOLS

CHARACTER BUILDING

	Oct.	Dec.	Feb.	Apr.	June
1. COOPERATION — Works and plays well with other children. Respects rights of others.	✓	✓	✓	✓	✓
2. RELIABILITY — Respects public and private property. Takes pride in being trusted, keeps promises, is truthful.	✓	✓	✓	✓	✓
3. COURTESY — Polite and considerate of others.	✓	✓	✓	✓	✓
4. INDUSTRY — Works well and steadily. Not given to idleness.	✓	✓	✓	✓	✓
5. PROMPTNESS — Obeys promptly. Does not keep others waiting.	✓	✓	✓	✓	✓
6. HEALTH HABITS — Sits, stands and walks correctly. Keeps clothing, hands, nails, face and teeth clean.	✓	✓	✓	✓	✓

RATING: A - Good; B - Improvement noted; C - Improvement necessary

SCHOOL WORK AND ATTENDANCE

SCHOOL WORK	Oct.	Dec.	Jan.	Feb.	Mar.	Apr.	May	Year
Art	85	—		A		A	A	
Language	100				90		C	B
Oral Reading Silent Reading	80	A+		96			A	A
Literature	—	—		—		—	—	
French								
Printing or Writing	98	A+		—			A	A
Spelling	100	A+		99		100	A	
Arithmetic	90	D		93		85	A	
Social Studies	99	B+		93		90	A	
Health, Nature or General Science	100	A+		94		80	A	
Music	66	—		97			A	A
General Shop								
Household Arts	—	—		—		—	—	
Total Marks	812			662				
Rank in Class	1	1		1			1	1st
Home Work	A	B+		A	A		A	A

ROTHESAY REGIONAL HIGH SCHOOL
HOME REPORT

Report of _Anne Maries Thompson_ of Grade _8_ for the _year_ ending _June_ 19_62_

Month Ending	Arithmetic	Algebra	Geometry	Writing and Drawing	Social Studies / Geography / History / English / Language	Spelling	Reading	Nature and Health	General Science	English Literature	French	Latin / Music C. / Chemistry	Physics / Biology	Shop	Home Economics	Average	No. Pupils in Class	Rank	Times Tardy	Days Absent	Deportment	SIGNATURE OF PARENT OR GUARDIAN
SEPT. 30																				0		
OCT. 31	85				89 78 85 100		91		89											0		Mrs. L. Thompson
NOV. 30																				½		
DEC. 31 (Grad'g)	70				87 86 93 86		97 92 87 98		A+							88.5 34		3		0		Mrs. L. Thompson
JAN. 31																				1		
FEB. 26/9																				6½		
MAR. 31																				0		
APR. 30 (Grad'g)	90				95 73 93 87		88 97 97 97									87 89.6 34		3		0		L. Thompson
MAY 31																				0		
JUNE 30 (Grad'g)					87 74 93 92		85 96 91 94	A+		9½						85 86.8 34				0		
Averages											A+					88.3		3				

Marks made in December, Easter and June Grading Examinations decide grading. Past Averages: Grade 7 & 8, 65%; 9 & 10, 60%; 11 & 12, 55%.

TO PARENTS AND GUARDIANS: Parents or Guardians will find it greatly to the interest of the pupils to see that they have no tardy or absent marks. Systematic and constant efforts will be made to prevent pupils and to stimulate them to a thorough and diligent exercise of their intellectual and moral faculties. Your co-operation will greatly aid in making the work satisfactory.

S. D. Patterson Principal _V. Mae McLellan_ Teacher

Community Halls

Gondola Point Community Hall:

The Village of Gondola Point's former Community Hall has a great deal of historical significance to the Village. The following information was found in a file entitled "Community Hall 1967-History."

> "Apparently Keirstead sold property to Flewelling. Flewelling deeded the property to three trustees of Garfield Temperance in 1896 or 1898 who were: Flewelling, James Logan and Lewis Trites.
>
> They started building the hall but for one reason or another could not finish. The Orange Lodge agreed to finish it for a 21-year lease during which time they used it.
>
> After the lease was up, the Temperance Group had ceased to exist so a Mr. Jim Smith of Gondola Point and a few others made some sort of arrangement through a lawyer (Carter-now deceased) to use it. They repaired the building, ran card parties, paid the taxes on it, etc. for a number of years.
>
> In the 1950's the Gondola Point Community Association was formed who took over the use of the Hall. They paid some taxes and let the hall weekly to a Mr. Ernie Marr of Gondola Point who hosted community card parties turning $1.00 per card party back to the Association.
>
> It was used for elections in 1967. The ladies of St. Luke's W.A. used the hall weekly for some years for their meetings and along with the association which had W.A. members on its executive looked after the hall, cleaning it etc."

The community hall was situated on the property where Randon's Store was previously located on the Gondola Point Road, near where the road intersects with Saunders Drive. The Community Hall was so close to the Gondola Point Road that the stairs ran parallel to the front wall so that they would not lead directly onto the road. Though the Community Hall does not stand today, it was once the location of dances, pie socials, showers, and card parties on Friday nights.

Quispamsis Community Hall:

The Old Community Hall in Quispamsis was located on the Old Coach Road not far from the Hampton Road. The Old Coach Road originally called the Station Road, and then the Quispamsis Road, prior to the Humpback Bridge's removal.

The Quispamsis Community Hall had no particular name. It was often referred to as the Quispamsis Community Hall, the Dance Hall, or the Quispamsis Community Club. The community hall was a very social place where town wide dances were held. In the 1950's, dances at the Community Hall cost 10 cents. Later on, dances at the community hall were priced at one dollar. Individuals who could not afford the dollar would stand out back and just listen to the music. Dances were also held to celebrate special occasions such as Easter. One resident of Quispamsis recalls that dances were not held at the community hall during Lent making the dance at Easter extra special.

For young teenagers there was a Jolly Youth Club located within the community hall. The community hall was also used for a variety of other purposes including community wide wedding showers. These showers were held for residents who had recently been married. The entire community would be welcome to attend such an event.

The above photo is of the Old Dance Hall located on the Old Coach Road in 1944.

Gondola Point Recreation Centre:

In the late 1970's the Louis Robichaud government was donating money to small communities for further development. The Village of Gondola Point submitted a plan to buy local property for the purpose of constructing a recreational centre. The Village of Gondola Point eventually purchased several acres of land from Jessie Rolfe.

Though the building had been completed a few months prior, the official opening of the Gondola Point Recreation Centre was on June 25, 1977. This opening was held in conjunction with a "Canada Week" celebration.

The following article appeared in The Kings County record, written by Barb Landry, concerning the opening of the Gondola Point Recreation Centre.

>Gondola Point's new recreation centre was officially opened Saturday, June 25. Presiding over the day's events was Mayor Lloyd Marshall.
>
>Harmon Saunders, Gondola Point's oldest citizen, cut the ribbon. Mr. Saunders is 87 years young and tends to 27 head of cattle everyday.
>
>In his opening speech he told the residents that in order to keep the community the happy place it has always been, the senior citizens of the community must keep on working along side the young generation not against each other.
>
>M.P., Gordon Fairweather, was on hand to help open the recreation centre. Mike Walton, student and a Queen's Scout read the opening prayer. Guest and residents then proceeded into the centre where the Lancaster Kiwanis Steel Band under the direction of Walter Ball provided the music. A chicken barbeque was held later and enjoyed by all.
>
>John Gardner of the Kennebecasis Scouting district served the mayor with a writ and the Rothesay Police then placed Mayor Marshall in the mock jail where he was later made an honorary member of the Gondola Point Scouting movement. The evening wound up with a dance for the whole family, which was also very enjoyable.

On October 18, 1979, a meeting was held between residents of

Gondola Point, the Village Council, and the Gondola Point Recreation Expansion Committee. It was decided that the Recreation Centre should be expanded at a cost of $180,000 to the Village of Gondola Point. On June 12, 1980 the Village asked the Capital Borrowing Board for $180,000 for the expansion at a rate of 14 percent for 15 years.

June 1977, Official opening of the Gondola Point Recreation Center, Meenan's Cove Road, Mayor Lloyd Marshall
Left to Right: John Gardner, Mike Walton, Bob Ross, Joe Scott, Malcolm Barry, Unknown, Jack Stevens, Unknown, Lloyd Marshall (Mayor), John Robinson, (Quispamsis Mayor), Harmon Saunders, Jordon Miller, Joe Streeter, Unknown.

Many recreation facilities were developed as part of the Recreation Centre complex including tennis courts, trails, a track, a playground and three fields used for soccer and softball. Numerous clubs and classes have been held at the Centre over the years including activities for seniors, after school programs, youth dances, gymnastics, and art and craft courses.

It is also the proposed site for the new QPlex Project (2008)

QPlex:

At the time of this writing, (2008), the new and innovative QPlex Project is in the design stage. It will be the largest project to date that the Town of Quispamsis has undertaken, and will go a long way to meet the needs of this ever-growing community. There will be something for everyone including an NHL sized ice surface operational 12 months of the year, designed for possible future twinning; an outdoor swimming pool, a trade and convention centre and an indoor walking trail to be located on the 80 acres of land at the Recreation Centre site. The project will be one of the first LEED Certification 'green' projects in Atlantic Canada.

Quonset Hut:

The land the Quispamsis Memorial Arena currently occupies was at one time used to host community clubs and the circus. Every year the county gave each community a portion of the funds that were collected from taxes the previous year. One year the community of Quispamsis decided to use a portion of these funds to build a rink house. Originally, the plan was to build a two storey square building, but, due to the limited budget, a Quonset hut was built. A Quonset hut is a round metal building made from prefabricated pieces of galvanized steel. The Quonset hut was used primarily to house the community clubs and bingo games. At this point the skating rink was still located outside of the building, and flooded by local volunteers.

Former Council Member, Ron Magee, was often seen on cold winter evenings flooding the outdoor rink for the young people of the community.

The Quonset Hut was dismantled and removed to make room for the Quispamsis Memorial Arena.

Civic Building:

In January of 1982 a two-story Civic Building was built in Quispamsis. This building contained the Community Centre, the Rothesay Fire Department's satellite station as well as the Ambulance Service. In recent years, the Civic Building underwent extensive renovations, with the upstairs used as a community hall, and the down stairs portion used as Fire Station No. 2.

Recreation & Culture

Winter Activities:

Skating and skiing were two outdoor activities that people enjoyed in the winter. Often people could be seen skiing down the Hampton Road as there was a limited amount of traffic on that street. McAfee Hill, on the corner of the Pettingill Road and the Quispamsis Road, was another beloved spot for skiing. There was also a little ski hill run by the Hardings that was located just prior to the Hammond River train tracks when heading towards Route 100. Hardings' ski hill was even equipped with a ski tow.

Mud Lake was a great place to go skating or to play hockey. Young people had a number of paths cut through the woods surrounding Mud Lake to the skating pond. The local boys could often be seen taking old tires down to Mud Lake to use when lighting bonfires at night. Ritchie Lake was also used for skating but one had to stay clear of where the springs fed into the lake, as these areas did not freeze well. The Rothesay Common was another popular spot for skating parties or hockey championships. Teachers often took their classes to the Rothesay Common to skate. Some residents remember returning to the school after skating and going to the home economics classroom for a mug of hot chocolate.

Spring, Summer and Fall Activities:

Traffic on the road was not a major concern prior to the 1920's and 1930's. Not many people owned a car in the Kennebecasis Valley in the 1920's and 1930's so roads would often be used for roller skating races. These races would begin in Rothesay and end at the Gondola Point Beach. Along the route, roller skaters would be required to stop and give one or two pennies. At the end of the race the person who won would receive all the money collected.

In the early to mid 1900's, activities enjoyed by youth were somewhat different than those of today. Young children would often build camps in the woods, without the worry of trespassing on land owned by someone else. Hister-sails was a popular game played by many children. According to one resident in order to play this game "you would go and hide, if you got caught, that's tough, but if you wanted to get on the base [home base] then you would run to it and say Hister-sails." There were other favourite games played by the children including Red Line and Baseball. Baseball was a popular sport that would be played without an official field, and often arguments occurred as a result of not having visible bases or foul lines. Versions of these games are still played by children today.

Cecil Johnston donated the above picture; the photo is of a homemade tent and is dated 1930.

Memorial Field:
      Memorial Ball Field was a project started by Provincial Police Constable Ned Sowery along with the Memorial Field Committee. Refer to the section entitled Distinguished Residents for more information on Ned Sowery. The field, which is still in use today, was constructed next to the Food Bank and the Quispamsis Memorial Arena. Mr. Sowery was very dedicated to ensuring the creation of this field, partly due to the fact it was to act as a memorial to the veterans of World War II. This is why the ball field was christened Memorial Field.

Kennebecasis Public Library:
      The Kennebecasis Public Library, a branch of the Saint John Regional Library system is located at 3 Landing Court. It was built in 1984 as another regional service amongst the Towns of Quispamsis and Rothesay and the Villages of Fairvale, Gondola Point, East-Riverside-Kingshurst and Renforth.

Below is an article that appeared in the December 30, 1983 publication of the Evening Times Globe:

"Library Plans Back on Track

Plans to build a Saint John Regional Library Branch in Quispamsis are back on the tracks, says the vice-chairman of the Kennebecasis Public Library Inc.

East Riverside-Kingshurst Village Councillor Peter Glennie says purchase of a 1.7 hectare property at The Landing Mall will likely be closed within the next two weeks.

It will be bought from the Bank of Montreal for $110,000 but $70,000 worth will be sold to the Rothesay Regional Board of Police Commissioners, he said.

The deal was held up until this week while Gondola Point, Fairvale, Rothesay, Quispamsis, East Riverside-Kingshurst and Renforth finalized the contract needed to bring the jointly-run Rothesay Regional Police Force into being, he said.

Although tenders for construction of the proposed library have been opened, a contractor has not yet been chosen, Councillor Glennie said.

The library facility will consist of a one-storey building and a 50 car parking lot with a total cost estimated around $266,000, he said.

Renforth will pay 3.4 percent of the cost, East Riverside-Kingshurst 3.4 per cent, Rothesay 8.3 percent, Fairvale 24 percent, Quispamsis 40 percent and Gondola Point 20 percent.

The Board of Directors for the library corporation consists of council members from the six communities."

"April 10, 1984, Evening Times Globe - OFFICIAL START; A sod-turning at The Landing Mall Monday marked the official start of building the Kennebecasis Public Library in Quispamsis as the seventh branch of the Saint John Regional Library system. Library officials hope to see the doors open by the middle of June. Here Saint John-Fundy MLA, B. J. Harrison mans the ceremonial shovel watched by East Riverside-Kingshurst Councillor Peter Glennie, left, vice-chairman of the Kennebecasis Public Library Inc. board of directors, and Richard McPhee, a former Quispamsis town councillor who is the town's representative on the board.

Quispamsis Memorial Arena:

With the opening of the Quispamsis Memorial Arena in 1983, both minor hockey and figure skating became very popular with young people in the community as well as public skating. Ice sports have continued to grow to the point that in 2007 the Quispamsis Town Council decided to build another ice surface.

Meenan's Cove Park & Beach House:

Located at Meenan's Cove on the Kennebecasis River along Model Farm Road, this park features a ballfield, beach volleyball courts, walking trail, picnic facilities and playground. In addition, it has a popular public beach, boat launch, docking facilities and a beach house.

Peat Drive Park :

This Park was originally developed as part of a Development Scheme By-law in the 'down town' area of the Hampton Road in the late 1980's and consisted of a beautifully landscaped green area with flower beds and park benches. The land was subsequently sold with proceeds of the sale going towards development of the new Arts & Culture Park, directly across the street, where the gardens were relocated.

Quispamsis Arts & Culture Park:

Below is a Press Release issued from ACOA, August 7, 2006 concerning the opening of the new Arts & Culture Park located behind the Town Hall, Landing Court:

FOR IMMEDIATE RELEASE
August 7, 2006

Arts and Culture Park to stimulate tourism in Quispamsis

Quispamsis, New Brunswick - The Town of Quispamsis celebrated today the grand opening of its new Arts and Culture Park. The event took place in conjunction with festivities for the Town's 40th Anniversary Celebration and New Brunswick Day events.

"I am confident that the Town of Quispamsis will see the positive impact of this new Arts and Culture Park as families and tourists use it year-round," said MP Moore, on behalf of the Honourable Peter MacKay, Minister of Foreign Affairs and Minister of the Atlantic Canada Opportunities Agency (ACOA). "Canada's new government supports projects in New Brunswick that will benefit generations to come."

MLA Brenda Fowlie said, "as MLA for Kennebecasis I am very pleased to be sharing in this important occasion with ACOA and the Town of Quispamsis. People from our Town and the surrounding area have a beautiful new central place to celebrate our vibrant arts and culture community and to host a wide range of regional events.

"We are very pleased to officially open our new Quispamsis Arts and Culture Park," said Quispamsis Mayor Ron Maloney. "The park has created a real sense of pride in our community. It will always remain a focal point where residents and neighbours can gather and enjoy all the delights that this park has to offer."

The Arts and Culture Park is an open-air art gallery where local artists can display their works and promote their talents. The Park will also provide a new and unique venue for art workshops, festivals, musical performances, outdoor movies and markets designed to bring the community together and attract more visitors to the area. During the winter months, an outdoor rink with music and lighting will be a festive addition to the town's existing outdoor activities.

The Government of Canada invested a total of $488,284 in the project under ACOA's Strategic Community Investment Fund. The Province of New Brunswick also supported the project contributing $60,000, through the Environmental Trust Fund and the Family and Youth Capital Assistance Program. Other financial contributors include J.D. Irving, Limited, the Greater Saint John Community Foundation, the Sobey's Foundation, the Quispamsis Island View Lions Club and the Rotary Club of Rothesay-Kings.

Below is the plaque located in the Arts and Culture Park that recognizes the sponsors that made the creation of this beautiful Park possible.

Arts and Culture Park
2006

FOUNDING PARTNERS - PARTENAIRES FONDATEURS
Atlantic Canada Opportunities Agency
Agence de promotion économique du Canada atlantique
Town of - Ville de Quispamsis

COMMUNITY PARTNERS - PARTENAIRES COMMUNAUTAIRES
J.D. Irving, Limited   Rotary Club of Rothesay-Kings   Sobey's Foundation
Environmental Trust Fund - Fonds en fiducie pour l'environnement
Province of New Brunswick - Province du Nouveau Brunswick
Greater Saint John Community Foundation
Quispamsis Island View Lions Club

Arts & Culture Park, late summer, 2006

Winter Scene, Arts & Culture Park, 2006
Photos by Megan Lucas

Trails:
Over the years Quispamsis has put resources towards the creation and maintenance of walking trails throughout the community. There are currently, (2008) four trails maintained by the Town of Quispamsis- the Hammond River Nature Park, Mud Lake Nature Park, Saunders Brook Trail and Matthew's Cove Trail located at the Gondola Point Recreation Centre, and trails along portions of Ritchie Lake. Due to their popularity with residents of all ages, trails will continue to expand throughout the community.

Youth Organizations:
One of the youth organizations in the community was Cadets, which is still a strong organization in Quispamsis today. The following is a picture of Phyllis Bettle, an Army Cadet member, dressed in her uniform. The uniform consisted of a navy skirt, a white shirt, and a black tie.

Other:
Over the years the school gymnasiums and fields and church halls were used as gathering places for many youth activities, whether it be basketball, floor hockey, brownies, guides, scouts or youth choirs. Baseball has continued to be popular sport in the community as well as in later years a growing interest in soccer, rugby and football. Ice Hockey has also continued as a favorite sport in the community.

Teen Centre:
In 1992 the Town of Quispamsis, along with the Rothesay Regional Police, established the first teen centre in Quispamsis. This was to be a fun and safe place for teens to call home. In 1995 the sport of skateboarding took off in Quispamsis so it was decided that an indoor skate park would be added to the teen centre. This new complex became known as the Warehouse Skate Park/Teen Centre, and was the first of its kind in New Brunswick. The Warehouse Skate Park/Teen Centre has since closed.

Beaches

Ritchie Lake:

      The Ritchie Lake swimming area was originally on the Maple Grove Court side of the lake, where the railway tracks run (on the opposite side of the lake from current beach). At the original site there was a little swimming area and a sandy beach. The easiest way to get to the beach was by walking down the tracks. Other popular activities that took place at Ritchie Lake were fishing, boating, and skating.

Patsy Briggs and Barb (Allison) Williams enjoying a day at Ritchie Lake.

This is Frank Cameron, and on the bow, his wife, Elsie in a rowboat on Ritchie Lake, 1922. The woman and baby at the stern of the boat are unidentified.

From left to right: Florence Carvel, unknown relative, and Minnie Mathews Carvel (Florence's mother). Taken with the view of Ritchie Lake in the background. Year unknown.

Gondola Point Beach:

The Gondola Point Road, prior to the creation of the arterial, connected directly to the Gondola Point Beach. The pictures below are of the Gondola Point Beach, the ferry landing at the beach, and the Golden Slipper.

253

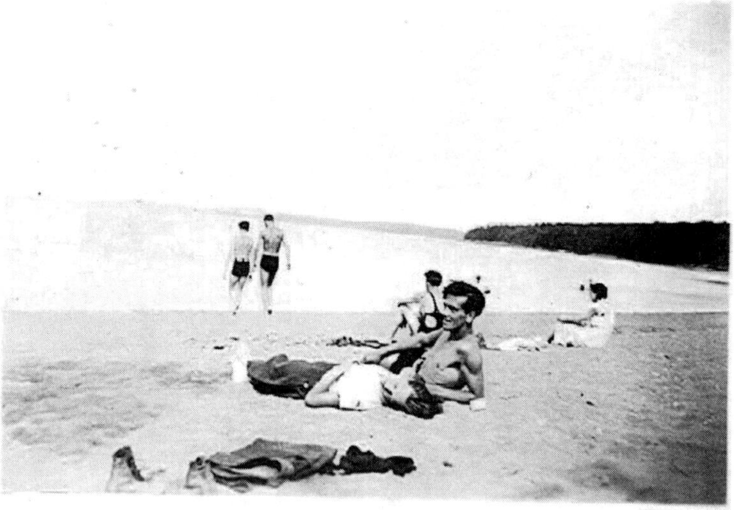

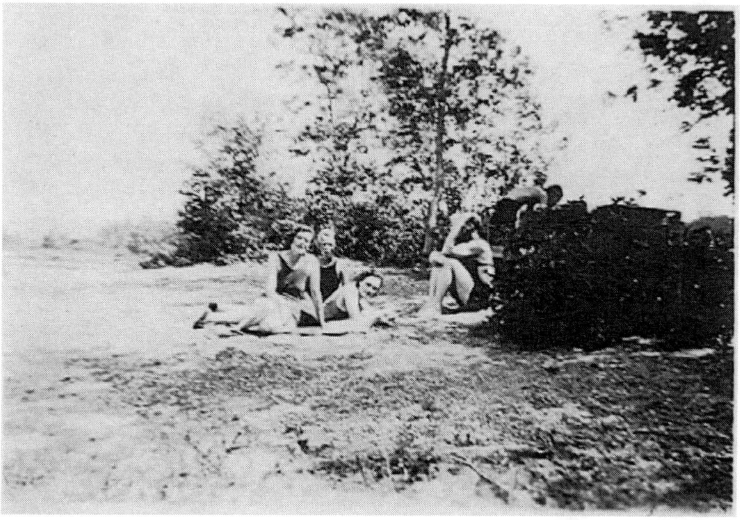

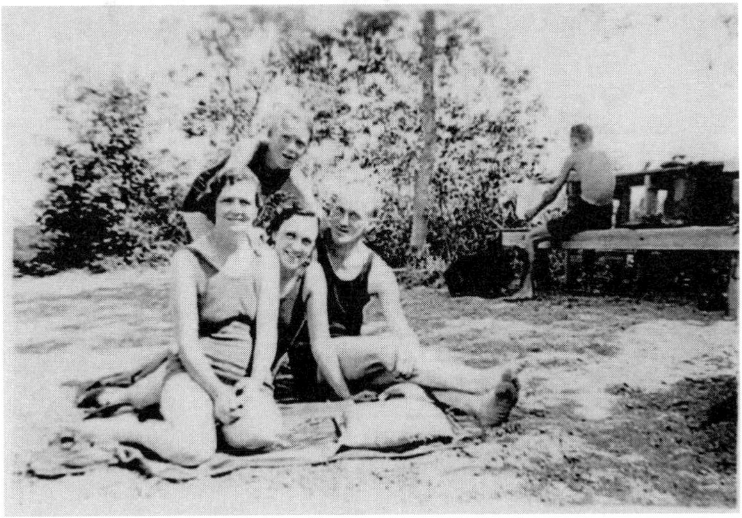

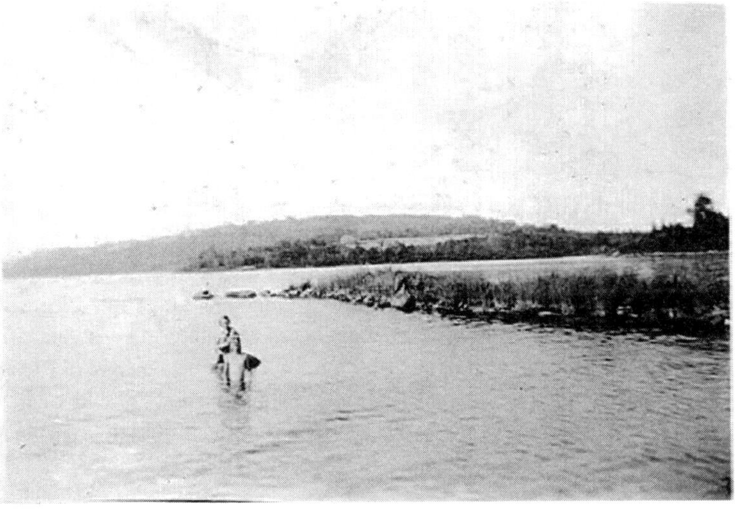

The Golden Slipper, winter of 1931

      In the 1920's and 1930's, a pavilion called the Golden Slipper drew people to Gondola Point Beach. People were attracted to the Golden Slipper, which was constructed on poles to prevent flooding in the springtime when the river rose, for its game machines and dances.

      In the mid 1900's, an attendant was available to park cars for visitors to the beach who arrived by automobile. The D .J. Purdy was later located at the Gondola Point Beach shortly after the end of the Second World War. Refer to the sections entitled Entertainment and Transportation by Water for more information on the D. J. Purdy.

*Vera & Oscar Saunders, Gondola Point Road
near the Ferry Landing, 1944.*

Meenan's Cove Beach:

The original Meenan's Cove Beach was located on the property owned by Jack Meenan at the end of Chamberlain Road. A walking path, which began at the Chamberlain Road, was created through the woods to the beach. Mr. Meenan would charge people 25 cents to swim at his beach. Young people would often pack a picnic lunch and spend the day at the beach. The unofficial changing rooms were in the bushes.

Jack Meenan's old home no longer exists at its original location. When Gordon Peacock purchased the property, he moved the old Meenan's farmhouse up to a corner lot and built his house where Jack Meenan's house once sat. The old farmhouse has since been torn down. Today the Peacock family privately owns the water front property.

The property the beach is on today was purchased by the Town at a cost of approximately $45,000 in the 1970's. Once the Town purchased the land, they employed crews to dive and remove whatever logs and debris they could find, that may have been left by the Irving logging company, in order to provide the public with a safe and pleasant place for swimming. Today on the property there is a baseball field, volleyball court, barbeque pit, walking trail, playground, boat launch, beach house, canteen equipped with changing rooms, and monitored swimming facility.

Entertainment

Drive-In Movie Theatre:

In Quispamsis in the mid to late 1900's a drive-in movie theatre existed between the Pine Valley and Hillcrest Trailer Parks, and was owned by the McKinney's. Each parking spot at the drive-in was equipped with a set of speakers to allow the passengers in the car to listen to the movie. A canteen was located on the site to fulfill the moviegoers snacking needs.

The D.J. Purdy:

The D. J. Purdy was a popular entertainment spot for residents of the area. The Purdy was an old Saint John Riverboat that had been beached at Gondola Point Beach in 1946 at the location known as the "Frog Pond." It became a place to dance and to socialize over food. At the Purdy, customers would be served hamburgers before dancing the night away to swing and early rock and roll music from the jukebox. A few local residents joked that it was a task to find the meat in hamburgers at the Purdy because the burgers were so small. Refer to the section entitled Transportation by Water for more information on the D. J. Purdy.

Located at the beach before the Purdy was a pavilion called the Golden Slipper. The Golden Slipper was a canteen that attracted people to its dances and game machines. For more information on the Golden Slipper refer to the section entitled Beaches.

Dances and Card Parties:

Between the 1930's and the 1960's, two of the most popular activities in Quispamsis were dances and card parties. Neighbours would often gather at each other's houses or at the local community halls on Friday nights to play cards. Square dancing and card games were events that were held frequently at the local community halls in Quispamsis and Gondola Point.

Dances were popular from the 1930's to the 1960's. Several people met their significant others at the community dances. People would often attend the dances in surrounding communities as well, sometimes traveling as far away as Kingston, Norton and Nauwigewauk. On Thursday nights dances were held at Golden Grove, Friday nights in Nauwigewauk, and Saturday nights at the Quispamsis Community Hall. The Quispamsis Dance Hall, which was located along the Old Coach Road between the Hovey Road and the Hampton Road, typically hosted square dances on Saturday night. The Community Hall also hosted round dances and ballroom dances on a number of Saturday nights. A live band would provide the music on these occasions.

Wedding Activities:

Community Wedding Showers were generally held at the Quispamsis Community Centre. A Community Wedding Shower was a shower held for anyone who had recently been married. The entire community was welcome to attend these events.

A shivaree, the word being the common corruption from the French word charivari, was a very common event following a wedding in the community. A shivaree is the term used to describe a noisy mock serenade (made by banging pans and kettles) for newlywed couples. On these occasions, community members would often gather outside the home of the newlyweds, on the night they were married or over the honeymoon period, with noisemakers such as pots, pans, and bells. The residents of Quispamsis also took the shivaree one step further by playing practical jokes, inside the home of the newly married couple.

Creating a Local Newspaper:

One form of entertainment that local families, such as the Leonard's and their friends, enjoyed in the summer was the creation a local paper they called the Quispam Herald. The paper was solely for entertainment value and was only circulated amongst family and close friends. The following pages are examples of the newspapers created by the Leonard family, their friends, and their neighbours in the early 1900's.

QUISPAM HERALD
— XMAS EDITION —

Dec 25, 1919.   FREE. Count Faraway paid for YOU.

A VERY MERRY CHRISTMAS TO YOU ALL.

It is again the privilege of the Editor to quietly seat himself in the old chair and try to go over the many events that have transpired during the past year.

Politically our town has been very quiet. William Hayward was again elected Mayor. He had the entire support of the women voters. Roy Sipprell was elected Chief of Police over his father-in-law by one vote. Lloyd Farquhar was elected Truant Officer for the third time. He was also elected Chicken Inspector. Sid Jones by some kind of a pull was elected Pound Keeper. It is reported that he will take charge of all the calves found astray. Jack Leonard, our genial Doc, had no difficulty in obtaining the entire support of the ladies and was elected Supt of the Sunday School.

Socially the season was a success with the exception of the night Edna Leonard and a crowd of of other hoodlums would not let Sid Jones keep his date with a charming young lady.

The only event that really marred the season was the theft of one of our beloved girls by the Editor of the Eastport Sardine.

Many thanks are due the Senior Leonards for the many pleasant times spent at their residence. The Editor takes it upon himself to express to them that the town would be DEAD without their hospitality.

It is with pleasure that the Editor again wishes you all A Merry Xmas and A Happy New Year.

The crops during the past year have been exceedingly good and the cellars are filled for winter.

For the past two years the Editor has been watching with much interest the garden of Willie Hayward.

He has come to the conclusion that the Mrs has more to do with it than Bill.

Good work Al. We will elect you Matron of the range at the next Annual meeting.

Poor Dad.

WELCOME

Since our last edition our numbers have been increasing and we take great pleasure in announcing that our esteemed friend and neighbor Knowles has taken upon himself a wife. Welcome Wifey.

Doc Leonard has purchased a new car. One man power. Containes a milk tank, capacity one half pint, and all other modern conveniences. The last time he was seen on the street with it a distinct rattle was heard.

Although only with us for a short time we wish to announce the election of the Count's mother as an Honorary Member of our Clan.

The Editor of the Eastport Sardine Has been admitted to our midst by marriage. He didn't have to do that as we would have elected him anyway.

EXPOSED

Doctor John Gould Leonard was seen at The Clifton House for supper a few evenings ago. While there a boy delivered him a note, which was picked up after he had left. While we do not beleive in going into family affairs it may be of interest to some and a good tip to the married women of our community. Hence we are printing copy of note.

Dec 12th, 1919.

Dear Jack:-
Come home. Forgive and forget. I have destroyed my cook-book of war recipes. Will use Mother's cook book in the future.
Your devoted wife.

Note: The Editor would suggest that the single girls also take notice. Even Kitchen Hounds have a keen sense of taste.

SERVICE

We wish to announce that we are now taking telephone orders for all of our wares. This has come about by the admission of a new member to our firm (Silent partner) namely Willie Weeks, who will carry your parcels ordered by phone.

HAYWOOD & STRAW.

OH! GIRLS

On December First a large number of our citizens, mainly young ladies, made a trip to St John to participate in the celebration of St Andrew's night. The entertainment was good. The dancing was up to the regular standard but the crowd was really disappointed as they expected to see our friend Burpee in the kilt.

It is with pleasure that the Editor announces that through a pull with a close relative of our friend, a picture, taken only a short time ago, has been procured. This we are reproducing for the benefit of all who do not remember when it was a common sight to see him starting over the hill with the bag pipes.

It may be of interst to note that since this picture was taken Burpee has lost Three pounds and four ounces.

P.B. GUM HAS THE SNAP.

On account of what the Editor knows about his past life we recommend that you all trade with

FATHER THE CANDY KID.

It has been reported on good authority that Percy has seen Father and was received with welcomed arms.

(Note bank book under arm and Victory Bonds in left hand.)

The school teacher had punished little Margaret so often for talking during school, and the punishments had been apparently without effect, that, as a last resort, she decided to notify Margaret's father of his daughter's fault. So following the deportment mark on her next report were the words:

"Margaret talks a great deal."

In due time the report was returned with her father's signature and under it was written:

"Your ought to hear her mother."

HAMPTON SPECIAL

Brown: Hello Smith. Met you on the road to Sussex the other day.
Smith: That so. Didn't see you.
Brown: Does your car pick up pretty quickly now?
Smith: Well on a good night I can pick up one in a block or so.
Brown: Thought so.

The Editor with Doughnuts saw the famous play "Aunt Ed's Beau" at the Dime last Saturday night. This play was written by herself and he was grand.
We understand that Auntie is about to put on another play "A Women's Mind" in four parts. The only comment we can make is that she largly underestimates th number of parts.

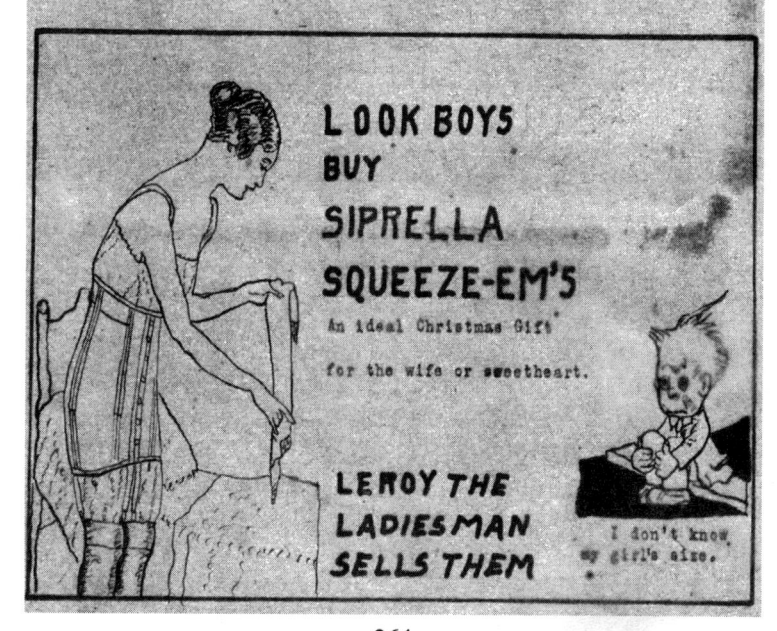

LOOK BOYS
BUY
SIPRELLA
SQUEEZE-EM'S

An ideal Christmas Gift
for the wife or sweetheart.

LEROY THE LADIES MAN SELLS THEM

I don't know my girl's size.

~QUISPAM CHRONIC~

Edited by Faith and Hope

Fee---The Sunshine of Your Smile.   Fee Delivered---A Little Love, a Little Kiss [Payable in Advance]

Editorials

This is not a TRY-yearly publication but is DO once in a life-time.

To the members of Clan Quispam, we extend our heartiest greetings. We do not ask your support as we feel that you have all you can do to support the Editor of the Quispam Herald.

What's This!! What's This!!!!!

The Road Commissioner, Mr. Roysie Sipprelli has demanded the recall of Mayor Bill Haywood. It is understood that there is a great deal of dissatisfaction over the way he has dealt with some important matters. There is some talk of electing a lady mayor, and it is rumored that this is Mr. Sip's suggestion.

Welcome

Miss Jane Leonard is welcomed into our clan and has the distinction of being the youngest member. At a very early age she proved herself a true member of the Clan by risking one eye on Mr. Sid Jones, the popular Editor of Sunday School Times.

Lost

Somewhere between 268 Princess Street., St. John and New York last August, a pale pink Dresden Powder Bag. Finder will kindly return in person to owner and receive reward. Shorty.

A. R. Badges Awarded

A certain young lady in our Community has been awarding "A. R." badges to a number of so called "Honest Men" who have applied in answer to her ad. in the Quispam Herald. The ad. is still running and the young lady is still hoping.

We are sorry to report that Mr. Jones still sees visions of bars in spite of the untiring efforts of the Quispam W. C. T. U.

Announcements

Inasmuch as there has been a change of faith in our little Faith, we feel it only too fitting and proper, out of due respect to her that further meetings of th' Clan be held on evenings other than Saturday. Since then circumstances have arisen that show her that "Old Time 'Ligion" is good enough for her even she can't have picnics on Sunday.

Applicants whose applications to the V. A. D. School were filed last October will report to Headquarters in August for their first lesson on the full of the moon. These lessons start with your first quarter and end with your last quarter.

Shorty is going to open a cafeteria at Quispam during August.

Issie. Rachael says she was twenty-four last Sis day.

Vassie. Yes, twenty-four marked down from twenty-nine.

Diogenes Loses Hope

We have just learned that Diogenes has given up his quest in disgust. He could not find an honest man so he sold his lantern and with the proceeds bought several hundred shares in the V. A. D. School. (We advise our little Ed. to do likewise. They are not to be found even among Baptist ministers).

Styles

The very latest word from New York is "Bustles, Bustles, Bustles!" all shapes and sizes. I think we are a little behind New York in this style. On the other hand, the bustles are behind many of us. Rose sweaters with khaki belts are in vogue. We note the shortage of skirts has been overcome. Striped stockings have been imported from New York and when introduced by a dashing young divorcee made quite an impression on the masculine minds of Quispam.

What puzzles the small boy is how mother can wear such a hot slipper.

The Christian Herald reports the discovery of a safety pin 3,000 years ago. This proves that fashions for infants are time-honored at least (Bill Haywood kindly take note of this as we understand that he is interested in antiques).

St. John Street Railway has instituted a new style of 6 cent car fares.—(Shorty please take note).

Notice

Service will be held in the Quispam Tabernacle Sunday morning at 11. Sermon—"The Prodigal Son."

Society Notes

Harvey will be at home to eligible young men most any evening.

Clan Quispam has recently enjoyed a very pleasant visit from a representative of the Passamaquoddy Tribe, and all feel that our hearts are made brighter and our wits much sharper after coming in contact with Big Chief Emery.

Knowlsie is still with us but for how long we cannot tell. By gorry.

Miss Rachael Haywood is in Halifax organizing a branch of the "Sisters of Israel."

Our little Ed spent Peace Day in Clifton.

Queries

1 What is love? Rachael—Ans. Love is faith in a jewelled setting.

2 Is it proper for a young lady to make dates with a young man on the Bridge at 12.15? Lois. Ans. I should say yes.

Little beams of moonshine,
Little hugs and kisses
Make a little maiden
Change her name to Mrs.

QUISPAM CHRONIC

3 Why does firelight make one think of the past and moonlight of the future? Sid—Ans. Ask Rachael.

4 Where do parrots come from? Faith—Ans. Jerusalem by the look of their beaks.

5 Should a young lady kiss a captain of the ship farewell after a pleasant voyage to the Tropics? Ans. Not if Harvey is near.

Music, Literature and Science
Favorite Songs

Al.—I wonder what will William Tell.
Jen.—Father get the hatchet, there's a fly on Baby's nose!
Grace—Where is my wandering boy tonight?
Carrie—A serenade in a Major.
Leora—I won't go home with Riley any more.
Faith—Love's Sorrow.
Vera—It's nice to get up in the morning but it's nicer to lie in bed.
Lois—Every little girl can teach you something.
Edna—Heaven is my home.
Bill—Daddy did a wonderful thing.
Jack—I'd love to be working in the Zoo.
Roy—I can dance with everybody but my wife.
Lloyd—I'm a 12 o'clock fellow in a 9 o'clock town.
Herbert—Good-bye, girls, I'm through.
Percy—As a Romeo I'm an onion.
Major Weeks—Chi rafferna il mio furore?

New Books

"How to Approach Father" by Count Faraway.
    Illustrated by Harvey.
"Villains After Dames, or Reminiscences of a Yankee Settler," by Sid Jones.
"Quispam Then and Now," by Willie Haywood, Sr.
"From Safety Pin to the Grave," by J. G. Leonard.
    With illustrations. Bound with kid.
"How I Won the Battle of Quispam in Spite of Shortage of Arms," by Major Weeks.
"The Goat of Quispam" by Shorty.
    Bound with calf.
"Short Stories,—How to Cultivate a Short Memory, Cabbageheads," etc., by P. Brigham Y. Leonard.
    Ill. by author.

A wonderful new specimen of bug life was found by Prof. Emery of Eastport not long ago at Matthews Cove. It has been called Twigorum Edna-cuss. He has also made some other very marvellous discoveries recently.

We are very anxious to know if Prof. Jones has yet discovered if Quispam is a flower or a disease. If it is the latter we hope he may become a chronic sufferer with the malady.

A Pome by Jack Entitled
Alice

She opens her window
    And looks on the lake.
O'er its slumbering surface
    No murmers awake.

Afar o'er the hill top
    The moon has long set;
The morning breeze freshens,
    Why tarries Bill yet?

A sound in the distance,
    A slow moving train,

Yes! yonder's a searchlight,
    I think I'll remain.

'Tis Bill! Safe returning!
    Joy leaps to her eyes!
And clasped to her bosom,
    "My Husband" She cries!

Another Pome
By Shorty

I'm a little New York flower
    Growing wilder every hour.
No ones cares to cultivate me,
    I'm wild, wild, WILD ! ! !

Query by Ed. (for male readers only): Can you tame wild wimmen?

"Honest" Diogenes Exposed at Last!
by H. I. Knowles, F. R. S. C. Q.

I smile and wink at that ancient tale,
    Of Diogenes' search for an honest male,
For, in sooth, 'tis plain as plain can be
    That the old chap himself lacked honesty.
If honest, why should he search the wild world o'er
    With an honest man at his very door?
No! he had been fooled by a covey of girls,
    Chorus ladies, perhaps, or society whirls,
And his quest, therefore, the result of cruel fate,
Was really a search for an honest mate.
Hence, historians have no right to re-tale
As original Diogenes' search for an honest male.
To whom this honor belongs, I can readily tell.
'Tis to that honest-man-searcher named.
    Peggy O'L.

A Mellow-Drama,—
Ending In Tragedy

(Describing a frequent occurrence in the career of the famous Ed.)

A maid and man sat underneath
    The large Quispamsis moon.
And did what maids and men will do,—
    They soon began to spoon.

His arm was long and large and strong
    No Lantac did he need.
He swept her into his embrace
    —The time did swiftly speed.

Thought he: "I cannot better do
    Than make this maid my wife.
The happiness that now I feel,
    —Why can't it be for life?"

"Oh be my sweet Quispamsis bride!"
    —He cried, and then he kissed her.
(Editor's note,—here's where the tragedy comes in)
"I cannot be your bride" said she,
    "But I'll be your Quispamsis-ter."

ADS.

A Marvelous Cure

I have suffered all my life with a terrible handicap, namely, short arms. I had despaired of ever being cured until my friend Sid advised using Lantac. After using two bottles I noticed a great difference in the length of my arm. I have since used several bottles and can now thoroughly enjoy the company of any young lady regardless of waist measurement. You may publish this letter if you think it will be of any help to others who have suffered as I have. I heartily thank Lantac for giving me the opportunity to hold my own.

Yours till you hear otherwise,
Bill.

Important Notice

Mr. Sidney Jones wishes to announce that the coming of peace forgoes the necessity of a V. A. D. School, which was essentially a war-time institution. His dearest wish however is to establish a Peace Academy and in a very short time there will be some very interesting announcements regarding the faculty of this new project. Among the subjects dealt with will be cooking, making of "apple pie beds," dressmaking and all other domestic arts and sciences. Mr. Jone's idea is exceptionally practical and there is no doubt that he intends making this institution a huge success of it. It is rumored that already he has a position ready for one of the first graduates.

A Letter From His Reverence

St. John, N. B., Mar. 27, 1918.
To Whom It May Concern,

I, Bishop of Ballarat, take the keenest delight in availing myself of this opportunity to express to all my appreciation of all features of the Quispamsis Hotel. The beauties of its location, the unexcelled cooking, the entertaining companionship of the aristocratic guests, and the charming hostess could not but appeal to the most fastidious. I have found it a most restful place to which I may retire to prepare my addresses in peace and quiet. But naturally as an eminent divine I have been most particularly impressed with the high moral and religious standards maintained throughout the establishment and by the reverential atmosphere which invariably pervades. I attribute this largely to the excellent example of the most pious landlady. All forms of profanity are discountenanced and it is this worthy woman who has herself established the forms of speech by which one may obtain satisfaction in moments of tense emotion without offense to one's conscience. Thus, all reference to the hereafter is studiously avoided unless the noun applied by the wicked and vulgar to the locality of high temperature can be camouflaged by incorporation into a word of unquestioned standing. Such words as Helma, help, and hello can be made very effective if pronounced slowly with a pause between syllables. The last mentioned word is particularly satisfying if repeated a number of times with longer pauses between syllables than between words. If at times of great excitement one is unable to think of sufficient words of this character the range of choice may be greatly extended by adopting a cockney English accent, when such words as elegant, elbow, elm, etc. become available. Also by a special arrangement justified by certain circumstances the word in question may be actually uttered undisguised provided it can be made to refer to the calyx of a strawberry or a city in the Province of Quebec elsewhere known as Hull. I as a Bishop desire to place a stamp of approval on these forms of verbiage which are a most efficient means of eliminating profanity, one of the curses of our modern civilization. On this account I heartily commend the Quispamsis Hotel to those desirous of reforming without foregoing the undisputed pleasures of sin.

I might mention that there are other respects in which the Quispamsis dialect differs from that encountered elsewhere. One is surprised to hear in this secluded region new words, or common words used in unique sense and construction. For the guidance of prospective guests I will append a list of a few of the most common.

Map—the anterior surface of the head.
Yap—an orifice in the map used for the reception of nutritive substance and slaps, and whatever it is that someone is going to get if he does not bee-hive, and for the ejection of large volumes of hot air and the words herein defined in frequent repetition.

QUISPAM CHRONIC

Bee-hive—equivalent to the English word behave. The relation is possibly suggested by the fact that someone is going to get stung if he thinks he is going to get what he has been told he is going to get if he does not bee-hive.

Illustration of a "Map" With "Yap" Exposed

Tummy—the reason why the landlady's profits are so scanty.

Honesty—a quality sometimes possessed by married men, very rarely and to a limited extent only, by engaged men, and never, though the reward of virtue in this case is priceless, by single men unattached.

Trains—conveyances designed to stimulate vigorous exercise and measure the maximum velocity of unaided human motion. Afternoon trains are always on time so that you are unable to catch them, evening trains returning to the city are always late so that you are usually unsuccessful in missing them.

Squash-blossom—a peculiar flower, blooming late.

Geranium—a plant. Garden geraniums are very small with brownish green leaves, one on each stalk, and short stems attaining a maximum length of 3 inches in as many years. They are admired for their rapid and vigorous growth. Potted geraniums are characterized by stems 8 to 10 feet long and 1 inch thick without leaves or branches except at the extreme top. They are valued for their rare grace and beauty.

Waiting for the Rest of the Clan

I trust these definitions may be an aid to strangers. In closing I cannot express too enthusiastically my opinion of our combined manager, cook, landlady, hostess and friend. Her abilities are large, her talents various, and her willingness to help you on any and every occasion absolutely unlimited. Helping others and taking what is left herself, if there is any, has become her unconscious habit. And her rates are low. No reference to this delightful watering place (during showers) would be complete, either, without mention of the manager's sister, a child of most winning ways and charming personality. We predict many broken hearts in the coming seasons as she is growing up.

Very sincerely,
Bishop of Ballarat.

Map of Africa

Paying for Chronic. (See Terms, Title Page).

❈❈❈❈❈❈❈❈❈❈❈❈❈❈❈

Another Ad

Our Hair Tonic needs no eulogy. Just look at this picture and let it speak for itself. Price $2.50 per bottle. Ask your grocer for it. If he does not carry it, apply to Nashiwaak Pulp and Paper Mill, St. John, N. B.

❈❈❈❈❈❈❈❈❈❈❈❈❈❈❈

～ THE ANNUAL BUST ～

Terms: Same (Only please pay this year)

Whether:- Mostly fresh, not much change in humor, a bit breezy (we hope)

St. John's All-Year Port
"Good to the last drop"

EDITORIALS

Once again the Queens are being led into the precincts of the "Sphinx" club. This annual event is anticipated and looked forward to for many moons (twelve, to be exact!).

In reviewing the events of the past year, there are a few outstanding events, which I would like to bring to your attention. Not the least of these, is the New Contract our little Gracie has taken on,—Percy having bid a Diamond and having been Doubled. And we all thought he was Invulnerable! We greatly regret three (3) Take-outs,—Bros. Knowles, Ford and Tot Leonard, their arduous duties having superseded the Ancient and Honorable Game of Bridge. We bid for future Happy Days with them up on their Re-entry. Mr. Hal. Sims-Black-Sims is responsible for the Squeeze Play, which is very popular with the Queens, particularly the Triple Squeeze. Mr. Sims-Black-Sims has kindly consented to demonstrate this Triple Squeeze at the Annual Blow-out of the Club, and is he proficient! We also wish to draw your attention to Mr. Jamieson's One Suit, Mrs. Allen's Major, and Mrs. J. Goold Leonard's Jack. We gladly welcome one new Queen and three new Jacks into the Pack; they are not strangers, but we will take them in just the same!—With Spring just around the Corner, Spades will be much in Demand, Clubs will be discontinued for the summer, when Short Suits wil be Established.—Happy Days and a New Deal to each and all. We hope there will be no more Losing Hearts in the Clubs and any Slams given on these pages will be Passed.

A Pome

There was a young lady named Grace
Who had a sweet and angelic Face
She took our dear Perce
For better or worse,
Says she—"For the good of the Race."

New Books

1. Educating a Husband for a Church Wedding.
   Al. Wayward
2. Ten Nights in a Bar-room   S. F. Jamieson
3. Hands I Have Held.
   Eddie Dickson, R.N., D.S.O., O.B.E.
4. The Norman Invasion   E. L. Farquhar
5. Montague, P. E. I., Then and Now
   L. Mac Farquhar
6. Whoa! Rex! or Black Beauty Mrs. L. T. Allen
7. The Story of My Life   Genevieve
8. Fines, and How to Collect Them   H. G. Black

Egg Laying Contest

A very keen contest is going on just at present between Mr. W. Hennery Hayward and Mr. N. Hennery Ford. Last week Mr. Ford was three (3) cackles ahead of Mr. Hayward, who says he is waiting for his hen to lay the Golden Egg. Mr. Ford's hen is off the Gold Standard. A nickel a piece would look good to him!

Lucky Laurie!

He has a wife and a cigarette lighter,—and they both work.

Wives of great men oft' remind us,
As we read their memoirs bright,
We should never leave behind us
Better halves who like to write.

Notice

My spouse, Ellie B. has left my bed and board without just cause, so I will no longer be responsible for her debts, either in Saint John or Moncton.
—H. GLADSTONE BLUE.

THE ANNUAL BUST

Notices

BIRTHS:—None. Dr. A. R. Dafoe investigating.
DEATHS:—O. M. DePression, Jan. 1, 1935, of starvation.
MARRIAGES:—Leonard-Sipprell. In New York City, March 16.

George Percy Leonard and Grace Keans Sipprell were joined in the bonds of holy matrimony. The bride looked very winsome in a smart Miami bathing costume of midnight blue, and the groom wore his customary ha"""" smile and a white necktie spotted with black. They were unattended and no one gave the bride away. After a honeymoon spent on Broadway the happy couple are living quietly at their home in Saint John. Welcome Home! and may we extend our Felicitations! The groom is the son of poor but honest parents of Loyalist stock, but he has lived that down. He began life as a baby boy but gradually overcame that difficulty and became a caddie on the Westfield Golf Course. In due course of time he came to hold the responsible position of Treasurer of the Club and Official Chaperon at the Saturday Night Dances. The bride is noted for her charming hospitality.

Vulcanize Before NOT After!

Radio Programme

6.15 p. m.—Don Hazel's Flap-jacks. Tooth Organ solo by Bucky.
6.30 p. m.—Hi-Ho Everybody,—Rudy Brenan and His Disconnected Yankees.
7.00 p. m.—Health Talk.—Subject: Bugs, Bugs and More Bugs. By Miss Eddie Dickson, R.N., D.S.O., O.B.E. Solo by Mike Robe.
7.15 p. m.—Singing Stan. Radio's gift to the Ladies. Sponsored by Golong's Peppermints.
8.00 p. m.—Drama. Why Men Leave Home. L. M. Farquhar.
9.00 p. m.—Bridge Talk.—Mrs. Ely Culblackson.
10.00 p. m.—News Commentator.—G. R. Leonard.
12.00 p. m.—Chidren's Hour.

Little Joan Hayward was taught to close her evening prayer during the absence of her father with: "Please watch over my papa." But she made her mother blush when she added, "and you had better keep an eye on mother, too."

Ads.

WANTED—Extra Saturdays during summer for Picnics. Must be fine. Apply, The Gang.
WANTED—Meetings to attend. Hazel.
WANTED—Some knee-action. Apply, Our Little Ed.
WANTED—Squeakless Shoes for church weddings. Apply, W. H. Hayward.
LOST—At Ononette, last summer, one night's sleep,—E.I.F.
LOST—Between noon and midnight, every day,— one wife, answering to name of Genevieve. Anyone found harboring same will be persecuted. Phone 3-4274.
FOUND—On Kingston Road, at Ford's Picnic. Two well-fed calves. Owner can have by proving ownership.
SWAPS—Will exchange Mechanical Bridge Table for large-sized Pram. Apply, Sec. of Westfield Golf Club.
TOO LATE FOR CLASSIFICATION—L. M. Farquhar.

Social and Personal

Social—Mrs. H. Gladdy Black has again visited Moncton.
Personal—Why does she never take H. G. B. on these tripes?
Social—L. McIntyre Farquhar often visits Hub.
Personal—How come!
Social—Allen's moving from Hill.
Personal—On level at last.
Social—Percy's close relations have been visiting the Bride and Groom.
Personal—Query from Bride: "Have you any distant relatives?"
Social—We welcome Spring again.
Personal—Why did Spring linger so long in the lap of Winter? Ask old Bill Hayward.

All Set

Herb. B.—"I've arranged so as not to be caught by any drought next summer."
Jack—"What have you done?"
H. B.—"I've planted onions and potatoes in alternate rows. The onions will make the potatoes' eyes water and irrigate the soil."

New Bridge Auditorium to be Started at Once

The following announcements regarding the new Auditorium have been received. Work to begin immediately, if not sooner, to be finished in time for season beginning Oct. 1, 1935. Following contracts and appointments have been awarded:

Financing—S. F. Jamieson
Architect—H. S. Brenan
Building Supplies—R. M. Farquhar
Office Furnishings—L. J. Allen
Glass—W. H. Hayward
Telephone Service—H. G. Black
Chairman of Privy Council—G. P. Leonard, Specialist
J. G. Leonard, D.D.S.—Director of Dining-room Service
Improvements and Suggestions—By Members of 100% Talkie Club.

And How!

What is the greatest known water power? Ans.: A woman's tears.

Reservation Notes

Heap Big Injun Pocohorace takes wigwam of Chief Ononette, for squaw, squaw's Papa and little Squawks.

Chief Perciononette joins Quispam Tribe with Gracie Catchum Hungarian Partridge.

Herbie Sitting Bull and squaw now selling May flowers in market.

Passamaquoddy Tripe will send Representatives to Old Home Week.

Chief Stanny Chewem-heap-big-peppermint gets Squatter's rights on Red Head Beach.

Larryhaha and Gennehaha open Tepee at Ononette Baskets for Sale.

Chief Johnny Pullumout and his Snookums at Quispamsis also Ole Bill Pain-in-the-Face and Papooses.

Did you hear the one about ——?
Important Notice

ELLIE B.—Please return home. All is forgiven. I cannot find my summer underwear.—H.G.B.

Hazel—"What is your husband's average income?"
Edna—"From one to two, a. m."

Notices of Meetings

Revival Meetings will be held as usual Sunday evenings after church at Farquhar's. Mrs. Allen will be the speaker at next meeting. Topic, "The Rise and Fall of the Roaming Umpire."

The annual meeting of the Ladies' Aid will be held in Centenary Church. Report to be given by Mrs. W. H. Hayward.

The Hays and Beans Committee will meet next Friday night at home of Dr. J. G. Leonard.

L. T. A.: "The horn on your car must be broken."
L. M. F.: "No, it's just indifferent."
L. T. A.: "Indifferent! What do you mean?"
L. M. F.: "It just doesn't give a hoot."

Bill—A wife is an expensive luxury.
H. G. B.—So is an automobile.
B.—Sure. But you can get a new model every year.

Country-house host (to arriving guest)—H'lo, Jack! Drove over with Miss Cuddles, eh? Ripping sleighing but cold going, ain't it?
Jack (cheerfully)—Oh, didn't notice it.
Host—All right, then. Come in and thaw that earring out of your mustache.

Ain't Nature Grand!

Elsie said sadly: "Men are too mean for anything."
"What's the trouble now?" asked her best friend.
"Why, I asked Herb for a motor-car to-day, and he said that I must be content with the splendid carriage that Nature had given me."

Typographical Errors

And they were married and lived happily even after.

Send mother a gift of hardly ever-blooming rose bushes.

Dig the ground over thoroughly and then pant.

I—I didn't know you cared for me . . . I've always thought of you as just a great big bother.

Wanted—position in cabaret; no bad habits; willing to learn.

The evening was spent in an infernal way, a radio program being the main diversion.

She doesn't kiss or neck or anything—she is nobody's fuel.

THE ANNUAL BUST

A Smile

Jen—"Who can name one important thing we have now that we did not have 100 years ago?"
Jack—"Me."

Which Was—

Girls, when they went out to swim
Once dressed like Mother Hubbard;
Now they have a bolder whim,
And dress more like her cupboard.

My! My!

Ze Americaine he is ver' funny. Ze Frenchman can nev' understan' hem—jus' like ze Americaine cocktail. Firs' he put in whiskey to make ze drink strong, zen he put in water to make her weak, zen he drop in some sugar to make her sweet, nex' he put in lemon to make her sour, zen he say "Here's to you," and he dreenk her hi'self!

No Chance

"Nurse," said the patient, "I'm in love with you. I don't want to get better."
"Don't worry, you won't," Edna D. said, cheerfully. "The doctor's in love with me, too, and he saw you kiss me this morning."

AN ENGINEER

is said to be a man who knows a great deal about very little and who goes along knowing more and more about less and less until finally he knows practically everything about nothing; whereas,

A SALESMAN

on the other hand, is a man who knows a very little about a great deal and keeps knowing less and less about more and more until he knows practically nothing about everything.

A PURCHASING AGENT

starts out knowing practically everything about everything, but ends up knowing nothing about anything, due to his association with engineers, salesmen and architects.

"This is the only life you will have on this earth; make it go as far as you can."

Ellie,—overheard on Westfield Course: "Really, I can't play golf, I don't even know how to hold the caddy."

THE TALE OF A FORD

A natty wee Ford one bright summer day
Came purring along in his usual way
When his eye got a glimpse of Miss Nan Henrietter
And he said as he stepped on the gas ("I must get her").

I've been looking, and waiting to give you a ride
So hop in beside me, sit close by my side.
I have not much to offer, but thank the good Lord
I can show you the latest in Model A Ford.

Nan looked him all over, his clutch was alright
He had no flat tires, his lamps were so bright
His starter was all that a maid could desire
He could drive it like H——, and never back fire.

So they travelled along all these years many miles
With their ups and their downs, their tears and their smiles
And they managed despite the depression and grind
To carry two little FORD TRAILERS behind.

MARRIED WOMAN'S CAKE

1 lb True Love
1 lb Perfect Trust and Confidence
1 lb Cheerfulness
A pinch of Unselfishness
A sprinkle of Interest in all your husband does
Method:—Mix all these well with 1 gill of oil of sympathy, put into a tin of Contentment. Spice with a bright fireside and bake often all your life.

Gen—"You kept the car out rather late last night. What delayed you?"
L. T. A.—"Had a blowout."
Gen—"Huh! Tire or roadhouse."

Big accident.—Machine skidded and hit a lady in the safety zone.

Sambo, giving an account of his sea voyage, said: "All de passengers was heavin', and, as if dat wasn't enough, de captain gave orders fo' de ship to heave to."

Grace—"This bathing suit I bought here won't do. I was in the water only an hour and it shrunk five inches."
Modest Clerk (examining the garment)—"Lady, it's a good thing you came out when you did."

Plays:

Another popular form of entertainment residents enjoyed was theatrical productions. Young people would often dress up and present plays to younger siblings, parents, grandparents, neighbours or guests. The local residents pictured in the photographs below may be dressed up for that exact reason.

This Photo was titled Masquerade Quispamsis, 1937-1938

Photo was titled Masquerade Quispamsis, 1937 - 1938

Special Occasions

Hallowe'en:

Hallowe'en activities of the early to mid 1900's were very similar to those of present day. The night was full of fun and excitement, which sometimes transformed into mischievous behaviour. On more than one occasion an outhouse would be toppled over or odd objects would appear on barn rooftops. No charges were laid and these incidents became stories that local residents still laugh about today, especially if they were the culprits who pulled pranks. Some common pranks pulled on Hallowe'en included breaking mailboxes, putting roosters in mailboxes, tarring pigs, pulling cabbages out of the garden, knocking over outhouses, putting Charlie Marr's wagon on his roof, and soaping people's windows.

Christmas:

Christmas was a time of year when the community always pulled together to help out families that were in need. A local resident of Quispamsis would make rounds on Christmas Day to spread cheer dressed as Santa Claus. His exact identity remains a mystery but it is known that he worked for the Telegraph Journal for a number of years. He would pass out barley toys and ribbon candy. He would especially make a point to visit individuals who had difficulties leaving their homes.

For more information about how Christmas was celebrated in the mid 1900's refer to Donna (Buckley) Harriott's poems in the section entitled Capturing What Life Was Like Through Art and Poetry.

At the Quispamsis Civic Centre there used to be a Christmas party for the children every year, in the 1980's and 1990's. Children from all over Quispamsis would come to the Christmas party to see Santa Claus. A local resident would play Santa and give toys to the young children. During this time span, residents and the Cadets would gather outside the Quispamsis Memorial Arena for a Tree Lighting Ceremony, then proceed to walk down to the Kings Valley Manor carolling to the residents along the way.

Other activities sponsored by the Town at Christmas time included an annual Christmas Property Decorating Contest with the Quispamsis Beautification and Environment Committee acting as judges for the contest. Cash prizes were awarded to the individuals who won this contest each year. Records show that for 1991, Mr. and Mrs. Edward O'Brien who lived at 363 Quispamsis Road won the one hundred dollar cash prize for that year. Mr. and Mrs. Guillaume Doucette, from 20 Ashfield Drive, won the second place prize of seventy-five dollars, while Mr. And Mrs. Harold Isnor of 32 Millican Drive won the third place prize of fifty dollars.

In more recent years, the Towns of Quispamsis and Rothesay organize the annual Kennebecasis Valley Santa Claus Parade, which begins at the Kennebecasis Valley High School, and travels down the Hampton Road to the Rothesay High School. With the opening of the new Arts & Culture Park in 2006, the holiday season begins with a magnificent Tree Lighting Ceremony which illuminates the whole Park into a magical winterland wonder. Many gather for the occasion, followed by skating and music at the outdoor rink.

Gondola Point Dominion Day/Week:
(Dominion Day name changed to Canada Day on October 27, 1982)

To mark Canada's Birthday in 1977 the Village of Gondola Point held a weeklong celebration in conjunction with the opening of the Gondola Point Recreation Centre, (refer to the section entitled Community Halls for more information on the Gondola Point Recreation Centre). The events planned for that week were the following:

Saturday:	Official opening ceremonies at 2:30 p.m. at the Recreation Center Chicken barbeque and a concert by the Kiwanis Steel Band Family Dance (evening)
Sunday:	Softball game, ladies versus men (afternoon) Box Social (evening)
Monday:	To be announced
Tuesday:	Gondola Point Frolics at 8:00 p.m.
Wednesday:	Kiddies Day (morning and afternoon) Giant Bingo at 8:00 p.m.
Thursday:	Car Rally and Talent Show
Friday:	To be announced

An article written by Barb Landry in The Kings County Record stated the following about the celebration:

> "Gondola Point celebrated both the opening of its new recreation center and Canada Days last week.
> On Saturday night after a chicken barbeque, a family dance took place and on Sunday the men and women of the village got together for a softball game, the score was tied.
> Tuesday evening some of the villagers put on a two-hour show which made for a very enjoyable evening with a lot of good talent in Gondola Point. Wednesday was kiddies' day, where the children dressed up for fun, games and contests. Prizes were awarded.
> In the evening, a giant bingo was held.
> On Thursday the Gondola Point youth group sponsored a car rally with Dave Anderson in charge."

Quispamsis Field Day:

Quispamsis Field Day was an annual event held to celebrate Canada Day. The following article written by Barb Landry appeared in The Kings County Record on Wednesday, June 29, 1977,:

> Quispamsis Field day got under way Saturday with a parade at 1 p.m. There were floats, horses and clowns, with the Quispamsis new ambulance leading it off. The parade wound through the Village and ended up at the recreation center where games, booths, and judging took place.
> M.P. Gordon Fairweather officially opened the Field Day.
> Donald Sherwood was organizer for the day's events. John Bone, Mrs. Milton Downey and Kay Ramsay of CFBC were the judges for the parade and various events.
> There were pony rides, horseshoe, log sawing and egg throwing contests.
> The winning floats were: 1. Quispamsis Brownie and Guides, 2. Kindergarten; 3. Residents of Millican Drive and 4. The Kinsmen
> Costume winners were 1. The Dutch Girls, 2. The Fat Girls and 3. Clown and Bunny and

honourable mention went to the Hotdog.

For the best-dressed bicycles, winners were Alice Ann O'Neill, Sharon McFate and Sean Nightingale.

The best of the pet show went to Randy for first, David and Goliath second and third place went to Barry Howes and Fluffy. They all received trophies donated by various business firms and friends of the area.

Ribbons were presented in the automotive category. They went to the Moonduster for first, 7 Up for second and third place went to the Rothesay fire truck.

In the wagon's category, ribbons went to Chocolate and Philip for first place, Chuckwagon took second and Sonny Hamilton and old wagon took third.

The prince and princesses for the day were Paul Betteridge and Sharanda Crouse.

One place that saw a lot of activity was the Kinsmen Mock Jail. One woman Mrs. Eddie Sherwood, a district 19 school bus driver spent a lot of time in there. The day's events wound up with a dance held at the Legion.

In later years, Canada Day festivities were celebrated at Meenan's Cove Park. Often the evening was concluded with large fire works displays that brought crowds from Quispamsis and the greater Saint John area.

Family Life

Every member of the family had a particular chore or task that they were required to do. Chores that were commonly done by children included putting hay down for cattle, gathering kindling for the night, and washing dishes. Women were often the ones responsible for doing the laundry. Most people did not own a dryer and had to hang their clothes outside even in the winter. The clothes when brought in during the winter would be as stiff as boards and would have to thaw in the house. The clotheslines used by these women were also stationary, meaning that they had to walk along the line and hang out the clothes. The clotheslines did not move on a set of reels like they do today.

Doctors and Homemade Remedies

Doctors:

The role the community doctor played in the early to mid 1900's was drastically different than the role they play today. Patients would rarely call on doctors in the early 1900's; however, when doctors were summoned, they would often make house calls. The two most common reasons for calling a doctor were births and deaths. It was not uncommon for a woman to give birth at home in the early to mid 1900's. Usually a sister, mother, or grandmother would assist the pregnant woman until the doctor arrived which, in most cases, would be after the baby was born.

Mr. John Darling says that a Doctor would have been present when he was born, but if he wanted to see a doctor he would have to travel to Hampton by horse and buggy. The three doctors that served the Quispamsis area were Dr. Leatherbarrow, Dr. Wetmore, and Dr. Snow. The dates of when these doctors practiced are currently under research, but it would have been in the early to mid 1900's.

Some of the doctors who practiced in this area over the years include: Dr. O. R. Peters, Dr. George Bate, Dr. Barry King and Dr. Roy Fanjoy. Dr. Peters had an office in his home on Peter's Lane near St. Paul's Church and practiced from the 1920's to the 1950's. He was followed by Dr. George Bate who later became a surgeon and moved his practice to Saint John. Dr. Barry King then set up his practice. Both Dr. Bate and Dr. King lived and had their offices in the house on the Rothesay Common. One resident can remember Dr. King making house calls in the 1960's. Dr. Roy Fanjoy was an ear, nose, and throat specialist who also practiced in Rothesay.

In extreme occasions when a person was required to go to the hospital, it was always a long journey. John Darling can recall when he had to go to the hospital to have his appendix removed when he was two years old. He was loaded on the back of a hay pile and taken by horse and wagon to the Saint John General Hospital. He can remember his mother holding onto him in the back of the wagon. After the operation he had to learn to walk all over again, because operations in the early 1900's were much more invasive than they are today with modern medicine.

In a file entitled Tales of The Kennebecasis located at the

Provincial Archives of New Brunswick in Fredericton, the following caption on doctors was written. The blurb summarizes the author's idea that people from the 1920's, 30's, and 40's had a higher standard of endurance in comparison to today's population. The date or author was not recorded.

"DOCTOR SELDOM SEEN"

"The doctor was seldom seen in the villages. Too often he was called in too late, but on the other hand the men and women of the country were skillful in dealing with common forms of injury, and, right or wrong, they depended much upon themselves in dealing with ordinary ailments. If work was hard, food was plentiful and wholesome. There was a high standard of endurance, among both men and women. Nearly all children went barefoot from spring till fall. Religion "took hold" strongly. The sermons were long, and mostly full of fire and brimstone. The amusements were few and simple. In the early days of baseball the players, even the catcher, wore no gloves."

Homemade Remedies:

Homemade remedies were very common, as doctors were not called upon frequently. Homemade remedies have been in existence since the beginning of time and are still used today. Many however, that were common in the 1920's and 1930's are no longer used in the medical world today.

Some of these remedies were very simple to make, but few were pleasant tasting. They could be made at home or bought from a peddler as he or she traveled through the area. Listed below are some examples of homemade remedies that were used by residents of Quispamsis.

1)   Molasses and sulfur were mixed together to cure spring allergies.

2)   Mustard, flour, and water were mixed together as a paste (or

poultice), to rub on the chest of a person who was suffering from a chest cold. Sometimes this mixture would also be patted onto a piece of cloth and pinned to someone's chest and back. According to the residents interviewed the remedy worked, but cautioned that it burned.

3) Bread poultice was also used for colds.

4) Rawleigh's Medicated Ointment was used for chest colds. This product is still available in some drug stores.

5) A spoonful of castor oil was taken to loosen bowels.

6) Hot and cold compresses were used to reduce swelling.

7) Goose grease from a roasted goose was used to treat croup or bronchitis. The grease would be heated on the stove to make it a liquid. Sometimes sugar would be added to make it taste more favorable; however, the sugar did not mix well with the oil. The individual who was sick would drink the grease off the spoon.

8) Friar's Balsam was a substance that was inhaled to treat bronchitis. A pot containing the mixture would be heated on the stove and the sick individual would place his or her head over the pot with a towel covering the head and pot. The person would then inhale the steam that was rising out of the pot. This home remedy was said to have a bad smell.

9) Gold Thread was used to cure arthritis and rheumatism.

Other remedies that were mentioned included dandelion wine, sulfur, baking soda, and lavender.

The Depression Years

In the 1920's, Canada experienced a boom in industry and finances. The 1920's were commonly referred to as the Roaring Twenties as unemployment was low, and earnings for the individual and businesses were significant. However from 1929 to 1939 the economy and stability of the country was catastrophically altered. Hardships were experienced with the collapse of the stock markets in New York, Toronto, Montreal, and around the world. The country entered into the period of history that is now known as The Great Depression.

During the depression the capital income in New Brunswick between 1928 and 1933 decreased by approximately 39%. Unemployment rates reached as high as 27% in 1933 in Canada. Men of all ages were out of work but were still required to support their families, which, on average, were much larger than today's family size. One saving grace for the people who resided in Quispamsis was dependable vegetable gardens that would produce decent crops. Individuals could also rely on their neighbours and friends for help when it was required.

Tramps:

During the depression, men and women who were jobless and homeless would often go door-to-door looking for food. The residents of Quispamsis often referred to these individuals as tramps. By definition, a tramp was a person who travels about, generally on foot, making a living by doing odd jobs. Houses were physically marked to indicate whether or not one would be guaranteed to receive a free hand out from the residents of that particular home. It is suggested that the homeless men and women may have marked trees along the road to indicate which houses were approachable. Many residents in Quispamsis were known to give these people a sandwich or a meal before they continued on their way in search of work or their next meal.

Involvement in the Wars

Honour Roll:

"To the glory of God and in ever grateful memory of those of the Parish of Rothesay who gave their lives for King and Country in the Great Wars of 1914 - 1918, 1939 - 1945 and the Korean War 1950 - 1953.

C. Donald Richards
C. Thomas Smith
Edward Saunders
Wallace W. Brown
James S. Braley
James W. Holly
Cyril Harriott
Ruth S. Arnold
A. Gerald Burnham
Donald F. Dobbin
Alvin Warren Duffy
W. Walter V. Foster
F.L.H. Gooday
Duncan A. Hewitt
Frank C. Beyea
John D. Brock
R. Heber H. Daniel
Gerald Glenwood Knorr
Frank Harris
Melvin C. Harrison
Joseph R. Johnston

Rae Mackay
Alexander McKinnon
J. Adord Peters
George A. Peirce
Ernest W. Saunders
Percy Saunders
Joseph T. Gallagher
John A. Gallagher
Robert C. Legge
Lawrence A. LeBlanc
Usher H. Miller
Hugh K. McAvity
Earle W. McCrae
John David Rodger
Wilfred Reinhart

MAY THEIR NAMES LIVETH FOREVER"

The Boer War:

There was no one cause for the Boer War; however, the general causes were centered on the hostilities between two republics in South Africa and Great Britain when Great Britain tried to unite all of South Africa under the British flag in the late 1890's. The two republics in South Africa were the South African Republic (Transvaal) and the Orange Free State. This war is sometimes referred to as the South African War but is more commonly known as The Boer War, which occurred between the years 1899-1903. The British did not anticipate much resistance from the two small South African republics, however there was a large conflict. The British eventually won the war, but at a higher casualty rate than the South Africans.

There were mixed opinions regarding Canada's participation in the overseas war. The Canadian Government was encouraged to join the war by Pro-Empire Canadians, (English Canadians), while the majority of French Canadians and recent immigrants were in opposition and believed Canada should stay out of war that was occurring halfway around the globe. Despite Prime Minister Sir Wilfrid Laurier's initial desire to insure political favor and national stability, ties to the Empire were strong and public pressure grew. At this point Canada was still a part of the British Empire. To settle the public dispute, the Prime Minister promised to send a battalion of Canadian volunteers to fight in South Africa.

Approximately 7,000 Canadians volunteered to serve in this war, of which 217 were killed. The first batch of Canadian troops were dispatched from Quebec and traveled to Cape Town in South Africa aboard the SS Sardinian in 1899. Three Canadian regiments served in the Boer War: the Royal Canadian Dragoons, the Royal Canadian Regiment, and Lord Strathcona's Horse, (Royal Canadians). Lieutenant-Colonel William Otter commanded the Royal Canadian Regiment.

Otty Sherwood can recall his father, Walter Sherwood (born 1885), telling him a story about the end of the Boer War. Walter Sherwood had walked over the Perry Point Bridge to a store on the Kingston Peninsula to buy some groceries. The storekeeper was having a celebration with the men of the community to commemorate the end of the Boer War (1899-1903). The storekeeper had some brand new chamber pots on the shelf in his store, which he used to make a big bowl of lemonade for the men. The men looked in the chamber pot and made a fuss about drinking out of what they thought was a used chamber pot.

The above picture is of the Pompom Section of the Canadian Scouts taken some place in Africa during the Boer War. Roy A. Harrison is the 4th from the left in the back row. Mr. Harrison was from Gondola Point, and was the uncle of Grace Harrison McLeod.

World War I:
    The First World War officially began in 1914 and ended in 1918; however, there were conflicts and hostilities leading up to the official beginning of the war. The number of Canadians who served in the war was 619,636. Approximately 66,655 were killed, and 172,950 were wounded. The Canadian Corps was comprised of four Divisions in World War I. Battles in which Canadian troops fought in during World War One include Arras, Amiens, Passchendaele, Sommes, Vimy Ridge, and Ypres.
    (Source Kings County Museum, the Valour Remembered Canada and the First World War)

The following names are members of the community who served in the First World War. These soldiers were listed on a plaque in the Anglican Church of Holy Trinity in Quispamsis. Please contact the Town Hall with any other names of soldiers from Quispamsis so that we may remember their contributions as well.

Alexander, George
Allen, Lawrence
Appleby, Irving
Barnes, Otty
Blakeney, Lee
Bland, Arthur
Bonney, Rorg
Buckley, James
Clark, James
Dickson, Edna
Dickson, Willard
Duffy, Charles [November 6, 1911]
Farmer, Geoffrey
Flewelling, Edgar
Fowler, Grant
Gibbs, Andrew
Grimis, George
Henderson, Clarence
Henderson, Harold
Henderson, William
Heywood, Leslie
Houston, James
King, Thomas
Leslie, John
Lloyd, George
Love, Cecil
Martin, Malcolm
Merrithew, Gary
Nickerson, Harry
Porter, Arthur
Saunders, William
Scovil, Edward
Slater, Edward
Smith, Eugene
Smith, Jacob
Smith, Roy [September 26, 1916]
Thompson, James

Cecil John Drayden Love fought in the First World War. Mr. Love spent his seventeenth birthday on the front line in France fighting against the Germans.

War Brides From the First War:

A number of Canadian soldiers brought home wives from overseas. One such soldier was William E. Saunders, whose nickname was Soldier Bill. William E. Saunders married Grace Jane Hawkins from England during the First World War. Their first son, Howard Saunders, was born in England. They lived on Chamberlain Road upon arrival into Canada from Europe.

The above picture is the engagement picture of Grace Hawkins and Williams Elias Saunders, 1917.

This picture is one of the houses in England where Miss. Grace Hawkins lived, prior to her engagement to this Canadian soldier.

World War II:

The Second World War lasted from 1939 to 1945. The Canadian Army, the Royal Canadian Navy, the Canadian Merchant Marine, and the Royal Canadian Air Force all served in this war. About 1,000,000 Canadians served in World War II, and over 45,000 were killed during the war. It is estimated that 55,000 were wounded. Individuals who served in the militia from Quispamsis were called up to Camp Sussex at the beginning of the War while some individuals from the area chose to join a regiment called the New Brunswick Rangers.

(Source: Valour Remembered Canada and the Second War, Kings County Museum.)

The following is a list of individuals from our community who served in the Second World War. The primary source for this list of names was a plaque at the Quispamsis Memorial Arena.

FOR KING AND COUNTRY MEMBERS OF QUISPAMSIS COMMUNITY WHO HAVE VOLUNTEERED FOR ACTIVE SERVICE WITH CANADA'S FIGHTING FORCES

MEN WHO SERVED

Alexander, H.E
Alexander, R.C.
Ball, S. M.
Bell, Dalton
Bettle, Charles
Bettle, Daryl S.
Brittian, D.W.
Brittian, F.W.
Brayley, G.A.
Brayley, H.A.
Brayley, J.S.
Brayley, L.L.
Briggs, W.
Brown, W.W.
Brownlee, P.A.
Burnside, J.T.
Burnside, H.A.
Burnside, M.R.
Cairns, J.J.
Campbell, N.M.
Carpenter, H.J.
Carpenter, J.L.
Carpenter, J.W.
Carter, W.T.
Catheline, R.A.
Chamberlain, D.M.
Chamberlain, R. A.
Copp, E.C.
Cotton, R.
Cowan, J.R.

Craft, F.H.
Craft, L.D.
Darling, John.A.
Dickson, James D.
Dickson, John H.
Dickson, Laurence A.
Diggle, A.N.
Diggle, W.W.
Dobbin, A.A.
Donovan, B.
Duffley, G.G.
Duffley, N.P.
Duffley, R.L.
Fowler, Rosewell
Fraser, W.C.
Fulton, Cecil
Gates, W.
Gilliland, James.W.
Gilliland, King
Glenn, W.
Gorton, A.E.
Gould, H.
Hamilton, B.G.
Hamilton, M.L.
Harding, Harold
Hatfield, A.B.
Hayward, W.H.
Hazelwood, E.
Hazelwood, M.
Heirlehy, E.A.
Henderson, Earle
Herrington, E.
Herrington, N.J.
Hodgson, D.
Hodgson, P.
Hughes, B.
Hughes, B.E.
Hughes, J.W.
Hughes, John
Johnson, C.
Jones, P.G.

Joudry, A.W.
Kelly, K.G.
Kelly, Ron B.
Kelly, Wallace
Kelter, G.T.
Kelter, James W.
Kelter, Jos. F.
Kelter, John F.
Ketchum, G.W.
Ketchum, W.F.
Laye, E. A.
Lawrence, F.E.
Lawrence, L.B.
Lawrence, P.E.
Lee, J.G.
Lester, Allan
Lester, Harold
Lindsay, G.
Love, E.A.
MacKim, M.J.
Markham, C. (Rev.)
Marr, Ken W.
Matheson, D.H.
McAvity, R.
McBurney, Jos.
McEachern, R.D.
McFarlane, J.R.
McKinnon, B.F.
McLean, I. M.
McLean, R.
McQuinn, F.V.
Miller, H.D.
Miller, J.W.
Miller, U.H.W.
Moore, H.A.
Moore, R.A.
Phillips, M.R.
Pollick, J.A.
Pollick, J.S.
Reinhart, G.H.
Reinhart, W.H.

Richards, D.P.
Robertson, G.C.R.
Rogerson, Ralph.
Saunders, A.M.
Saunders, B.R.
Saunders, D.M.
Saunders, Edward M.
Saunders, Myles
Saunders, T.
Saunders, W.K.
Scott, J.A.
Scribner, R.R.
Scullion, Wallace
Sherwood, L.M.
Sipprell, J.M.
Smith, Donald
Smith, Eugene
Smith, Roy
Stephenson, W.J.
Stuart, A.J.N.
Thomson, W.
Tonge, J.S.
Tonge, R.
Warman, R.
Whittaker, Bennett.
Whitehead, H.A.
Wood, D.G.
Wyman, R.S.

WOMEN WHO SERVED

Bettle, Barbara
Darling, Alice
Glenn, Thelma
Henderson, Carol
Hughes, K.
Kelly, Leslie
Love, Florence
Saunders, Ruth
Whitehead, Daisy
Whitehead, Ferne

Below is a list of names of individuals from Quispamsis who would have served in one or more of the following wars: World War II, Korean War, Vietnam War, as well as other peace keeping missions:

Alison, James R.
Bourque, Joseph C.
Brooks, Lawrence D.
Cairns, Murray L.
Carroll, Henry J.
Casey, Roger V.
Cipryk, Arthur J.
Clarke, George B.
Cooper, George R.
Cormier, Paul J.H.
Cuming, Donald V.H.
Curran, Robert John
Dempster, Leonard E.
Despres, J.A.
Dollar, Andrew
Eisan, Brian G.
Fitzgerald, Michael M.
Foggo, Francis R.
Foggo, Graham C.
Friars, Gordon G.
Gaillard, Norman J.
Gallant, Tilmon J.
Gallop, G. Allison
Galloway, A. Ross
Gilbert, Lawrence B.
Gillis, Joseph B.
Gordon, Maurice J.
Griffin, Dianne
Griffin, John Ian
Hall, Norman R.
Holland, Alfred H.
Jennings, Granville R.
Johnson, Harold D.
MacDonald, Robert
MacKenzie, Robert E.
Maher, Harold E.
Marginson, R.B.
Masson, Kenneth L.
McKinnon, Harold M.
Mosher, Ray
Murphy, Gary Roy
Neilson, Brain C.

Pollock, A
Pollock, Margaret P.
Pyne, Oswald W.
Ranger, Kevin J.
Reinhart, Wilfred H.
Renshaw, James
Ritchie, W.J.
Robert, Maurice J.V.
Saunders, Chris
Savage, David L.
Savoie, Joseph E.
Severin, Wayne G.
Sleep, Cecil C.
Thomson, Donald
Wall, Robin F.
Walton, J.C.
Yaschuk, Ronald J.

Troop trains left from Saint John taking troops to basic training camps all over Canada. Those individuals who wished to join the Navy were taken to Halifax for basic training. Those who desired to join the Air Force, such as Edwin Love, were shipped to Moncton. Individuals who were in the militia would often receive basic training at Camp Sussex or in Fredericton.

John Darling joined the Army in 1938. He was stationed in Halifax and at a camp located in Ontario. For part of his service he was a recruiter for the Army. He belonged to the First Engineers Regiment. During the Christmas of 1939, he recalls that he was aboard the first boat of Canadians headed over to Europe. He eventually became an officer, and in 1945 he returned home.

Ron, Ken and Wallace Kelly all served in the Armed Forces. They lived on the Pettingill Road. Daryl Bettle, Charles Bettle, Barb Bettle, Myles Saunders, Ken Marr, and Jack Hughes all served in the Air Force. Daryl Bettle fought in Africa, Italy and Europe. Myles Saunders and Jack Hughes were both paratroopers who fought at the Battle of the Bulge.

The Battle of the Bulge lasted from December 1944 to January 1945. It was the last German offensive in the west during World War II and pushed a 'bulge' into Allied lines in the Ardennes in Belgium and Luxembourg. The Allies cut off the German advance near the Meuse River.

Sergeant Edward Saunders, son of Mr. and Mrs. W. Harmon Saunders of Gondola Point, served two years in the Canadian Army. While on leave from Newfoundland, he drowned in a canoeing accident in the Kennebecasis River on a Sunday afternoon in August of 1942. He had set out with his brother-in-law, Arthur Beardsley, from Gondola Point for Long Island in a small canoe with the intention of visiting his brother, Stanford, who was haying on the island. A strong breeze and choppy waves overturned their canoe. They were about 500 to 600 yards from the shore when it capsized. A nearby yacht was able to rescue Mr. Beardsley, but Sgt. Saunders drowned while waiting to be rescued, as he could not swim. Sgt. Saunders was in his twenties when he died.

The two images above are of Myles Saunders. The photo is of Myles Saunders who served in the First Parachute Platoon. He jumped in to Normandy on D-Day. The newspaper article has a caption that reads, "D-Day WARM-UP-Hard hitting Canadian paratroopers, waiting for the invasion signal, set up a ring and take turns belting each other around. Private Andrew Hogarth, Toronto, and L.-Cpl. A. M. Saunders, New Brunswick, are entertaining their buddies in this period bout."

    Stories about the war from Veterans are very rare as many of the experiences were horrifying. For many of the men, their time overseas was hell. Phyllis Bettle can recall a few stories that her brother, Myles Saunders, told her about the Second World War. Myles Saunders experienced a broken ankle as a result of jumping out of a window of a two-storey house. The Jerries, German soldiers, were approaching the house and there was no other way out. He told his fellow comrades to leave him behind as he could not walk, but they quickly found an old bike and pushed him to safety.

    Mrs. Bettle can also remember, once her brother was back in Quispamsis after the war, the sound of a car back firing would cause Mr.

Saunders to dive for the nearest ditch. The men who fought for our Nation were truly heroic, ordinary people in extraordinary times.

James Donald Dickson, better known to his family and friends as Don Dickson joined the air force in World War II like his two brothers Lawrence and John. Donald Dickson was one of the greatest pilots to come out of New Brunswick during the Second World War.

Donald Dickson received a number of titles and honors while serving in the RCAF. These titles included D.F.C. (Distinguished Flying Cross), A.F.C. (Air Force Cross), B.E.M. (British Empire Medal), D.F.M. (Distinguished flying Medal), C.D. (Canada Decoration), and the position of Squadron Leader.

Don Dickson was a well-liked individual; many people can recall fond stories of Don. He was also a well-respected flyer, and as such was given the honor of being one of the first Canadians to fly the Comet jetliner. E. Louise Dickson relates an interesting tale of how Don Dickson would fly low over his home in Hammond River, in effect buzzing the house. His mother would race out of the house each time and wave to him.

Don Dickson (right) in the cockpit of a de Havilland Comet aircraft at the Moncton airport in 1953, with his cousin Ed Titus (left)

The following obituary, which was found in a scrapbook kept by E. Louise Dickson, summarizes some of the highlights of Donald Dickson's career before he died overseas from an attack of poliomyelitis. Poliomyelitis, or polio as it is better known as, is a viral paralytic disease that causes muscle weakness, paralysis, and sometimes death. The newspaper clipping was dated July 26, 1953, but it could not be determined from which newspaper the clipping was taken.

"One of Canada's leading airmen of both war and peace, Squadron Leader J.D. Dickson, died Saturday night at the Royal Air Force Station at Houlton, England it was announced in Montreal by Air Defense Command Headquarters Sunday. Squadron Leader Dickson had been ill for only a short time following an attack of poliomyelitis. The thirty-two year old pilot had served with the RCAF during the Second World War a native of Hammond River, Kings Co. he was stationed with #412 Squadron at Rockcliffe Airport, near Ottawa where he was second in command of the squadron. He was one of the first Canadians to fly the RCAF's new Comet jetliner acting as Pilot on the flight to this country of the first Comet last May. His wartime decorations include DFC, DFM, AFC, BEM. In 1943 at the time he received the DFC, the investiture was made by the late King George VI at Buckingham Palace.

James Donald Dickson was the son of H. Allen Dickson and the late Mrs. Dickson of Hammond River. Following his outstanding wartime service, Squadron Leader Dickson became one of Canada's most experienced pilots in the peacetime force. In the fall of 1952, he was one of 60 Canadians to go to England for advanced training on flying the famous Comet jet airliner.

Previous to this he had flown the large jet on familiarization flights between Britain and Singapore. He was also one of 30 Maritime airmen who took part in the 1950 Korean air lift.

His most recent decoration came early in June of this year when he was one of two Maritimers and 17 Canadians to be included in the Queen's Birthday Honors List. He was awarded the Air Force Cross at that time. Squadron Leader Dickson was senior officer among Maritimers who took part in the post-war operation "Sweet Briar", a combined Canada - United States military exercise in 1950.

As recently as last month, Squadron Leader Dickson brought attention to his native province when he piloted the first Comet jet liner ever seen here, to Moncton from Ottawa.

Surviving are his wife the former Marguerite Hanlon of Barnesville; two sons James and Richard all of Cambridge, N.S. His father, two brothers Laurence A. Hammond River and John H. of Ottawa, three aunts and two uncles.

The funeral is expected to take place tomorrow in England with interment at North Luffingham, England."

James Donald Dickson's funeral procession.

Ray

...ing is another obituary for Donald Dickson that was ...k that was kept by E. Louise Dickson. The date of ... source of the clipping are unknown.

Death Of A Hero
...eath Comes too soon for heroes.

...ut it is an even greater tragedy that ...Leader J.D. Dickson of Hammond River ...truck down after having passed through so ...ers of war, by a dreaded disease like ...tis which offered the young flier no

He brought a good deal of glory to New Brunswick, and during the course of a brilliant wartime career as an RCAF pilot he won first as a non-commissioned officer the Distinguished Flying Medal and the Distinguished Flying Cross as an officer. He was also awarded the British Empire Medal, and the Queen recently authorized the Air Force Cross for him in recognition of his services in the Korean air lift and his part in helping to develop Canada's jet power. Such a record is one rarely excelled.

Squadron Leader Dickson was in England on transport duties when he died. He was at the height of his career, youthful and vigorous. But perhaps his most valuable asset--like that of so many of the young men in the flying services--was vision. He and that comparatively small group of airmen in the RCAF helped pave the way to peace. Others will follow down the road with less difficulty. We know well enough that few of us are indispensable and that the family of Canadians is getting larger. But we still have none to spare, and certainly none such as Squadron Leader Dickson.

Like every community in Canada who had men and women who went to war to serve their country, the community of Quispamsis also experienced losses. Several men and women did not return home as a result of the horrors associated with war. Saint John held a parade in honor of the men of the Greater Saint John area who served in the war.

The Ladies Auxiliary hosted a dinner on the D.J. Purdy while it was beached in Gondola Point for the men who had come home from fighting at the end of the war. The community of Quispamsis held celebrations and victory dances every time a man from the community returned home.

During the time of the war, residents who lived in this area were under strict rationing orders in an attempt to help out with the war efforts. Items such as butter, sugar, tea, meat, molasses, tires, and gasoline were rationed. Families were provided with ration stamps that they would take to a store to receive their portion of essential items such as sugar or meat. In the fall when preserves were being made, the allotment of sugar given to each person was increased. Storekeepers had to collect the ration stamps and paste them onto a sheet. Once the sheet was full, the storekeeper would send it away to the distribution store so that they could purchase more items for resale. It was common to trade food among neighbours in order to make sure everyone had an equal share. Below are some examples of the ration coupons that were used in the Quispamsis area.

PERMIS—*Suite*

1946, conformément à la téneur des coupons contenus dans le carnet de coupons de rations, et sur remise desdits coupons. Chaque coupon donne droit à la quantité d'essence classée que le Régisseur des huiles autorisera de temps à autre.

9. Toute altération, oblitération ou mutilation, en tout ou en partie, de ce permis d'essence avec carnet de coupons de rations ou du numéro de série ou du numéro de plaque de licence de véhicule automobile inscrit sur la couverture de ce permis l'annulera et rendra invalides les coupons qui y sont attachés, et toute altération, oblitération ou mutilation d'une unité ou d'une fraction d'unité de coupon rendra invalide respectivement l'unité ou la fraction d'unité de coupon, et personne ne devra livrer ou obtenir de l'essence en échange d'un coupon ainsi altéré, oblitéré ou mutilé.

10. Le présent permis sera annulé pour toute infraction aux présentes conditions ou à une ordonnance du Régisseur des huiles (y compris les ordonnances qu'il pourra rendre par la suite), que cette infraction soit commise par le propriétaire dudit véhicule automobile ou par toute personne qui l'a en sa possession et qui en a acquis la possession avec le consentement explicite ou implicite dudit propriétaire.

mCottrell
Régisseur des huiles pour le Canada.

AVERTISSEMENT: Quiconque participe à une infraction auxdites conditions ou à une ordonnance du Régisseur des huiles est coupable d'un délit et passible des peines prévues par la loi.

Le timbre gommé remis avec votre permis d'essence avec carnet de coupons de rations doit être apposé à l'intérieur du pare-brise avant que vous puissiez acheter de l'essence classée en échange de vos coupons.

GASOLINE LICENCE AND RATION COUPON BOOK
LICENCE

The owner of the motor vehicle bearing the provincial licence plate number imprinted on the cover of this book (having been registered for the purpose of gasoline control) IS HEREBY LICENSED to purchase graded gasoline for use only in the operation of such motor vehicle, subject to strict compliance with the following

CONDITIONS

1. It is understood and agreed that this licence and the attached ration coupons are issued in respect of the said motor vehicle and are and shall remain the property of the Oil Controller and are not transferable, and may be cancelled or varied at any time.

2. The attached coupons are not valid for exchange for graded gasoline until the motor vehicle licence plate number shown on the front cover hereof has been written in ink on each and every coupon. This must be done immediately upon receipt of the book. *Provided that if* a one-half coupon is tendered in exchange for graded gasoline, the entire motor vehicle licence plate number shown on the front cover hereof shall be written in ink on each one-half coupon.

3. The only gasoline used to operate the said motor vehicle shall be graded gasoline (as designated by the Oil Controller), which gasoline shall be obtained in accordance with the orders of the Oil Controller, including any order hereafter made, and shall be used in compliance with the provisions of the said orders and of this licence and the attached ration coupons.

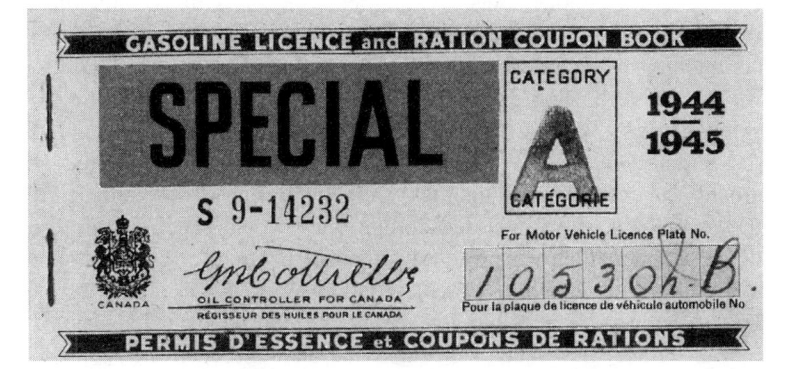

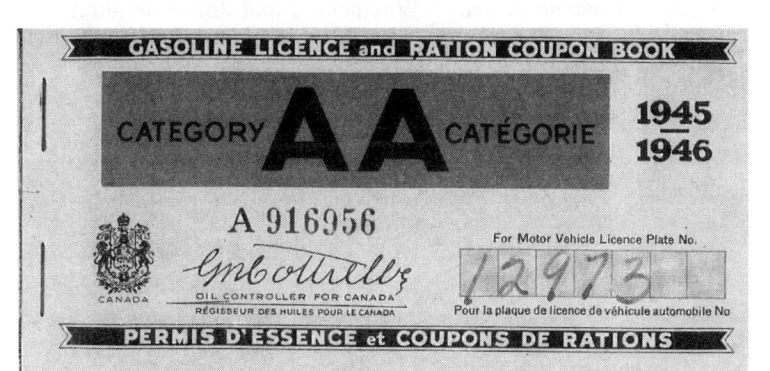

The war symbolized a huge financial burden to the Canadian Government. Money was needed for equipment, troops, training facilities, and most of all to win the war. Prior to the war Canada's military expenditure was approximately $500 million per year. In less than a year, the military expenditure doubled. During the war Canadians were encouraged to buy war stamps and Victory bonds. The war stamps were 25 cents each and the money raised went towards the war effort. The Victory bonds helped cover the debt incurred by the war, and once it was over; these bonds were converted into savings certificates. The campaign was highly successful, raising a total of $8.8 billion during the war. Young people were also encouraged to help the war effort by collecting tinfoil and old scraps of metal. Like so many other communities across the country, Quispamsis was mobilized for the war.

Air raid blackouts were enforced in several communities, especially along the coast of the province. Several Quispamsis community members can remember air raid rehearsals. The curtains would have to be closed tight and absolutely no light was permitted to shine through. William E. Saunders and Henry MacFaren were two of the volunteer Air Raid Wardens for Quispamsis. These men would go around and ensure that no light was shining out from anyone's home. If they saw light or an unclosed curtain, they would stand outside the house and blow their whistles. It was considered to be a very important and serious job to hold. Each Air Raid Warden had six or seven houses he was responsible for in his neighborhood. The air raid rehearsals may have been scheduled and announced on the radio, or random and unannounced. Whether or not the community of Quispamsis was in direct danger is very debatable, but for people of all ages at that time, it was a frightening experience.

The image below depicts the specific set of directions community members were expected to follow during an air raid, or an air raid practice.

PLEASE HANG UP!

NEW BRUNSWICK CIVILIAN VOLUNTEER CORPS

AIR RAID PRECAUTIONS

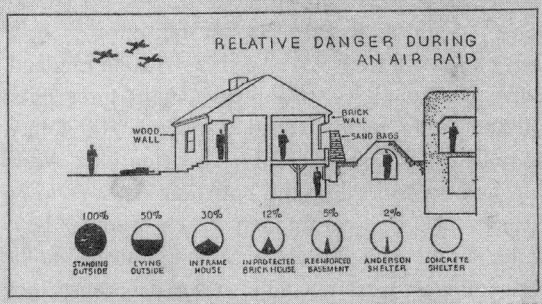

RELATIVE DANGER DURING AN AIR RAID

Standing Outside	Lying Outside	In Frame House	Unprotected Brick House	Reinforced Basement	Anderson Shelter	Concrete Shelter
100%	50%	30%	12%	5%	2%	

IN THE EVENT OF AN EMERGENCY

1. **If you are in your own home or place of employment "STAY PUT".** You will be safer there and will lessen the possibility of confusion. Keep away from windows.

2. **If you are on the street—seek cover at once.** There is much less danger of being hurt from the effects of bombing or shell fire under cover.

3. **If you are in a car, immediately pull into the curb or some convenient parking place, and if you do not wish to remain in the car, seek cover elsewhere.** Remember, the streets must be kept clear for the movement of troops, fire-apparatus, ambulances and other authorized vehicles.

4. **Lights out—Remember the black-out instructions. Lights must be obscured so that they will not be visible to aid as a landmark for the enemy. ALWAYS insure that lights are out when you leave your home unoccupied.** Don't oblige the enemy by lighting up his target for him.

5. **Avoid the use of the telephone unless it is a case of real emergency.** False rumours and faulty information can be spread only too quickly by telephone. Your line should be kept free to receive orders or instructions from competent authority. If you are suspicious of the message hang up and ring back to make sure.

6. **Obey orders and follow out instructions promptly and completely.** Make their task easier and prevent confusion by obeying the orders of competent authority who have been appointed to take charge.

7. **Above all—think before you act—do not become confused or stampeded.** The enemy will try his best to spread confusion—avoid helping him.

8. Do it now—become acquainted with the C.V.C. A.R.P. Warden on your street.

9. Advise him at once if you have any sick or infirm people in your house or in the case of an emergency.

10. The nearest First Aid Centre is located at:—

....
....
....

Your Block Warden is Mr. ....
Address.. Phone No. ....
C. V. C. Headquarters control room at ....

Make it your business NOW to fill in the spaces above.
Issued by the N. B. Civilian Volunteer Corps in co-operation with the Defence Forces

305

Children from war torn countries were sent to Canada during World War II. Bon Harriett was one child who came to Quispamsis on April 26, 1930 from England. He was ten years old when he and his three older brothers were evacuated to Canada. The story of his experience as written by Valerie Evans, appeared in the Telegraph Journal on Thursday, July 4, 2005, in an article entitled "I told them I was going to school on a horse."

Derrick Ronald "Bon" Harriott was born Derrick Ronald Harriot on April 26, 1930 in England. When he was 10 years old, he and his three older brothers were evacuated to Canada. His father, Alfred Lennox Harriott, had been in the First World War and he decided he did not want his boys to go through what he went through. There were six boys in the family. The four oldest came to Canada but the two youngest were not able to come because they were not in school. Bon returned to Canada after the war and settled in New Brunswick. He is married to the former Ann Lord and they have two children: Deborah Jane and John Kent.

I was 10 when we left to come here. The blitz had already started but hadn't got to the real rough part. We sailed in a convoy from Liverpool and landed here on August 15. Everything went off fine but I don't think I had one day when I wasn't seasick.

There were about 200 kids on board. There were lots of women looking after all of us. Those coming to New Brunswick went as far as Sackville - Mt. Allison University by train. From there we went in a motorcar. Alfred, one of my brothers was let off in Hampton; and Cib in Nauwigewauk. My oldest brother and I came to the J.M. Robinson family at Stoneycroft just above Rothesay. He stayed with me for two months and then he went to Hampton.

One of the biggest surprises, disappointments really, was my mother had told me in Canada I would be going to school on a horse. They had horses at Stoneycroft and when it was time to go to school, I was waiting and waiting for the horses. When they told me the bus was there, I told them I was going to school on a horse. I stayed there for about six months. J.M. had lost his wife before I arrived and there had to be a wife present. Miss Purdy, the lady who was in charge of all these kids in and around the Rothesay area, looked after us pretty well. She sent me down to his cousin, Beverly Armstrong. It was a lovely house, one of the biggest in Rothesay and here I was out of a little tiny place. I stayed there for pretty near three years. They were awfully good to me there.

In Nauwigewauk, they were kind of using my brother Cib as someone to do the work. He was a rugged little lad and did what he was told. He wouldn't complain but Miss Purdy decided to take him out of there. After Colonel Armstrong died, Cib and I ended up at Shadow Lawn and went to R.C.S. We also went to summer camps. We weren't suppose to know but I know who paid for it. Dad had to send a pittance to keep us out here. They bought war bonds and stamps with the money and when I went back home, they gave it all back.

My three brothers joined the army when they became of age so I was the only one sent back to Britain. I told Mom and Dad right off, there is no place for me here and they understood. They said as soon as the young boys are ready, we are coming out to Canada, too. Mom made it but Dad didn't.

I used to catch the train every Saturday and go to London and go through all the shipping companies to see if I could get back here. All the army wives were coming to Canada and it was just a waste of time so Dad decided to come with me. He was one you didn't argue with. My 18th birthday was coming up and it was compulsory that I would go into the army. Dad went right to the top and told them he would get me out if he had to smuggle me out. We got home, there was a notice there on Friday I could go on the Empress of Canada.

I started a little business making hand throws in Hampton. I came to St. Andrews about 1950 and worked with Cottage Craft for four years. Margie's dad had an electrical business, E.C. Lord Electric and I helped him after work. Finally I decided to do this for a living so I worked with him until his death when I fell heir to the business. Later I was working for the Biological Station in St. Andrews and through them I did the fish illustrations for The Fishes of the Atlantic Coast of Canada, Pacific Fishes of Canada, Atlantic Fishes of Canada and Whales of the Bay of Fundy. There are some funny looking critters on the bottom of the ocean.

I often say I am one of the luckiest people. Most people who were in charge of me when I came here during the war are probably all passed on but they were awfully good and I would like to say thank you to all of them.

On December 7, 1945 many residents from Quispamsis can remember being glued to the radio listening for the announcement that would indicate that the War in Europe was over. This announcement came in the morning of December 7, 1945.

Taxes

In the 1930's, there were three main types of taxes that residents of Quispamsis had to pay: school tax, road tax, and poll tax. Mrs. Steele of Rothesay, who was formerly a Kennedy, would often collect the school tax. The road tax did not have to be paid in cash; instead it could be worked off by digging ditches. When sufficient labour had been completed to pay off the road tax, the road supervisor would issue the worker a slip that indicated the road tax had been paid. Every male over the age of 18 was required to pay a poll tax. The poll tax was for being a resident of the community and it cost five dollars. There was also a fee of approximately three dollars a year that had to be paid to gain access to fire protection.

Elections

Elections were held in community halls such as the Quispamsis Community Hall on the Old Coach Road, and the Old Gondola Point Community Hall on the Gondola Point Road. The older residents would often provide meals for the voters. If an individual were voting Conservative, then the Liberal supporters would not feed him or her and vice versa. The following is a two-page list of 420 names of everyone eligible in the Parish of Rothesay, which at this time included Quispamsis, to vote in 1938 in the election. Beside each person's name his or her occupation is listed as well as the location he or she would have cast a ballet. Some of the occupations listed vary from widows, overseas, carpenters, farmers, clerks, seamstresses, and longshoremen. The document is titled "The Dominion Elections Act, 1938 - Rural Preliminary Lists of Electors."

THE DOMINION ELECTIONS ACT, 1938
RURAL PRELIMINARY LIST OF ELECTORS

Electoral District of Royal.   **Rural Polling Division No. 11-C, Rothesay**

Comprising the remainder of the Parish of Rothesay.

1 Arnold, Mrs. Edith, widow, Fair Vale Station.
2 Arnold, Douglas, timekeeper, Fair Vale Station.
3 Alexander, Mrs. William, widow, Fair Vale Station.
4 Alexander, Gordon, mechanic, Fair Vale Station.
5 Alexander, Mrs. Gordon — Fair Vale Station.
6 Alexander, Horace, carpenter, Fair Vale Station.
7 Alexander, Mrs. Horace — Fair Vale Station.
8 Breen, Mortimer, farmer, Fair Vale P.O.
9 Breen, Mrs. Mortimer — Fair Vale P.O.
10 Breen, Miss Ardis, telephone operator, Fair Vale P.O.
11 Beamish, John, express Co. empl., Fair Vale P.O.
12 Beamish, Mrs. John — Fair Vale P.O.
13 Beemish, Miss Margaret, hairdresser, Fair Vale P.O.
14 Ball, Stanley, overseas, Gondola Point.
15 Ball, Mrs. Stanley — Gondola Point.
16 Burger, Frank, carpenter, Fair Vale P.O.
17 Buckley, Percy, longshoreman, Fair Vale P.O.
18 Buckley, Mrs. Percy — Fair Vale P.O.
19 Beyea, Mrs. James, widow, Fair Vale Station.
20 Barry, Miss Marjorie, nurse, Gondola Point.
21 Belyea, Mrs. Bernice, housekeeper, Gondola Point.
22 Byers, Trueman, Telephone Co., Fair Vale Station.
23 Byers, Mrs. Trueman — Fair Vale Station.
24 Beyen, James, overseas, Fair Vale Station.
25 Beyea, Mrs. James — Fair Vale Station.
26 Burnett, Gillis, retired, Fair Vale Station.
27 Burnett, Mrs. Gillis — Fair Vale Station.
28 Banks, Mrs. William, widow, Fair Vale Station.
29 Banks, Walter, farmer, Fair Vale Station.
30 Blair, William, labourer, Fair Vale Station.
31 Blair, Mrs. William — Fair Vale Station.
32 Bateman, Fred, Govt. employee, Fair Vale Station.
33 Bateman, Mrs. Fred — Fair Vale Station.
34 Bateman, Miss Joan, stenographer, Fair Vale Station.
35 Breen, Harold, carpenter, Rothesay RR. 1.
36 Breen, Mrs. Harold — Rothesay RR. 1.
37 Beyea, George, overseas, Fair Vale Station.
38 Beyea, Mrs. George — Fair Vale Station.
39 Brayley, Lex, skipper, Rothesay RR. 1.
40 Brayley, Mrs. Lex — Rothesay RR. 1.
41 Brayley, Miss Dorothy, clerk, Rothesay RR. 1.
42 Brayley, James, overseas, Rothesay RR. 1.
43 Brayley, Harold, overseas, Rothesay RR. 1.
44 Brayley, Lex, overseas, Rothesay RR. 1.
45 Bishop, Mrs. May, housekeeper, Rothesay RR. 1.
46 Breen, Fred, building contr., Rothesay RR. 1.
47 Breen, Mrs. Fred — Rothesay RR. 1.
48 Burns, James, labourer, Rothesay RR. 1.
49 Burns, Mrs. James — Rothesay RR. 1.
50 Carter, Mrs. Edward, widow, Fair Vale P.O.
51 Carter, Miss Royce, householder, Fair Vale P.O.
52 Casey, Ernest, retired, Gondola Point.
53 Casey, Mrs. Ernest — Gondola Point.
54 Cooper, Mrs. May, widow, Gondola Point.
55 Creamer, Mrs. Kay, housekeeper, Fair Vale P.O.
56 Colwell, Alonzo, 'phone Co. empl., Fair Vale P.O.
57 Colwell, Mrs. Alonzo — Fair Vale P.O.
58 Chamberlain, Andrew, upholsterer, Fair Vale Sta.
59 Chamberlain, Mrs. Andrew — Fair Vale Sta.
60 Chamberlain, Miss Ada, stenographer, Fair Vale Sta.
61 Coleman, Harry, city traveler, Fair Vale Sta.
62 Coleman, Mrs. Harry — Fair Vale Sta.
63 Cameron, Miss Mary, maid, Gondola Point.
64 Cooper, Thomas, driver truck, Fair Vale Sta.
65 Cooper, Mrs. Thomas — Fair Vale Sta.
66 Chamberlain, William, baker, Fair Vale Sta.
67 Cameron, Donald, railway empl., Fair Vale Sta.
68 Cameron, Mrs. Donald — Fair Vale Sta.
69 Cochrane, William, labourer, Fair Vale Sta.
70 Cochrane, Mrs. William — Fair Vale Sta.
71 Clark, Robert, retired, Fair Vale Sta.
72 Clark, Mrs. Robert — Fair Vale Sta.
73 Clark, Gordon, clerk, Fair Vale Sta.
74 Clark, Russell, clerk, Fair Vale Sta.
75 Clark, Mrs. Russell — Fair Vale Sta.
76 Cosman, Ralph, bookkeeper, Fair Vale Sta.
77 Cosman, Mrs. Ralph — Fair Vale Sta.
78 Coates, Albert, labourer, Rothesay RR. 1.
79 Coates, Mrs. Albert — Rothesay RR. 1.
80 Cripps, Cecil, carpenter, Fair Vale Sta.
81 Cripps, Mrs. Cecil — Fair Vale Sta.
82 Copeland, Raymond, railway empl., Fair Vale Sta.
83 Copeland, Mrs. Raymond — Fair Vale Sta.
84 Dykeman, Mrs. Herbert, widow, Fair Vale P.O.
85 Dykeman, Miss Norma, school teacher, Fair Vale P.O.
86 Dykeman, Miss Constance, stenographer, Fair Vale P.O.
87 Dobson, John, school teacher, Fair Vale Sta.
88 Dobson, Mrs. John — Fair Vale Sta.
89 Dobson, Fleming, retired, Fair Vale Sta.
90 Dobson, Mrs. Fleming — Fair Vale Sta.
91 Dobbin, John H., carpenter, Fair Vale Sta.
92 Dobbin, Mrs. John H. — Fair Vale Sta.
93 Dobbin, G. Edward, carpenter, Fair Vale Sta.
94 Dobbin, Mrs. G. Edward — Fair Vale Sta.
95 Dobbin, George R., bldg. contractor, Fair Vale Sta.
96 Dobbin, Mrs. George R. — Fair Vale Sta.
97 Dobbin, Miss Annie, seamstress, Fair Vale Sta.
98 Dobbin, Aaron, florist, Fair Vale Sta.
99 Dobbin, Mrs. Aaron — Fair Vale Sta.
100 Dobbin, Cedric, gardener, Fair Vale Sta.
101 Dobbin, Cedric — Fair Vale Sta.
102 Dobbin, Anthony, labourer, Fair Vale Sta.
103 Dobbin, Mrs. Anthony — Fair Vale Sta.
104 Dobbin, Miss Jean, stenographer, Fair Vale Sta.
105 Dobbin, Thomas, overseas, Fair Vale Sta.
106 Dobbin, Mrs. Thomas — Fair Vale Sta.

107 Dobbin, Miss Margaret, stenographer, Fair Vale Sta.
108 Dobbin, Murray, overseas, Fair Vale Sta.
109 Dobbin, Stuart, overseas, Fair Vale Sta.
110 Daley, William, army Dist. 7, Fair Vale Sta.
111 Daley, Mrs. William — Fair Vale Sta.
112 Dykeman, Orland, wholesale grocer, Fair Vale Sta.
113 Dykeman, Mrs. Orland — Fair Vale Sta.
114 Dykeman, Muriel (Miss), school teacher, Fair Vale P.O.
115 Diggle, Norman, grocer, Fair Vale Sta.
116 Diggle, Mrs. Norman — Fair Vale Sta.
117 Diggle, William, overseas, Fair Vale Sta.
118 Diggle, Arthur — Fair Vale Sta.
119 Diggle, Agnes, clerk, Fair Vale Sta.
120 Diggle, Constance, nurse, Fair Vale Sta.
121 Dow, Burns, overseas, Fair Vale Sta.
122 Dow, Mrs. Burns — Fair Vale Sta.
123 Dickson, Lloyd, farmer, Rothesay RR. 1.
124 Dickson, Mrs. Lloyd — Rothesay RR. 1.
125 Dobbin, John A., mechanic, Rothesay RR. 1.
126 Dobbin, Mrs. John A. — Rothesay RR. 1.
127 Earle, Robert J., mechan. supt., Fair Vale P.O.
128 Earle, Miss Isabella M., householder, Fair Vale P.O.
129 Edwards, George, longshoreman, Fair Vale P.O.
130 Edwards, Mrs. George — Fair Vale P.O.
131 Ellis, James, labourer, Fair Vale P.O.
132 Ellis, Mrs. James — Fair Vale P.O.
133 Emmerson, Fred, machine shop, Gondola Point.
134 Ellis, William (Dr.) retired, Rothesay RR. 1.
135 Ellis, Mrs. William — Rothesay RR. 1.
136 Finley, Don, longshoreman, Gondola Point.
137 Finley, Mrs. Don — Gondola Point.
138 Frost, Clement, painter, Fair Vale Sta.
139 Frost, Mrs. Clement — Fair Vale Sta.
140 Frost, Harrison, overseas, Fair Vale Sta.
141 Frost, Mrs. Harrison — Fair Vale Sta.
142 Friers, Edgar, longshoreman, Fair Vale Sta.
143 Friers, Mrs. Edgar — Fair Vale Sta.
144 Filmore, Brundage, carpenter, Fair Vale Sta.
145 Filmore, Mrs. Brundage — Fair Vale Sta.
146 Gilliland, Arnold, farmer, Gondola Point.
147 Gale, William, commercial trav., Fair Vale P.O.
148 Gale, Mrs. William — Fair Vale P.O.
149 Garnett, William, retired, Fair Vale Station.
150 Gilliland, Fred, fishman, Fair Vale Sta.
151 Gilliland, Mrs. Fred — Fair Vale Sta.
152 Harvey, George, stevedore, Gondola Point.
153 Harrison, Ralph, farmer, Gondola Point.
154 Harrison, Miss Daisy, school teacher, Gondola Point.
155 Harrison, Budd, farmer, Gondola Pt.
156 Heenan, Arthur, film co. empl., Fair Vale P.O.
157 Heenan, Mrs. Arthur — Fair Vale P.O.
158 Henderson, Fred, carpenter, Fair Vale Sta.
159 Henderson, Mrs. Fred — Fair Vale Sta.
160 Henderson, Mrs. Viola, widow, Fair Vale Sta.
161 Hachey, Elzear, meat inspector, Fair Vale Sta.
162 Hachey, Mrs. Elzear — Fair Vale Sta.
163 Howell, Thomas, overseas, Rothesay RR. 1.
164 Howell, Mrs. Thomas — Rothesay RR. 1.
165 Haworth, Murray, barber, Rothesay RR. 1.
166 Haworth, Mrs. Murray — Rothesay RR. 1.
167 Hatfield, Percy, plumber, Rothesay RR. 1.
168 Hatfield, Mrs. Percy — Rothesay RR. 1.
169 Hatfield, Allan, overseas, Rothesay RR. 1.
170 Hill, Ralph, bldg. contractor, Rothesay RR. 1.
171 Hill, Mrs. Ralph — Rothesay RR. 1.
172 Hooper, Harry, plumber, Rothesay RR. 1.
173 Hooper, Mrs. Harry — Rothesay RR. 1.
174 Jones, Harold, farmer, Fair Vale P.O.
175 Jones, Mrs. Harold — Fair Vale P.O.
176 Jones, Allison, truckman, Fair Vale P.O.
177 Jackson, Sylvester, carman, Fair Vale P.O.
178 Jackson, Mrs. Sylvester — Fair Vale P.O.
179 Jackson, Marley, carman, Fair Vale P.O.
180 Jackson, Mrs. Marley — Fair Vale P.O.
181 Juvet, Stanley, overseas, Gondola Point.
182 Juvet, Mrs. Stanley — Gondola Point.
183 Keirstead, Leslie, labourer, Gondola Point.
184 Keirstead, Mrs. Fred, housewife, Gondola Point.
185 Kee, Mrs. Charles, engineer, Fair Vale Sta.
186 Kee, Mrs. Charles — Fair Vale Sta.
187 Koval, Michael, shoe repair shop, Gondola Point.
188 Koval, Mrs. Michael — Gondola Point.
189 Keating, Ernest, overseas, Fair Vale Sta.
190 Keating, Mrs. Ernest — Fair Vale Sta.
191 Kennedy, Gilbert, ironworker, Rothesay RR. 1.
192 Kennedy, Mrs. Gilbert — Rothesay RR. 1.
193 Logan, Weldon, meter reader, Fair Vale P.O.
194 Logan, Mrs. Weldon — Fair Vale P.O.
195 Lynch, Nesbitt, carpenter, Fair Vale P.O.
196 Lynch, Mrs. Nesbitt — Fair Vale P.O.
197 Lawrence, Percy, labourer, Rothesay RR. 1.
198 Lawrence, Charles, labourer, Rothesay RR. 1.
199 Lawrence, Mrs. Charles — Rothesay RR. 1.
200 Lawrence, Sydney, labourer, Rothesay RR. 1.
201 Lane, Mrs. Linda, widow, Fair Vale Station.
202 Lindsay, George O., overseas, Rothesay RR. 1.
203 Lindsay, Gordon, grocer, Rothesay RR. 1.
204 Lindsay, Mrs. Gordon — Rothesay RR. 1.
205 Landry, Murray, clerk, Fair Vale Station.
206 Landry, Mrs. Murray — Fair Vale Station.
207 Lyman, Henry, labourer, Rothesay RR. 1.
208 Lyman, Mrs. Henry — Rothesay RR. 1.
209 Lyman, Norville, longshoreman, Rothesay RR. 1.
210 Lyman, Mrs. Norville — Rothesay RR. 1.
211 Lowe, Richard, mechanic, Rothesay RR. 1.
212 Lowe, Mrs. Richard — Rothesay RR. 1.

213 Lee, Thomas, retired, Rothesay RR. 1.
214 Lee, Mrs. Thomas — Rothesay RR. 1.
215 Lawrence, Fred, overseas, Rothesay RR. 1.
216 Lawrence, Mrs. Fred — Rothesay RR. 1.
217 McCully, Seymour, bldg. contractor, Gondola Point.
218 McCully, Mrs. Seymour — Gondola Point.
219 McCumber, Mrs. Cora, widow, Gondola Point.
220 McLean, Ernest, army Dist. 7, Fair Vale Sta.
221 McLean, Mrs. Ernest — Fair Vale Sta.
222 McElwaine, Mrs. William, widow, Fair Vale Sta.
223 McElwaine, Miss Gertrude, postmistress, Fair Vale Sta.
224 McLean, Malcolm, overseas, Fair Vale Sta.
225 McLean, Robin, overseas, Fair Vale Sta.
226 McArthur, Percy, shipper, Fair Vale Sta.
227 McArthur, Mrs. Percy — Fair Vale Sta.
228 McMackin, Harold, truck driver, Fair Vale Sta.
229 McMackin, Mrs. Harold — Fair Vale Sta.
230 McLaughlin, James, mechanic, Rothesay RR. 1.
231 McLaughlin, Mrs. James — Rothesay RR. 1.
232 Mullett, Gordon, truck driver, Fair Vale P.O.
233 Mullett, Mrs. Gordon — Fair Vale P.O.
234 Mullett, John, truck driver, Fair Vale P.O.
235 Mullett, Mrs. John — Fair Vale P.O.
236 Mullett, Malcolm, carpenter, Fair Vale P.O.
237 Mullett, Mrs. Malcolm — Fair Vale P.O.
238 Mullett, Mrs. James, widow, Fair Vale P.O.
239 Marr, Ernest, carpenter, Fair Vale P.O.
240 Marr, Mrs. Ernest — Fair Vale P.O.
241 Marr, Robert A., carpenter, Fair Vale P.O.
242 Marr, Mrs. Robert A. — Fair Vale P.O.
243 Melvin, Miss Harriett, spinster, Fair Vale P.O.
244 Marr, Arthur C., retired, Fair Vale P.O.
245 Merrithew, Haldene, overseas, Fair Vale Sta.
246 Merrithew, Guy, Ord. Corps, Fair Vale Sta.
247 Morrithew, Winona, school teacher, Fair Vale Sta.
248 Monteith, Marjorie, school teacher, Fair Vale Sta.
249 Matthews, Ora, mail clerk, Fair Vale Sta.
250 Matthews, Mrs. Ora — Fair Vale Sta.
251 Myers, Raleigh, clerk, Fair Vale Sta.
252 Myers, Mrs. Raleigh — Fair Vale Sta.
253 Mullett, Robert, carpenter, Fair Vale Sta.
254 Mullett, Mrs. Robert — Fair Vale Sta.
255 Marshall, Ernest, bookkeeper, Fair Vale Sta.
256 Marsall, Mrs. Ernest — Fair Vale Sta.
257 Monteith, Albert, insur. agent, Fair Vale Sta.
258 Monteith, Mrs. Albert — Fair Vale Sta.
259 Marr, Arthur, mason, Rothesay RR. 1.
260 Marr, Mrs. Arthur — Rothesay RR. 1.
261 Marr, Oliver, labourer, Rothesay RR. 1.
262 Marr, Mrs. Oliver — Rothesay RR. 1.
263 Moore, Harold G., bus driver, Fair Vale Sta.
264 Moore, Mrs. Harold G. — Fair Vale Sta.
265 Mallette, Louis, clerk, Fair Vale Sta.
266 Mallette, Mrs. Louis — Fair Vale sta.
267 Moyse, William, gunsmith, Fair Vale Sta.
268 Moyse, Mrs. William — Fair Vale Sta.
269 Morrell, Albert, clerk, Fair Vale Sta.
270 Morrell, Mrs. Albert — Fair Vale Sta.
271 Marshall, Mrs. Janie, widow, Fair Vale Sta.
272 Marr, Esburn, labourer, Rothesay RR. 1.
273 Marr, Mrs. Esburn — Rothesay RR. 1.
274 Marr, Clarence, painter, Rothesay RR. 1.
275 Marr, Mrs. Clarence — Rothesay RR. 1.
276 Marr, Miss Helen, stenographer, Rothesay RR. 1.
277 Moore, Herbert, overseas, Rothesay RR. 1.
278 Nelson, F. E., storekeeper, Fair Vale P.O.
279 Nelson, Mrs. F. E. — Fair Vale P.O.
280 Northrup, Gerald L., watchman, Fair Vale Sta.
281 Northrup, Mrs. Gerald L. — Fair Vale Sta.
282 Northrup, Gerald, overseas, Fair Vale Sta.
283 Northrup, Ronald, overseas, Fair Vale Sta.
284 Phillips, Herbert, Civil Engineer, Fair Vale P.O.
285 Parsons, Avery A., plate shop worker, Fair Vale P.O.
286 Parsons, Mrs. Avery A. — Fair Vale P.O.
287 Pollock, Mrs. John B., housewife, Fair Vale P.O.
288 Peterson, Mrs. Ethel, housekeeper, Fair Vale P.O.
289 Price, Albert, longshoreman, Gondola Point.
290 Price, Mrs. Albert — Gondola Point.
291 Pollock, Mrs. Richard, widow, Fair Vale Sta.
292 Pollock, Miss Rachel, stenographer, Fair Vale Sta.
293 Peacock, Mrs. Walter, factory worker, Fair Vale Sta.
294 Peacock, Mrs. Walter — Fair Vale Sta.
295 Palmer, Roy, checker, Rothesay RR. 1.
296 Quick, Arthur, mechanic, Rothesay RR. 1.
297 Quick, Mrs. Arthur — Rothesay RR. 1.
298 Roberts, Eric, farmer, Fair Vale P.O.
299 Roberts, Mrs. Eric — Fair Vale P.O.
300 Roberts, Mrs. Frank, widow, Fair Vale P.O.
301 Roberts, Albert, retired, Fair Vale P.O.
302 Roberts, Miss Helen, spinster, Fair Vale P.O.
303 Roberts, Walter M., retired, Fair Vale P.O.
304 Roberts, Mrs. Walter M. — Fair Vale P.O.
305 Roberts, Guilford, storekeeper, Fair Vale P.O.
306 Roberts, Mrs. Guilford — Fair Vale P.O.
307 Rickard, James, mechanic, Gondola Point.
308 Rickard, Mrs. James — Gondola Point.
309 Roberts, Harold, overseas, Fair Vale P.O.
310 Roberts, Ernest, overseas, Fair Vale P.O.
311 Robertson, John Herbert, retired, Gondola Point.
312 Roberts, David, overseas, Fair Vale P.O.
313 Rankine, Mrs. Annie, widow, Rothesay RR. 1.
314 Ross, Mrs. Rose, widow, Rothesay RR. 1.
315 Stackhouse, Howard, manager store, Fair Vale Sta.
316 Stackhouse, Mrs. Howard — Fair Vale Sta.

317 Smith, Hugh, overseas, Gondola Point.
318 Smith, Mrs. Hugh — Gondola Point.
319 Smith, Miss Irene, bookkeeper, Gondola Point.
320 Smith, Charles E., salesman, Gondola Point.
321 Smith, Charles William, retired, Gondola Point.
322 Saunders, Sydney, farmer, Gondola Point.
323 Saunders, Mrs. Sydney — Gondola Point.
324 Saunders, Miss Audrey, clerk, Gondola Point.
325 Saunders, Byron, labourer, Gondola Point.
326 Smith, Mrs. Thomas, widow, Gondola Point.
327 Smith, C. Rutherford, farmer, Gondola Point.
328 Smith, Mrs. C. Rutherford — Gondola Point.
329 Smith, James A., farmer, Gondola Point.
330 Smith, Mrs. James A. — Gondola Point.
331 Saunders, Earl, oil en. employ, Gondola Point.
332 Saunders, Mrs. Earl — Gondola Point.
333 Saunders, Oswald, meat dealer, Gondola Point.
334 Saunders, Mrs. Oscar, widow, Gondola Point.
335 Saunders, Oscar L., farmer, Gondola Point.
336 Saunders, Mrs. Oscar L. — Gondola Point.
337 Steen, Earl, labourer, Gondola Point.
338 Saunders, Mrs. Walter Stirling, widow, Gondola Point.
339 Saunders, Horton, farmer, Gondola Point.
340 Saunders, Perry, farmer, Gondola Point.
341 Saunders, Mrs. Perry — Gondola Point.
342 Snodgrass, Thomas, longshoreman, Fair Vale P.O.
343 Snodgrass, Leonard, carpenter, Fair Vale P.O.
344 Snodgrass, Mrs. Leonard — Fair Vale P.O.
345 Smith, George, railway employee, Fair Vale Sta.
346 Smith, Mrs. George — Fair Vale Sta.
347 Smith, Miss Eileen, telephone oper., Fair Vale Sta.
348 Smith, Leroy, overseas, Gondola Point.
349 Stack, Thomas, shipper, Fair Vale Sta.
350 Stack, Mrs. Thomas — Fair Vale Sta.
351 Simpson, James, painter, Fair Vale Sta.
352 Simpson, Mrs. James — Fair Vale Sta.
353 Smith, James L., Telephone Co., Fair Vale Sta.
354 Smith, Mrs. James L. — Fair Vale Sta.
355 Seely, Howard, shipper, Fair Vale Sta.
356 Seely, Mrs. Howard — Fair Vale Sta.
357 Schofield, Aaron, carpenter, Fair Vale Sta.
358 Schofield, Mrs. Aaron — Fair Vale Sta.
359 Slocum, Cecil, delivery truck, Fair Vale Sta.
360 Slocum, Mrs. Cecil — Fair Vale Sta.
361 Slocum, Vernon, overseas, Fair Vale Sta.
362 Smith, Ralph, electrician, Fair Vale Sta.
363 Smith, Fred, clerk, Fair Vale Sta.
364 Smith, Mrs. Fred — Fair Vale Sta.
365 Sproule, Allie, mechanic, Rothesay RR. 1.
366 Sproule, Mrs. Allie — Rothesay RR. 1.
367 Scott, Wheaton, machinist, Rothesay RR. 1.
368 Scott, Mrs. Wheaton — Rothesay RR. 1.
369 Sproule, George, mason, Rothesay RR. 1.
370 Sproule, Mrs. George — Rothesay RR. 1.
371 Stuart, Noel, overseas, Rothesay RR. 1.
372 Stuart, Mrs. Noel — Rothesay RR. 1.
373 Sprague, Edmund, truckman, Rothesay RR. 1.
374 Sprague, Mrs. Edmund — Rothesay RR. 1.
375 Tufts, Andrew, retired, Gondola Point.
376 Thompson, Thomas, labourer, Gondola Point.
377 Touse, John, bookkeeper, Fair Vale Sta.
378 Touse, Mrs. John — Fair Vale Sta.
379 Vincent, Clarence, clerk, Fair Vale P.O.
380 Vincent, Mrs. Clarence — Fair Vale P.O.
381 Vincent, Alec, farmer, Fair Vale P.O.
382 Wilson, Bernard, carpenter, Fair Vale P.O.
383 Wilson, Mrs. Bernard — Fair Vale P.O.
384 White, Gervase, clerk, Fair Vale P.O.
385 Wyman, Mrs. Kenneth, clerk, Fair Vale P.O.
386 Wyman, Jesse, clerk, Gondola Point.
387 Wyman, Mrs. Jesse — Gondola Point.
388 Wyman, Miss Phyllis, hairdresser, Gondola Point.
389 Wilson, Charles, shipping clerk, Gondola Point.
390 Wilson, Mrs. Charles — Gondola Point.
391 Wilson, Mrs. Fred, widow, Gondola Point.
392 Wright, Mrs. John, widow, Fair Vale P.O.
393 Ward, Verner, railway employee, Fair Vale Sta.
394 Ward, Mrs. Verner — Fair Vale Sta.
395 White, Patrick, salesman, Fair Vale Sta.
396 White, Mrs. Patrick — Fair Vale Sta.
397 Wyld, Jonathan, clerk, Fair Vale Sta.
398 Wyld, Mrs. Jonathan — Fair Vale Sta.
399 Wilcox, Neil, overseas, Fair Vale Sta.
400 Wilcox, Mrs. Neil — Fair Vale Sta.
401 Ward, Malcolm, overseas, Fair Vale Sta.
402 Ward, Mrs. Malcolm — Fair Vale Sta.
403 Ward, Ronald, overseas, Fair Vale Sta.
404 Ward, Lester, overseas, Fair Vale Sta.
405 Walker, Ronald, overseas, Fair Vale Sta.
406 Walker, Mrs. Ronald — Fair Vale Sta.
407 Williams, George, clerk, Fair Vale Sta.
408 Williams, Mrs. George — Fair Vale Sta.
409 Waddell, George, truckdriver, Fair Vale Sta.
410 Waddell, Mrs. George — Fair Vale Sta.
411 Wetmore, Mrs. Leonard, widow, Fair Vale Sta.
412 Worden, William, policeman, Fair Vale Sta.
413 Worden, Mrs. William — Fair Vale Sta.
414 Worden, Mrs. Arthur, widow, Fair Vale Sta.
415 Wiggins, Jazen, labourer, Rothesay RR. 1.
416 Wiggins, Mrs. Jazen — Rothesay RR. 1.
417 Wiggins, Arthur, carpenter, Rothesay RR. 1.
418 Wiggins, Mrs. Arthur — Rothesay RR. 1.
419 Yenson, Herman, labourer, Rothesay RR. 1.
420 Yenson, Mrs. Herman — Rothesay RR. 1.

I hereby certify that the foregoing is the printed preliminary list of electors for rural polling division No. 11 C. of the electoral district of Royal, as prepared by the appropriate enumerator for use at the pending election.

Dated at Hampstead this 3rd day of May, 1945.

ARLIE L. PALMER,
Returning Officer.

Printed by the Maritime Publishing Co. Limited, whose address is Sussex, N. B.

Weather

Snow:

Residents of Quispamsis, who were born in the early 1900's, can remember there being some really terrible snowstorms in the winter during their childhood. After some of these storms the snow along the roadsides would be piled as high as the telephone wires. Vera Stephenson can recall that men in the community would get together in teams and drag chains through the snow to lower the height of the snow banks away from the telephone wires after some of these storms. Vera Stephenson also recalls that in the early to mid 1900's, there were no public snowplows in the area that she lived in (Forrester's Cove present day Meenan's Cove area); however, the Province did maintain some roads in Quispamsis. As the outlying areas of Quispamsis were incorporated into communities, their roads were serviced by the community snowplows but roads were still very often plugged with snow. In place of using the roads, residents would drive through the fields with their horses and sleighs. Before the use of the modern day snowplow, individuals, such as George Higgins, would plow certain roads using his horses and a wooden snowplow.

Jim McLaughlin, who was born in 1900, fondly recalls a particularly big snowstorm when he was young. After this snowstorm the snow was so deep people could sit on top of the telephone poles. He also recollected a train being caught in a snowdrift by McCaferty's Bridge in front of the McLaughlin Homestead after this snowstorm. Volunteers dug for three days before the train was finally freed.

Lightening:

Audrey Saunders, Joan (Saunders) Wheaton, Iris (Saunders) Bettle, and Phyllis (Saunders) Bettle. This picture was taken in the field that Audrey, Iris and Phyllis would have crossed on the way home on the night of the terrifying lightening storm.

In 1934 or 1935, Phyllis (Saunders) Bettle can remember being walked home one stormy night, by her older sister, Iris, and her cousin, Audrey Saunders, across the fields from her Uncle George Saunders' home. The reason Mrs. Bettle was eager to return home this stormy night was because there was a lightening storm occurring and she, like her mother, was terrified of lightening. Phyllis and her mother tried to sit out the storm, but by some freak chance a bolt of lightening came in the front door, struck both mother and child, and then proceeded out the back screen door. According to Phyllis, who has a vivid memory of that event "it took the fuses out of the fuse box on the porch!" Luckily neither Phyllis nor her mother was seriously hurt, but they were knocked unconscious for a short period of time. According to Mrs. Bettle that is why her hair is curly today.

Environment

Hammond River Park:

The Hammond River Park was first settled by the Acadians, and then later by the Loyalists. The land has since been a mixture of pasture and forest until the Village of Quispamsis purchased the 40 acres of hillside and 40 acres of adjacent marsh in 1976. The planning for Hammond River Park began in 1976 when Duncan Kelbaugh created the original design for the 80 acre park as part of a thesis for his forestry degree from the University of New Brunswick. Mr. Kelbaugh has been an active environmentalist in the community for a number of years and is the current owner of Brunswick Nurseries on the Model Farm Road.

When the Town of Quispamsis approved Mr. Kelbaugh's proposal to build a nature park, he applied for grants to aid in its construction, which began in 1977. During the next three years, several Canada Works grants allowed student work crews to build an extensive network of nature trails and a log cabin visitor center.

GRANT - A $30,000 Canada Works grant has been awarded for the construction of a pavillion at the Hammond River Park in Quispamsis. Above, are, from left: William Hickey, donator of the land for the park; park manager Duncan Kelbaugh; village manager Donald Scott; and Mayor John Robinson. (Photo by Bill Hart).

Poor maintenance and limited usage during the 1980's saw the trail system fall into disrepair. With the unprecedented environmental awareness of the 1990's, priorities changed. In 1991, the Quispamsis Beautification and Environmental Committee, the Town of Quispamsis, and the Federal Environmental Partners Fund cooperated in a major renovation of Hammond River Park, with an emphasis on its role in environmental awareness and education.

The park is located off Reynar Drive, just above the Hammond River Marsh, and is still in operation today. The trail system is open to the general public year round, dawn until dusk, with no admission fee. There are over 7.8 kilometers (3 miles) of hiking trails, clearly marked and mapped; a 61-meter (200 foot) boardwalk; a wooden bridge and two observation decks at the river.

In Hammond River Park there is a survey marker cut into a large boulder with the date 1714 clearly inscribed on it. The year 1714 predates the existence of Hammond River as a settlement, which was named so in 1783. There are also four squares inscribed on the boulder, possibly signifying that the land was divided at this location. A future study into the origins of the survey marker will hopefully uncover more information.

The above picture was taken in the summer of 2005

Mud Lake Nature Trail:
Mud Lake is a 25 acre bog surrounding two acres of open water and brook that flows about 4.8 kilometers, (3 miles), to Ritchie Lake. Like all wetland, Mud Lake has an important role to play as a wildlife habitat and reservoir of clean, fresh water for a large watershed including Ritchie Lake. Bogs have an interesting natural history that dates back to the last ice age over 10,000 years ago. When walking this trail, visitors will pass from upland forest, through more and more stunted trees and shrubs, onto a floating bog, and finally to the lake itself. In the past, Mud Lake has been an excellent spot for outdoor skating.

Ritchie Lake:
Ritchie Lake, is the lake referenced in the Maliseet name, "Quispamsis", which means 'little lake'. In the early 1950's, Ritchie Lake was deliberately poisoned with pesticides in an attempt to kill all of the 'garbage fish', as they were termed, which were probably pickerel. With the elimination of this fish, officials hoped to restock the lake with trout. The poisoning worked and all of the garbage fish were killed. The lake was closed to fishing for two years to allow the trout stocks to mature and develop. A warden was stationed at the lake to ensure that the ban was not broken. When the lake was reopened, fishing was excellent due to the plentiful trout population. A small dam had also been constructed during this time beside the train tracks to prevent the 'garbage fish' from returning to the lake as they came up the Kennebecasis River. However, the dam eventually collapsed and the 'garbage fish' were able to reenter the lake.

Ritchie Lake is a 58-acre lake that has been used by residents of Quispamsis for fishing, swimming and boating. There were two beaches on opposite sides of the lake, and a walking trail ran along a portion of the lake. A study conducted between July 1990 and February 1991 recommended that the Town prohibit further construction along this lake. In 1991 there were already twenty-seven homes located around the lake.

This recommendation came when it was discovered that high phosphate levels, caused by sewage and fertilizers, were causing algae blooms in the lake. These blooms were so toxic that they were killing the fish. It was believed the sewage was entering into the lake from possible leaks in the surrounding septic systems.

Quispamsis Beautification and Environment Committee:
When this committee existed from the 1980's until the mid 1990's, it made an impact on the promotion of environmental awareness. The mascot of the committee was Bob the Beaver, who was designed by Jonathan Gallant. Among the activities this committee sponsored were poster contests, roadside litter clean-ups, beautification works, and environmental information sessions. These information sessions were offered in 1990 and covered such topics as, groundwater pollution and local garbage issues.

Christmas Tree Mulch:
The first Christmas tree mulch in Quispamsis was held on January 6, 1990. The mulch was recycled and donated to the Cherry Brook Zoo for use in their animal enclosures. Prior to this date the Kennebecasis Valley held an annual Christmas tree burning which was discontinued due to the air pollution created by carbon and smoke. Another contributing factor to its termination was the close proximity of the burning to the Co-op gas bar.

Volunteers from the Rothesay Regional Fire Department have often helped out with the annual Christmas tree mulch. Sites in Quispamsis where this mulch has taken place in the past include the Co-op parking lot, the Daly's Store on the Vincent Road, Meenan's Cove ball field, Jimmy's Store on the Gondola Point Road, and the Village Place Mall parking lot.

Green Schools:
In 1992 Quispamsis Elementary School was designated a Green School. It was the third school in the Province, and one of 105 in Canada to earn this title. The school earned the title by performing acts such as planting a tree in recognition of Arbour Day, cleaning school property, recycling, and creating bird feeders from empty milk cartons. In order for a school to receive a Green School designation, students must complete at least 100 environmental projects. By 2006, both Lakefield Elementary and Quispamsis Elementary schools had received this honour.

Other:
In more recent years, the Town of Quispamsis has proudly

promoted responsible and environmentally conscious management of its community. The Town does not use pesticides on any public properties, and encourages residents to use alternatives to pesticides. Garbage is recycled separating the wet, (perishables), from the dry, (household garbage), with recycling bins provided for plastics, paper, cardboard and glass.

Quispamsis, in the late 1990's, became a member of the Federation of Canadian Municipalities' Partners for Climate Protection, which confirmed the community's commitment to reducing green house gas emissions. Retrofits and new construction since that time, have been done with sustainability and energy efficiency in mind.

CANADA/NEW BRUNSWICK INFRASTRUCTURE PROGRAM ANNOUNCEMENT
for Longwood Park Wastewater Treatment Plant Expansion - From left to right: Councillor Gordon Friars, Councillor Mary Schryer, MLA Brenda Fowlie, Mayor Ron Maloney, Premier Bernard Lord, MP John Herron, Deputy Mayor Murray Driscoll, Senator Joe Day, Councillor Daryl Bishop & Councillor Gerry Garnett.

The Longwood Wastewater Treatment Plant was given a significant $6.2 million upgrade in 2004 with the financial assistance of a Federal/Provincial Infrastructure grant, which saw the three levels of government equally sharing in the project's cost. The project involved the decommissioning of the Matthew's Cove Wastewater Treatment facility, construction of two sewage lift stations, and 1.5 kilometers of force main, 2.5 kilometers of gravity sewer lines and the expansion of the Longwood Wastewater Treatment Facility, (originally built in 1976). A further 3 kilometer collector line was built in the Monarch Drive area called the Eastern Collector System.

The decommissioning of the Wastewater Treatment Plant and the three lift stations were key in ensuring the Town met the main environmental target of eliminating potential point source contamination to the ecosystem, and positioned the Town well for sustainable growth in the future.

As the Town continues to develop, we will see more and more environmentally sustainable projects come to fruition, like the proposed new Wellness Centre to be built at the Gondola Point Recreation Centre site, and is, at the time of this writing, (2008), in its design stages. Plans for the Centre include an NHL size arena, and an outdoor swimming pool. The LEED (Leadership in Energy & Environmental Design), facility will consist of a geothermal heat recovery system, solar energy for water heating, collection of rainwater for gray water, and efficient lighting and equipment. It is expected to be one of the most 'green', sustainable projects of its time in New Brunswick.

Further reference to QPlex under "Recreation and Culture"

Road Maintenance

Unlike today, when Quispamsis was first being formed, the roads were all made of dirt and were often impassable. In the spring the roads were too muddy and in the winter the roads were not always plowed. Before improvements were made to the roads in the Quispamsis area, they were prone to the formation of ruts and holes.

This picture shows Joan (Allison) Tonge walking on the Hampton Road in 1946. This road was first paved in 1939.

In the mid 1900's George Higgins was the Supervisor of the roads. Many of the roads in the outlying areas were gravel so ditches had to be dug and the road re-graveled every spring. Mr. Higgins was in charge of hiring people to do this work, and to supervise the progress of the work being done.

The nine-mile stretch of road from Saint John to Rothesay was the first hard surfaced road in New Brunswick. When automobiles became popular, families would often travel this road when taking a relaxing afternoon drive. Farmers found it difficult to move livestock along this road due to the surface becoming slippery when wet.

Views of the area

The left hand portion of the photo is a view of the McAfee Farm located on top of the Pettingill Road hill. St. Augustine's Church can be seen in the woods in the bottom right hand portion of the picture.

A view of Meenan's Cove Covered Bridge from Meenan's Cove Road. The picture was taken before 1982.

A view of the Gondola Point Road prior to 1920. Jean (Mullett) Wilson's house is located in the upper right hand corner. Her family home burnt in 1920. Jean (Mullett) Wilson would have been three at the time. The location of these homes would be near present day Lionel Drive.

Left to Right: James Breen (John's brother), Bert Breen (Mort's brother), John Breen (Mort's father), Lawrence McCarthy, Mort Breen. Lawrence was the son of Mort's sister. This photo was taken from Mather's Island looking toward Long Island.

An aerial view of the Meenan's Cove Road, taken May 30, 1974, for military training purposes.

Long Island, New Brunswick

Mayors and Councillors (1966 - 2008)

The following is a list of Mayors and Councillors from the communities of Quispamsis and Gondola Point. In 1998 Quispamsis, Gondola Point, and a portion of Wells amalgamated to become the new Town of Quispamsis. Prior to amalgamation, Quispamsis and Gondola Point were incorporated as Villages in 1966, and then, in 1982, Quispamsis was incorporated as a Town, while Gondola Point remained a Village.

Mayors of Quispamsis:
1966 - 1968	Mayor Alan E. Kelly
1968 - 1970	Mayor Keith S. Settle
1970 - 1972	Mayor Keith S. Settle
1972 - 1974	Mayor Sterling E. Gilmore
1974 - 1977	Mayor Sterling E. Gilmore
1977 - 1980	Mayor John F. H. Robinson
1980 - 1983	Mayor Gary G. Smith
1983 - 1986	Mayor Emil T. Olsen
1986 - 1989	Mayor Emil T. Olsen
1989 - 1992	Mayor Emil T. Olsen
1992 - 1995	Mayor Emil T. Olsen
1995 - 1998	Mayor Bob A. Peters, Ed. D.

Mayors of Gondola Point:
1967 - 1969	Mayor Otty S. Sherwood
1969 - 1971	Mayor Gerarda R. Connors
1971 - 1974	Mayor Joseph G. Scott
1974 - 1977	Mayor E. Lloyd Marshall
1977 - 1980	Mayor E. Lloyd Marshall
1980 - 1983	Mayor James F. Watt
1983 - 1986	Mayor James F. Watt
1986 - 1989	Mayor James F. Watt
1989 - 1992	Mayor James F. Watt
1992 - 1995	Mayor James F. Watt
1995 - 1997	Mayor Leslie Hamilton-Brown

Mayors of the Amalgamated Town of Quispamsis:
1997 - 2001	Mayor Leslie Hamilton-Brown
2001 - 2004	Mayor Ron Maloney
2004 - 2008	Mayor Ron Maloney
2008 - 2012	Mayor G. Murray Driscoll

Quispamsis Councils

1966 - 1968	Mayor Alan E. Kelly
	Councillor John A. Higgins
	Councillor Donald B. Bursey
1968 - 1970	Mayor Keith S. Settle
	Councillor Edward L. Beckwith
	Councillor George A. McAfee

1970 - 1974   Mayor Keith S. Settle (1970 - 1972)
                Mayor Sterling E. Gilmore (1972 - 1974)
                Councillor George A. McAfee
                Councillor Howard A. Saunders
                Councillor Edward L. Beckwith

1974 - 1977	Mayor Sterling E. Gilmore
Councillor J. Gordon Anderson
Councillor Donald E. Kennedy
Councillor William R. McLaughlin
Councillor John F. H. Robinson
Councillor Donald R. Sherwood
Councillor Edward L. Beckwith
Village Manager, Donald G. Scott
Village Engineer, Thomas Jepson

1977 - 1980   Mayor John F. H. Robinson
              Deputy Mayor Donald R. Sherwood
              Councillor J. Gordan Anderson
              Councillor E. Diane Fleet
              Councillor James W. Renshaw
              Councillor Roger H. Nesbitt
              Village Manager, Donald G. Scott
              Village Engineer, Thomas Jepson

1980 - 1983   Mayor Gary G. Smith
              Deputy Mayor Roger H. Nesbitt
              Councillor Ronald A. Magee
              Councillor Joseph McCarten
              Councillor Donald R. Sherwood
              Councillor Richard F. McPhee
              Village Manager, Donald G. Scott
              Village Engineer, Thomas Jepson
              Works Superintendent, Ralph Breen

1983 - 1986   Mayor Emil T. Olsen
Deputy Mayor Brian Blaikie
Councillor Willard Carr
Councillor Ronald Magee
Councillor Joseph McCarten
Councillor Donald Sherwood
Town Manager, Donald Scott
Town Clerk, Catherine Cameron
Works Superintendent, Ralph Breen

Quispamsis Council
1983-1986

1986 - 1989   Mayor Emil T. Olsen
Deputy Mayor Shirley Corkum
Councillor Brian Blaikie
Councillor Joseph McCarten
Councillor Donald Sherwood
Councillor Garry Duperreault
Town Manager, Donald Scott
Town Clerk, Catherine Snow
Works Superintendent, Ralph Breen

Emil T. Olsen
- Mayor -

Shirley Corkum
- Deputy Mayor -

Donald Scott
- Town Manager -

Catherine P. Snow
- Town Clerk -

Quispamsis Council
1986-1989

Ralph Breen
- Works Superintendant -

Brian Blaikie
- Councillor -

Joseph McCarten
- Councillor -

Donald Sherwood
- Councillor -

Garry Duperreault
- Councillor -

1989 - 1992   Mayor Emil T. Olsen
               Deputy Mayor Stephen Campbell
               Councillor William McLaughlin
               Councillor Ronald Magee
               Councillor Donald Sherwood
               Councillor Daniel Dobson
               Councillor Bob Peters, Ed. D.
               Councillor Garry Duperreault
               Councillor Leo Bonnevie

Quispamsis Council
1989-1992

1992 - 1995   Mayor Emil T. Olsen
Deputy Mayor Anne Downey
Councillor Leo Bonnevie
Councillor William McLaughlin
Councillor Bob Peters
Councillor Cindy Swetnam
Councillor Gerry Garnett
Councillor Ron Magee
Councillor Mike LeRoy

QUISPAMSIS COUNCIL
1992 - 1995

1995 - 1998   Mayor Bob Peters, Ed. D.
Deputy Mayor Ronald Magee
Councillor Gerry Garnett
Councillor John van Kralingen
Councillor Brenda Fowlie
Councillor Bob Wisted
Councillor Douglas Lee
Councillor Donald MacQuarrie
Councillor Micheal Reinhart

Village of Gondola Point Councils:

1967 - 1969	Mayor Otty S. Sherwood
	Councillor Lionel A. Hodges
	Councillor D. Horton Saunders
1969 - 1971	Mayor Gerarda R. Connors
	Councillor D. Horton Saunders
	Councillor Michael A. Sheppard

Otty S. Sherwood
Mayor
1967-1969

Gerarda R. Connors
Mayor
1969-1971

Lionel A. Hodges

D. Horton Saunders

D. Horton Saunders

Michael A. Sheppard

1971 - 1974   Mayor Joseph G. Scott
                 Councillor Stanley R. Boyle
                 Councillor Gerarda R. Connors
                 Councillor Donald W. Cooper
                 Councillor E. Lloyd Marshall

1974 - 1977   Mayor E. Lloyd Marshall
Councillor Stanley R. Boyle
Councillor Donald W. Cooper
Councillor David M. Driscoll
Councillor Joseph G. Scott

1977 - 1980   Mayor E. Lloyd Marshall
Councillor James E. Davis
Councillor Robert G. Ross
Councillor Joseph G. Scott
Councillor John. G. Walton

1980 - 1983   Mayor James F. Watt
Councillor Martha McCully
Councillor Ronald E. Roberts
Councillor J. Douglas Templeton
Councillor John G. Walton

1983 - 1986   Mayor James F. Watt
              Councillor Joseph B. Gillis
              Councillor Wayne N. Lavallee
              Councillor Donald W. McElman
              Councillor Robert G. Ross
              Councillor Robert D. Taylor

1986 - 1989		Mayor James F. Watt
				Councillor Yvonne B. Gibb
				Councillor Robert G. Ross
				Councillor Noreen P. Russell
				Councillor Robert D. Taylor

1989 - 1992   Mayor James F. Watt
Councillor Yvonne B. Gibb
Councillor Carolyn J. LeBlanc
Councillor R. Douglas Lee
Councillor Robert G. Ross
Councillor Noreen P. Russell
Councillor Robert D. Taylor

1992 - 1995   Mayor James F. Watt
              Councillor Robert D. Taylor
              Councillor Carolyn J. LeBlanc
              Councillor R. Douglas Lee
              Councillor Robert G. Ross
              Councillor Donald W. McElman
              Councillor Stephen Flynn

1995 - 1997   Mayor Leslie Hamilton-Brown
Councillor Robert D. Taylor
Councillor Carolyn J. LeBlanc
Councillor R. Douglas Lee
Councillor Robert G. Ross
Councillor Donald W. McElman
Councillor Stephen Flynn

Amalgamated Town of Quispamsis Councils:

1997 - 2001   Mayor Leslie Hamilton-Brown
Deputy Mayor Ron Maloney
Councillor Beth Thompson
Councillor Brenda Fowlie (1997-1999)
Councillor Carolyn LeBlanc
Councillor Mary Schryer (1999-2001)
Councillor Daryl Bishop
Councillor Gerry Garnett
Councillor Ronald Magee

2001 - 2004   Mayor Ron Maloney
Deputy Mayor G. Murray Driscoll
Councillor Beth Thompson
Councillor Daryl Bishop
Councillor Mary Schryer
Councillor Gordon Friars
Councillor Lisa Loughery
Councillor Gerry Garnett

2004 - 2008   Mayor Ron Maloney
                Deputy Mayor G. Murray Driscoll
                Councillor Mary Schryer (2004-2006)
                Councillor Daryl Bishop
                Councillor Pierre Rioux
                Councillor Emil Olsen
                Councillor Lisa Loughery
                Councillor Beth Thompson
                Councillor Gerry Maher (2006 - 2008)

Centre Photo includes: Town Administrator, Michael Brennan (back row, 2nd from right); Town Engineer, Gary Losier (back row, 1st from right); Town Treasurer, Jo-Anne McGraw (back row, 3rd from right); Community Services Director, Dana Purton Dickson (front row, 1st from right); Town Clerk, Catherine Snow (front row, 2nd from right); PAC Secretary, Margie McGrath (back row, 2nd from left); and Town Solicitor, Richard McPhee (back row, 1st from left).

Quispamsis Town Council & Management 2008

Murray Driscoll, Mayor

Emil Olsen, Deputy Mayor

Gary Clark, Councillor

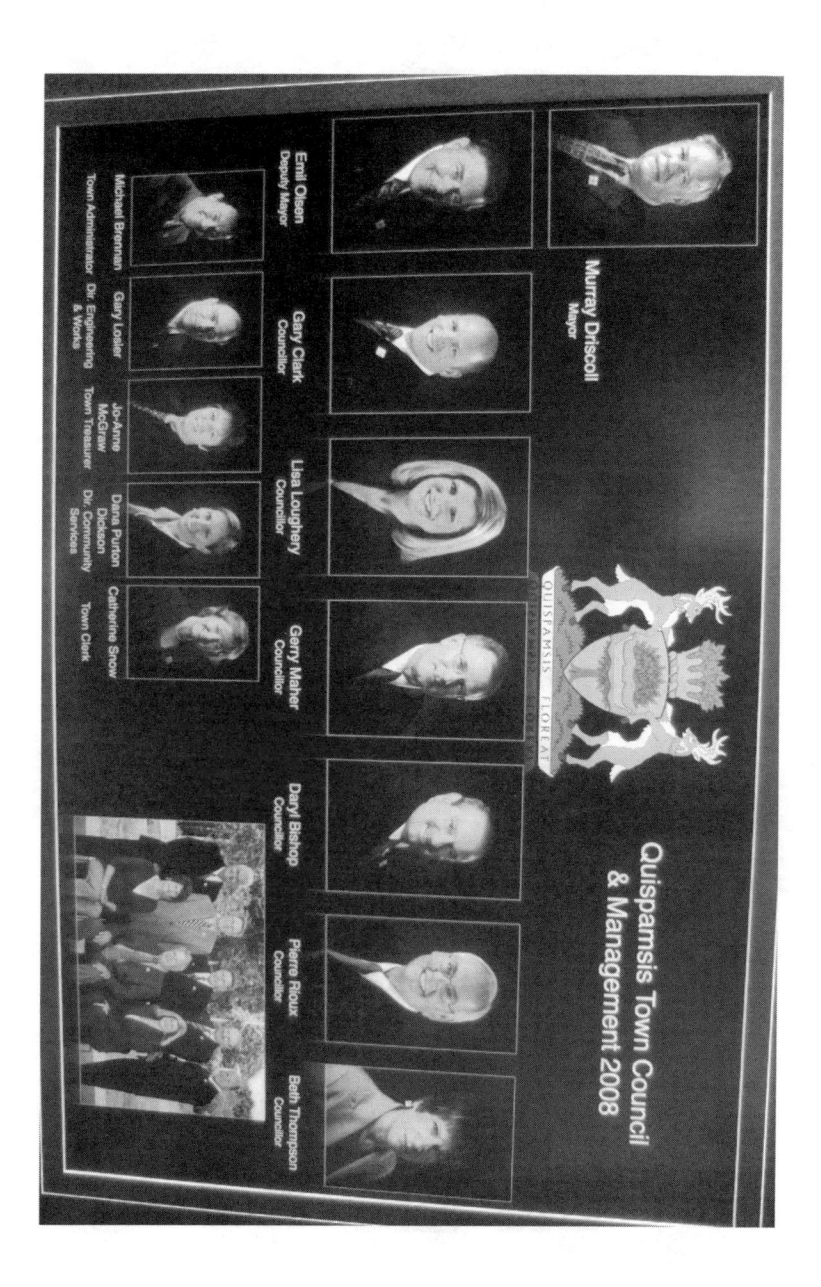

Lisa Loughery, Councillor

Gerry Maher, Councillor

Daryl Bishop, Councillor

Pierre Rioux, Councillor

Beth Thompson, Councillor

Michael Brennan, Town Administrator

Gary Losier, Dir. Engineering & Works

Jo-Anne McGraw, Town Treasurer

Dana Purton Dickson, Dir. Community Services

Catherine Snow, Town Clerk

2008 - 2012   Mayor G. Murray Driscoll
Duputy Mayor Emil Olsen
Councillor Daryl Bishop
Councillor Gary Clark
Councillor Lisa Loughery
Councillor Gerry Maher
Councillor Pierre Rioux
Councillor Beth Thompson
Town Administrator Michael Brennan
Dir. Engineering & Works Gary Losier
Town Treasurer Jo-Anne McGraw
Dir. Community Services Dana Purton Dickson
Town Clerk Catherine Snow

Amalgamation

When amalgamation was proposed, the majority of Quispamsis and Gondola Point residents were not satisfied with the options presented to them. Many political analysts felt that the McKenna provincial government was driving a wedge between Saint John and the surrounding communities. Skip Cormier, the provincially appointed commissioner, was responsible for examining options to reorganize local municipalities. Five proposals were put forth outlining possible scenarios on how the outlying municipalities would be joined together. The Kennebecasis Valley municipalities joining the City of Saint John, and the Kennebecasis Valley Municipalities uniting together to form the Kennebecasis Valley City were two of these proposals. None of the above proposals were realized. Instead the municipalities of Quispamsis and Gondola Point, and a portion of the LSD area known as Wells joined together to form the new Town of Quispamsis, while the municipalities of Fairvale, Rothesay, East Riverside and Renforth joined together to form the Town of Rothesay. These amalgamations became effective in 1998.

Amalgamation takes another progressive step
'This is a piece of history'

LONG ROAD AHEAD:
The first meeting for the merged town of Quispamsis may have been a short one, but it's certainly not a sign of things to come.

Two things are for sure: The inaugural meeting of the new council that will direct the destiny of the merged town of Quispamsis will surely be remembered as the shortest in the four years of council sessions that lie ahead.

There was first a speedy swearing-in ceremony by acting transitional council legal officer Robert Creamer - composed of Mayor Leslie Hamilton-Brown, Deputy Mayor Ron Maloney and councillors Brenda Fowlie, Daryl Bishop, Gerry Garnett, Carolyn leBlanc, Beth Thompson and Ron

Magee. Then came 25 minutes of business and then council and many guests settled in for a reception and refreshments of punch, coffee and Timbits.

The other thing, as Ms. Thompson put it, was that "this is a piece of history. It's very significant for the community and the Valley. Things have changed".

And there is much to do ahead.

Mrs. Hamilton-Brown said among other things, the transitional council must find appropriate staffing levels when it takes over the reins of three merged communities on Jan 1, 1998. It will also have to settle on a new tax rate, amend bylaws, do liaison work with Saint John and the new towns of Grand Bay-Westfield and Rothesay, and help set up the new regional commissions. "We have our work cut out for us," she said.

Mrs. Hamilton-Brown is wasting no time in getting down to that work. Last night, council voted to appoint Catherine Snow as Clerk and to name Councillors to specific committees, with Mrs. Hamilton-Brown and Mr. Maloney being the representatives on the sensitive budget and personnel committees.

They also voted to seek capital borrowing of $155,000 for repaving of the Neck Road, $45,000 for the Gondola Point Road, while deferring decisions on moneys for the collector-connector road and Quispamsis's share into the regional salt shed.

Council has an "orientation night" at the Hilton Hotel later this week with special input from Kennebecasis MLA Peter Leblanc, on infrastructure funding.

The next council meeting is on July 23, with subsequent meetings to be held in the Gondola Point Recreation Centre the first and third Mondays of every month.

The mayor also said that beginning tomorrow, she would meet with existing staff and said that she has already had a letter from Saint John Mayor Shirley McAlary and Grand Bay-Westfield suggesting the communities trade ideas.

She also said there would be the closest cooperation possible between Quispamasis and the new transitional council of Rothesay.

Glen Allen

The Town Crest

In 2008, the Town obtained a grant of armorial bearings for an official Coat of Arms from The Canadian Heraldic Authority, which contains symbolic elements of both the former Quispamsis and Gondola Point crests.

Concept for Armorial Bearings for the town of Quispamsis -
Explanation of the Symbolism:

Arms:

The gold colour of the shield represents the sunlight that is the life-giving force to all. The green colour of the tree places some importance on the natural vegetation of the area. The blue wave alludes to the name Quispamsis, meaning "little lake" in the Maliseet language. The blue wave also represents the Kennebecasis River, which has been the major influence in the region for the aspects of historical transportation of goods and lumber as well as modern recreation. The gondola is a raft that was used in the logging days on the river and carried passengers, goods and people on the river. This style of transportation gave its name to Gondola Point, one of the component municipalities merging to form the new town of Quispamsis.

Crest:

The maple leaves support the municipality's identification as Canadian. The crown vallary presents an image of both a Town and a fenced area of appreciation.

Supporters:

The deer represents the Province of New Brunswick, which also has such supporters. Each is differenced from other such supporters by the masoned circlet. The masonry design represents the idea of a town. In addition, it can allude to the portion of the Local Service District of Wells that was also merged to form the new town.

Compartment:
The green grassy mound also represents the verdant area.

Michelle Pelrine, a former Kennebecasis Valley High School student, designed a Quispamsis Crest in 1997. The crest consisted of six symbols signifying the joining of the former communities of Gondola Point, Quispamsis, and Wells, as part of amalgamation in 1998. The red and yellow of the rainbow represented the Province of New Brunswick. The maple leaf represented Canada. The tree signified the original beautiful parks and forestland, and was part of the original Quispamsis Crest. The water represents the scenic Kennebecasis River, which borders the Town. The gondola was part of the original Gondola Point Crest and was used to signify the gondola (raft) used in the logging days of the river. The sun represented the sun shining upon us all.

The pre-amalgamated Village of Gondola Point crest. The maple leaf symbolizes Canada, the ship symbolizes New Brunswick, and the gondola symbolizes the travel used in the logging days of the river.

The pre-amalgamated Quispamsis crest. The tree and green areas symbolized the verdant area of the community, the natural vegetation and park areas. The water symbolized Ritchie Lake, the lake referred to in the Maliseet name, 'Quispamsis', 'little lake'.

Development of Quispamsis

Quispamsis: From a Village to a Town:
The following article appeared in the Telegraph Journal on Saturday February 19, 1983 shortly after the Village of Quispamsis was made into a Town. The article discusses the benefits for Quispamsis upon becoming a Town.

Benefits Follow 'Promotion' From Village

Increased influence with higher governments and a growing sense of local identity are cited by Quispamsis residents and businessmen as possible after effects of the recent conversion of their community from a village to a town.

"This could mean that more money will be coming from the (provincial) government," said Jeannine St. Amand, 18, student president of Kennebecasis Valley High School, in Quispamsis. "Also, it makes me proud. I go down to the States and they ask me where I'm from and I would say Quispamsis. They would say 'What is that?' Now I can answer it's a town."

She concluded that Quispamsis Field Days, the local summer celebration, would be more successful.

Quispamsis Mayor, Gary Smith, and Town Manager, Don Scott, claim the Town will now be able to take a seat at the negotiation table equal to other New Brunswick communities of a similar size. Scott added that town status acted as a lobbying tool.

Daryl Bishop, Manager of the Kennebecasis Home Hardware store, agreed with Scott.

"Quispamsis is one of the bedroom communities that is finally going to be recognized," Bishop said. "It's not any longer going to be Rothesay and area, it's going to be Rothesay and Quispamsis and area."

Bishop speculated someday this and surrounding communities might be part of one large, residential city-similar to Dartmouth, N.S. He even volunteered a name: Kennebecasis.

"I've always called it a town automatically,"

said June Steeves, Manager of the Quispamsis Co-op store. Steeves, like Bishop, said she had not noticed any demonstrative outbursts from citizens celebrating municipal stratification. But she quickly added, "I certainly haven't heard anything bad."

Marg Melanson, Manager of the Rollertheque roller skating rink, said the attitude of the locals she deals with- the vast majority of whom are in their teens- has remained the same. And that attitude, she explains, can best be described as somewhat apathetic. Maybe the turn will spark some enthusiasm for existing recreational facilities, she added.

"The truth is that I think they are aware (of the present facilities), but they don't use them. It's a shame," Melanson said.

"I think becoming a town is great," said Eleanor Jones, local historian and a Quispamsis resident for over 40 years. "At first I thought they were going a little quick. I didn't think we were in a position to know what had to be done. It seemed that we grew too quickly. This all happened in the last 10 to 15 years."

Concluded Eleanor's husband, Percy "It's all for the good I guess. It's progress."

- From the Telegraph-Journal,
Saturday, February 19, 1983.

Quispamsis (until 1998):

Quispamsis was incorporated into a Town on December 22, 1982. Prior to this, on November 9, 1966 Quispamsis was incorporated as a Village by an Act of the Legislature in New Brunswick, and consisted of 3626 square kilometers. Prior to 1966 Quispamsis was often referred to as the community of Quispamsis, or was associated with the Parishes of Rothesay and Hampton.

Quispamsis has been one of the fastest growing communities in Kings County, especially in the 1970's and the 1980's. It is believed that this is due to migration from Saint John to suburban areas. Below in Table 1 is the population numbers for Quispamsis up until 2006. Note that in 1998 the population numbers would include those of Gondola Point and a portion of Wells due to the amalgamation.

Table 1: Quispamsis Population Numbers

Date	Population
1966	1,556
1971	2,215
1973	2,700
1976	4,968
1982	6,500
1986	7,185
1991	8,446
1998	13,521
2001	13,757
2006	15,239

In 1976 census data for families by number of children at home for Quispamsis show two to four persons per family was the average family size. It is also interesting to note that of the 1,250 families in Quispamsis, 285 did not have children. Table 2 clearly illustrates the facts.

Table 2: Quispamsis 1976 census data for families by the number of children at home.

Total Number of Children at Home	Number of Families	Percentage(%)
One Child	270	28
Two Children	365	37.8
Three Children	185	19.2
Four Children	85	8.8
Five or More Children	60	6.2
TOTAL	965	100

In the 1970's the majority of occupations in Quispamsis were in the service sector - managerial, teaching, medicine, sales, construction and transportation. In 1971 there were 125 jobs within the Village. Of these 125 jobs, local residents filled 72% and the rest were commuters.

Quispamsis (1998 - present):

On January 1, 1998 the Town of Quispamsis was amalgamated with the Village of Gondola Point and with a portion of a local service District known as Wells. These amalgamated communities became collectively known as the Town of Quispamsis. For more information on amalgamation refer to the section entitled Amalgamation. With the creation of the new Town came a new Town Crest that symbolized the amalgamated communities. Refer to the section entitled Town Crest for more information on the Town Crest.

Gondola Point (until 1998):

The name Gondola Point was likely derived from the dugout canoe-like boats that carried passengers and goods along the river. These small boats were called gondolas to distinguish them from the fishing boats and freight scows used on the river. There are references to gondolas in New Brunswick as early as 1768.

Gondola Point was one of six municipalities in the Rothesay parish. In 1966 Gondola Point officially became a village. Originally the Village of Gondola Point was strictly residential and like other municipalities, was the area where people came to spend the summer. Gondola Point even had a hotel, Hillhurst House, to accommodate some of these summer guests. Refer to the section entitled Businesses, Hotels, & Stores for more information on Hillhurst House.

Gondola Point was the second fastest growing community in Kings County. Below in Table 3 are the population numbers for Gondola Point until 1991. Note that Gondola Point's population numbers would be included with those of Quispamsis after 1997 due to amalgamation.

Table 3: Gondola Point Population Numbers

Date	Population
1966	479
1971	850
1976	1,846
1986	3,596
1991	4,218

It is interesting to note that while the Kennebecasis Valley communities were experiencing growth, the City of Saint John was losing population. Many residents were eager to escape the busy city life, favouring the slower pace of the suburban communities.

The population pyramid in Figure 1 shows the distribution of people based on age in the years 1971 and 1976. In 1971 there is a notably higher proportion of younger people (both male and female) in the community especially in the age groups 0-4 through 30-34. Young couples were migrating to this community with their young and teenage children. In 1976 there is a marked increase in the proportion of people in the age groups 25-29 and 30-34 (both male and female) in comparison to 1971 confirming a trend of young couples relocating to the community.

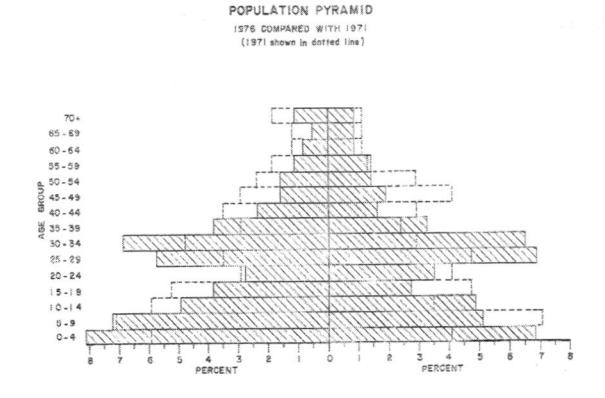

Figure 1: Population Pyramid for Gondola Point comparing the year 1976 with 1971. Note that the year 1971 is shown in dotted lines.

Family sizes in Gondola Point in 1976 were on par with the Provincial average of 1.8 children per family. However, there were more families with two children than any other category. Shown below in Table 4 is the size of families based on the number of children in each. Note that only the 370 families with children are represented while there were approximately 465 families in Gondola Point.

Table 4: Representation of family size in the Village of Gondola Point in 1976 based on the number of children in each family.

Total Number of Children at Home	Number of Families	Percentage(%)
One Child	105	22.4
Two Children	150	40.5
Three Children	70	18.9
Four Children	35	9.5
Five or More Children	10	2.7
TOTAL	1335	100

In the 1970's the majority of the labor force residing in Gondola Point commuted to work. There were only three commercial outlets, all convenience stores, in the Village at this time. From information obtained from Statistics Canada it was concluded that 87% of the resident employed work force in Gondola Point commuted outside the Village for work. These statistics can be seen in the Table 5 below.

Table 5. Gondola Point Journey to Work Data - 1971

Resident-Employed Labor Force	Number of Workers	Percentage(%)
Working in the Village	20	6.5
Working outside of the Village	265	87.0
Place of Work not stated	20	6.5
Total Labor Force	305	100

Of the 87% of residents who worked outside the Village, the majority (67%) worked in Saint John while 12% worked in Rothesay. The remainder worked at various locations outside of the Village.

The majority of the development that took place in Gondola Point prior to 1982 occurred between the years 1962 and 1981. It was during this period that major subdivisions came into existence. Prior to 1945 the developments in the community were primarily along the Gondola Point Road.

Quispamsis at a Glance:
In the years since amalgamation, the Town of Quispamsis has been in a permanent state of growth. As one of the fastest growing communities in New Brunswick, the Town is continually changing. Table 6 displays some notable figures about the Town as compiled by researchers in 2006 as well as by Statistics Canada from the 2001 Census.

Table 6. General Statistics About Quispamsis

Population	13, 757
Workforce	7, 530
Households	4,596
Housing Costs	Average value $118, 740
Household Income	Median $79,922
Residential Taxes (2006)	$1.25

Commercial Taxes (2006)	$4.14
Services	Fire, Police, Ambulance, Library
Places of Worship	18
Schools	1 high school, 1 middle school, 2 elementary schools
Cultural and Recreational	Nature parks, public beaches, walking trails, arena, ball fields, soccer fields, tennis courts

First Quispamsis Municipal Building, 346 Hampton Road 1976 - 1984

Village of Gondola Point Municipal Building (portion of the Gondola Point Recreation Centre off Meenan's Cove Road)

Quispamsis Town Hall 1984 - 2002; 18 Municipal Drive

Quispamsis Town Hall 2002 - Present

Emergency Services

Royal Canadian Mounted Police:

Before the Rothesay Regional Police Force began patrolling the communities of Quispamsis and Gondola Point, both communities were under the jurisdiction of the Royal Canadian Mounted Police (RCMP). The RCMP was stationed in Hampton but patrolled the Village of Gondola Point on a daily basis in 1982. Residents could reach the RCMP after hours using a Zenith number, which was a special type of telephone number introduced before the development of toll-free services. It would allow a subscriber to call a number at no charge by dialling the Operator and requesting the specified Zenith number

Rothesay Regional Police Force:

The only member of the Rothesay Police Department in 1951 was Chief Harry Miller. Chief Miller worked day and night, seven days a week and operated the police station from his home with the help of his wife and three daughters. For more information on Harry Miller please refer to the section entitled Distinguished Residents.

Despite the fact that Chief Harry Miller's jurisdiction was only in the Town of Rothesay where he resided, he was well known and respected by the residents of Quispamsis. Residents of Quispamsis depended on the RCMP for policing services until the late 1970's. At this point the Village of Quispamsis made an arrangement with the Village of Rothesay for joint police protection. In 1984 the communities of Rothesay, Quispamsis, Fairvale, Renforth, Gondola Point, and East Riverside-Kinghurst decided to create a regional police force. These communities came under the jurisdiction of the Rothesay Regional Police Force.

Since 1998, the Rothesay Regional Police Force polices both Rothesay and Quispamsis. A new police station was built at 126 Millennium Drive in Quispamsis in 2004. The police station was previously located at 3 Landing Court, next to the current Quispamsis Town Hall. The police force also has two other Community Offices, located in Rothesay and Quispamsis. The Quispamsis Community Office, which is staffed by volunteers, is located on Parkside Drive in the mobile home park. It was established in 1994 as the first

FINALLY SIGNED — An agreement setting up a regional police force to serve six Kennebecasis Valley communities was formally signed last night after several delays over the past number of weeks. Taking part in the ceremony were the mayors of the six communities. Seated, left to right, are Emil Olsen of Quispamsis, Donald Horne of Rothesay, Anthony McGuire of Renforth and James Watt of Gondola Point. Standing, left to right, are Gary Corscadden of Fairvale and John Brittain of East Riverside-Kingshurst. The new force will begin patrols Jan. 1.

community office for the Rothesay Regional Police Force. The office hosts various events for the community throughout the year such as Family Fun Days, Winter Carnival, and the annual visit from Santa in December.

The above pictures are of the Rothesay Regional Police Station located on Millennium Drive.

The above picture is of the old Rothesay Regional Police Station at 3 Landing Court prior to its closure in 2004.

The Rothesay Regional Board of Police Commissioners assists the overseeing of administration and organization of the police force. The Board is comprised of ten members, eight of which are appointed by the Mayor and Councillors of their respective Town Councils. As of June 2008 the Quispamsis Committee members included Councillor

Lisa Loughery, Jim Gillespie, Gordon Friars, and Danny Dobson. The Department of Public Safety appoints one member and the Chief of Police is appointed as an ex-officio member of the Board. The overall duty of the Board is to ensure that the police force is fulfilling its obligations to the community.

Since the Rothesay Regional Police began operation, six men have held the title of police chief. Listed below are the six police chiefs of the Rothesay Regional Police Force.

Rothesay Regional Police Chiefs:

Chief Harry Miller	1951-1975
Chief Grant Lewis	1975-1977
Chief Melvin Saunders	1977-1982
Chief Cyril Oram	1982-1986
Chief Thomas Gladney	1986-1998
Chief Stephen McIntyre	1998-Present

Not only are the members of the Rothesay Regional Police Force busy serving the Kennebecasis Valley, but they are also heavily involved in organizing and sponsoring several community events including the annual bike rodeo, local t-ball leagues, Rothesay Police Force Hockey Team, and other local sports teams.

Rothesay Regional Police T-ball Team

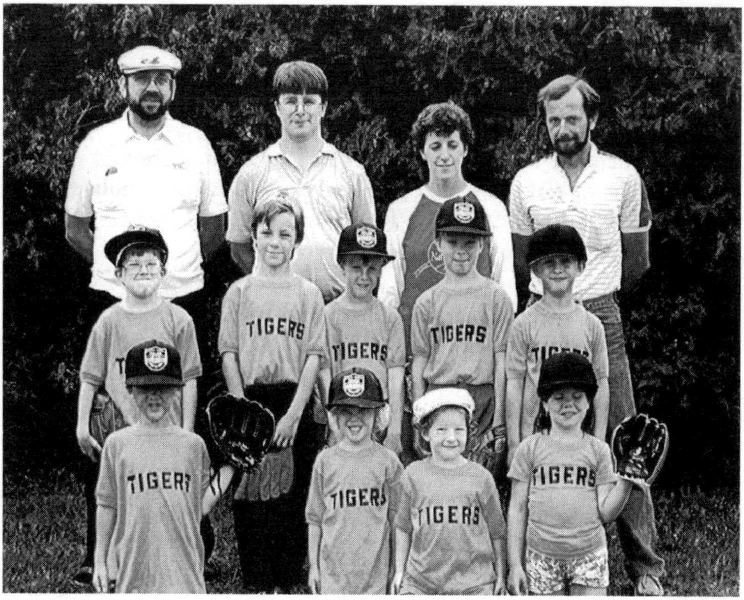
TIGERS

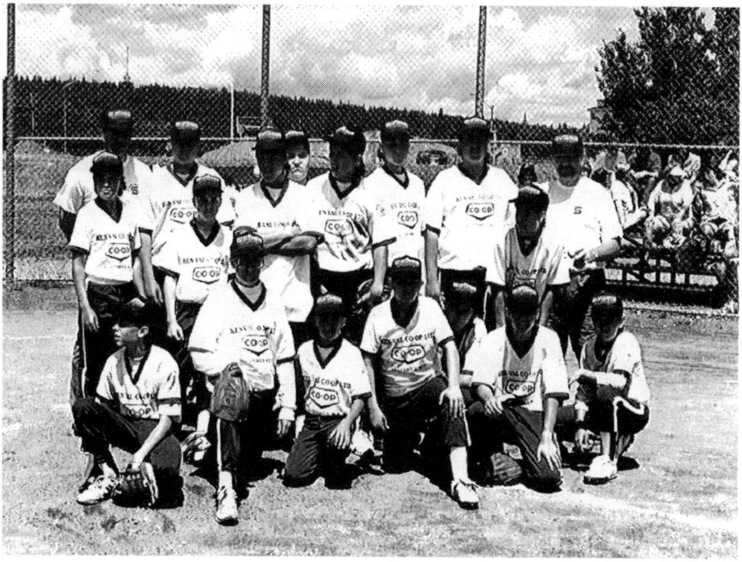
CO-OP

373

Various Rothesay Regional Police Force T-Ball Teams over the years.

Rothesay Regional Police Department Hockey Team

Hockey Jerseys are donated by Rothesay Regional Police to a local girls' hockey team.

Police Officer Norm McKay helps hand out jerseys.

The above picture is taken at the Olympic Stadium before an Expos Games with kids from the Rothesay Regional Police Force T-ball league.

An unidentified boy from the Rothesay Regional Police Force T-ball Team gets ready to bat at the Olympic Stadium.

The Rothesay Regional Police Force is composed of a number of departments or sections including Major Crime, Traffic, Truth Verification, Victim Services, Emergency Tactical, Public Safety, Court, Identification, Technology Crime, Media Liaison, Community Policing, Police Community Relations, Dispatch Centre, School Officers, Bike Patrol, D.A.R.E., Neighbourhood Watch, Firearms, K.V. Crimestoppers, Fundy Integrated Intelligence Unit, and Auxiliary Police. In 2006, staff included 32 police officers, including five females, seven civilian staff, and eight auxiliary members.

CORPORAL STEVE McINTYRE of the Rothesay police department keeps busy indoors dusting fingerprints.

The Citizen newspaper published various photographs of "The Boys in Blue" on June 17, 1986. The images included several photos and captions of busy police officers at work from across the province. Current Chief of Police, Steve McIntyre, was photographed for the paper dusting for fingerprints.

In 2002 Senior Constable Evan Scott was awarded the National Police Award for Traffic Safety in recognition of his outstanding dedication to improving safety on Canadian roadways.

Quispamsis Ambulance Service:

The Quispamsis Ambulance Brigade supplied an ambulance service in the 1980's administered by the Town of Quispamsis and operated by both paid employees and volunteers. Pictured below on the left is the Quispamsis Ambulance dated May 16, 1984. In 1983, Mayor Emil Olsen presented to Trevor Landry and Kelly Honeyman, both members of the Quispamsis Ambulance, the Youth of the Year Award. Mayor Olsen, Mr. Landry and Mr. Honeyman are pictured below on the right.

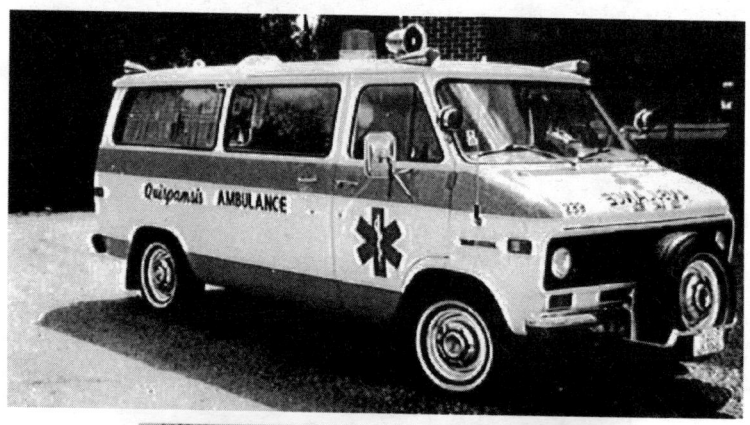

Rothesay Regional Fire Department:

The Rothesay Fire Department was formed in 1924 and was comprised solely of volunteers. Geoff Sayre and Fred Crosby purchased the department's first fire truck, a 1924 Ford Model T chemical unit, from Saint John. The very night the truck was acquired, Mr. Sayre's house caught on fire, and the truck was put to good use.

The original Model T chemical unit was put to good use when Mr. Sayre's house caught on fire the night the truck was acquired.

Over the years the department grew in size and changed locations several times. In 1966, when several of the surrounding villages were incorporated, the department began official fire protection to the six municipalities in the Kennebecasis Valley. In 1967 the first two career firefighters were hired, Chief Geoff Sayre and Deputy Chief Earl Carleton.

In 1982 the Quispamsis fire station at 12 Civic Drive was officially opened, providing the growing population in the area with a faster response time. In 1989 the department was regionalized and became jointly owned by all six municipalities. In the mid 1990's, the Rothesay Regional Fire Department responded to approximately 350 calls per year. That number increased to 733 responses in 2000 and

1069 in 2005.

The department currently provides services to the amalgamated towns of Quispamsis and Rothesay, as well as portions of three local service districts, encompassing a coverage area in excess of 120 square kilometres. With these changes, and the increasing size of the force and equipment, it was apparent a new fire station was necessary to house the organization. On April 22, 2001 a new fire station on Campbell Drive in Rothesay was officially opened.

The department is comprised of twenty-four career staff, five part-time fire fighters, and thirty volunteer fire fighters, currently (2006) under the direction of Chief Larry Greer and Deputy Chief Brian Jensen. Housed in the two fire stations are two rapid intervention vehicles, four pumpers, three tankers, an equipment van, a Boston Whaler rescue boat, an all terrain vehicle, three service vehicles, and two antiques including the original 1924 Model T.

Fire Station #1, Campbell Drive, Rothesay

Fire Station #2, Municipal Drive, Quispamsis

Services

Sewage:

In Quispamsis, the Longwood Park wastewater system was constructed in 1976. It connected homes within the more populated area of the community, which included most of the Pettingill Road, and the portion of the Hampton Road from the Rothesay boundary to KVHS, and the subdivisions that feed into these roads. The construction of the wastewater treatment system was necessary to address problems concerning contamination of well water and complaints about smells from septic systems in the rapidly growing subdivisions. It allowed for smaller building lots in the sewer serviced part of the community.

The Gondola Point sewage system lagoon was in full operation by September of 1977. The treatment facility consisted of an aerated lagoon located near Matthew's Cove. When first designed, it had the capacity to service a population of 4,000 with the ability to be easily expanded if necessary.

The Matthew's Cove system in 2005 was decommissioned after reaching its capacity. Sewer lines were extended to the newly expanded Longwood Lagoon, a six million dollar project made possible through an infrastructure grant from the Federal and Provincial Governments.

Water Supply and Distribution System:

At the time of this writing, most of the Town of Quispamsis is not serviced by a municipal water distribution system. Residents are dependent on individual wells for their water. The Town does have two small municipal water systems as well as a small privately owned and operated water distribution system that services the Mobile Home Parks. The two municipal systems include the Ridgewood Park system and the Downeast/Millennium Drive system.

The Ridgewood Park water system, located west of the Vincent Road was installed by the developer and includes two production wells, one backup well and two pump houses, and was designed to service 100 homes in this subdivision.

The first water tower in Quispamsis was built in 2006 on Market Street. The one million gallon water reservoir and storage tower provided fire protection and potable water supply to the upper residential areas of Cedar Ridge Park Subdivision and Sunset Acres Subdivision, as well as the Business Park area located along Millennium Drive, with the potential to develop in further areas of the community. The tower draws its water supply from the two production wells located east of the MacKay Highway on Downeast Drive near the Town of Quispamsis/Town of Rothesay municipal boundary.

Solid Waste Disposal:

In Gondola Point prior to 1982 the disposal of solid waste was done at a site located outside of the Village. The site was privately owned and the Village had use of the site on a contractual basis. The residents had private arrangements for pick-up and service.

At one point the Town of Quispamsis had a garbage dump by present day Shoppers Drug Mart. According to former Mayor Alan Kelly the smell released from the dump when the garbage was burned was terrible. The garbage dump was eventually relocated to the French Village Dumpsite owned by Mr. Frank McKinnon. In the 1990's, solid waste from the Greater Saint John Region was trucked by haulers to the Regional Landfill site at Crane Mountain in Grand Bay. The Landfill site is managed by the Fundy Region Solid Waste Commission.

Communication

Telephone:

In the late 1800's, Western Union began to string telephone lines from Saint John to Netherwood School for girls in Rothesay. In 1880 the Bell Telephone Company took over Western Union and eight years later constructed its own lines along the Post Road. However, telephones were not installed until the turn of the century. At this time the majority of the phones were crank telephones on party lines, which were lines that more than one family would use. There was also a toll to call Saint John.

The Supernatural and Legends

Ghosts and Hauntings:
  The Town of Quispamsis has had a long history of possible ghost hauntings of particular buildings and areas around the town. Two of the more famous rumoured ghost hauntings are the haunting of the old Town Hall and the haunting of Stoneycroft house. Some residents of Quispamsis have reported peculiar happenings in these buildings.
  The old Town Hall building, where the KV Food Bank is housed today, next door to the Quispamsis Memorial Arena, has a long history of being haunted. The article below, from The Kings County Record of Sussex, NB, was published on December 28, 1977 and claims that a ghost possibly haunted the building. Some past employees of the Town of Quispamsis claim that the ghost was a female in a red dress. This ghost was known to like the male employees of the Town but not the female employees.

Does supernatural citizen watch Quispamsis Council?

SPOOKED? — There are those who'll tell this old-time stagecoach house, now the Quispamsis Village Hall, is haunted by a girl with long, black hair, wearing a red dress. [Photo by Bill Hart].

By JOHN FOGAN

The Village of Quispamsis, which lays claim to being one of the fastest growing communities in the province, may have another but more dubious claim to fame.

It may have the distinction of being the only municipality in the province with a haunted municipal office. Yes, among other things, Quispamsis may have its own ghost.

And, while some village officials say they feel the municipal office is spooked anyway following winter storms or just before or after council meetings, this particular ghost has shown no interest so far in municipal politics.

While many acknowledge her existence, very little is known about her. One popular story has it that the ghost is a woman who likes men and has a strong dislike for other women.

While this ghost has not been known to move things around in the building, she has been known to make a lot of noise.

The building, located on the Old Hampton Road, was once a coach house and is located on what was part of a 500-acre parcel of land granted to a Calib Wetmore in 1820. While the exact age of the house is not known, records show that it is over 120 years old.

Village Manager Don Scott, a hardy sort who claims he is not usually bothered by things of the supernatural, says that on a couple of occasions he was "scared" by unusual sounds within the building.

Mr. Scott said that on two occasions while he was working alone in his office on the second-storey of the building he heard what he thought were footsteps coming across the lower hall and up the stairs.

He recounts the event. "I was all alone in my office and I heard the creaking downstairs and later on the stairway. The steps approached the office and I looked up expecting to see someone there. There was no one.

"I thought it might be one of the councillors or other staff playing tricks so I went downstairs to have a look and called out, but there was no one there.

"When it is very quiet in here at night you hear this creaking. And it happens not just in the winter when buildings are cold and do creak, you can hear it all year round," says the village manager.

But the Quispamsis ghost does not make herself known only in the evenings, but from time to time in the daytime can cause some havoc.

Both Mr. Scott and a village clerk Mrs. Melda MacMillan tell of hearing what sounded to them like the building being struck by a truck, but finding nothing.

Mrs. MacMillan said she was working at the counter on the lower floor when she heard "a loud rumble in the wall" of council chambers. "I thought a transport truck had hit us."

Mr. Scott who was in his office upstairs said he heard the noise and "looked out of the window first as I thought something had hit us."

Seeing nothing he went downstairs to the chambers "I came in and went to the front corner of the room where the sound had come from. It was vacant and there were no cracks in the wall."

This incident occurred on a hot summer day in June.

A similar incident occurred in July when a loud thump was heard in the front corner of the council room. This time Mr. Scott and another village employee went into the basement to check on the foundation and supports and found nothing out of place.

As though this was not enough to shake the most steady nerves, Mr. Scott and Mrs. MacMillan say that unexplainable cold drafts occur in this front room from time to time while all the rest of the building may be warm.

Mrs. MacMillan said one day she "walked into the room and it was really cold, I just felt a cold chill, and the rest of the building was beautiful. This room was really cold. I left and returned a few minutes later and it was as warm as the rest of the building."

Ever been alone in a second floor room at night and suddenly you hear knocking on the wall behind you?

Local residents have also thought Stoneycroft to be haunted. Many eyewitnesses claimed to have seen lights and heard strange noises coming from the house during the period it remained unoccupied. Refer to the section entitled Stoneycroft for more information on the history of Stoneycroft.

Ghost Rock is another site in Quispamsis that had a reputation for being haunted. On the way home from one of the many events held at the Gondola Point Community Hall, some residents would pass by what was referred to as "Ghost Rock" on the Meenan's Cove Road. Odd unexplainable things would occur when you passed by this rock making people believe that it was haunted. In actual fact all events could be linked to two brothers living on the Meenan's Cove Road who would purposely try to scare young couples as they passed by this rock on their way home.

Like the two brothers in the above story, there are similar stories of ghost hauntings that would usually turn out to be the result of a couple of youngsters out for a good laugh at the expense of someone else.

Legends:

Legend has it that a vessel was lost in the fog after leaving Saint John and ended up sinking in Matthews Cove. According to the legend, treasure was said to be aboard the ship. A local Gondola Point Resident found silver spoons in the river one day and speculated that they came from this ship.

In 1905 the Saint John Globe reported various expeditions taking place in search of Captain Kidd's treasure. This treasure was supposedly a Spanish chest filled with gold and jewels. One of the locations that treasure seekers searched was along the Kennebecasis River.

If any resident has any information on other interesting legends, such as the Hanging Tree located on the Model Farm Road, please feel free to contact the Town of Quispamsis with this information.

Capturing What Life was like Through Art and Poetry

Quispamsis is, and has been, home to a number of amateur artists which is one reason why the Town undertook the construction of an "Arts and Culture Park" next to its Town Hall. One amateur artist who will be highlighted in this section is Donna T. (Buckley) Harriott. Mrs. Harriott has graciously allowed the Town to replicate some of her work here in the compilation of our Town's history

Mrs. Harriott:

Donna T. (Buckley) Harriott painted the watercolour entitled "School Days," which is pictured below, in 1999. Her painting captures the daily activities that took place in the Model Farm community. The painting also reflects her cherished childhood memories of her beloved home. The Model Farm School, McQuinn Home, Clark Store, C.N.R, Model Farm Station, Crowley Home, and Buckley Homestead are all prominently shown in her painting. Across from the Clark's house and store was the location where the Clark's stored feed and flour. The sign for flour was located above the door of Clark's Store when Mrs. Harriott was attending school at the Model Farm Schoolhouse. All of these buildings played vital roles in this rural community.

Mrs. Harriott explained that in the painting there is a rock with a tree growing out of it, across the road from the McQuinn home, which caused the rock to split. This was a great conversation piece for the children and was often referred to in nature class at school as an example of how tree roots can burrow through stone. Mrs. Harriott believes that a portion of that rock is still there today and that it enhances someone's lawn. The artist's detail and attention to objects such as the milk cans on the morning milk train, and her cousin John Higgins in the blue truck with milk from his farm are all events that were carved into the artist's memory from childhood. Through her art, Mrs. Harriott hopes to be able to share her knowledge of the past with future generations.

Donna Harriott also writes beautiful poetry. More themes of the Model Farm community can be drawn from her poetic words. Mrs. Harriott has allowed three of her poems, A Place Called Model Farm (2005), Home and Happy Thought (1998), and Tea in the Parlor (1998) to be displayed in the Town's history.

A Place Called Model Farm

There once was a place called Model Farm
I want to tell you a little about.
Really a very special place in that there is no doubt
For within its hills and valleys it held a heavenly charm.

A wonderful place to grow up as a child
Where life was so simple on R.R #1 in the county of Kings.
For in it all, in everything laid, God's greatest blessings:
A run through a green field, a play in the brook and smell the roses wild.

Across the field and over the ditch, down the Montgomery Hill,
The little band of one, two, three had grown as Crowley's brown house we viewed.
Over the rail tracks, past Model Farm Station, went the little crew
To make it to Minnie's candy store was the greatest joy and thrill.

Though the underpass was there, we did not go that way,
But through Minnie's yard, down the hill and past the house McQuinn.
Soon to be there, a short distance of a mile, for 9 am school is in;
First a baseball or fox and geese game before we began our day.

First up with the flag, don't let it touch the ground now!
Teacher would be upset and that would not do.
There goes the bell. Line up in order; first grades one

then two.
Boys on the left, girls on the right, all in an orderly row.

Seats all in a row and we all standing beside them,
Waited for teacher to read a scripture and to pray.
She then bids us to be seated; BIG 5 notebooks out to begin the day.
Grades one to eight all in a room; what a great place for all to be in!

From the school, farms, churches, families and friends
To the train winding in and out of the way,
It all has a special meaning in our hearts today.
Final words of memories that have no end.

Many became graduates of the school of Model Farm;
Became teacher, nurse, banker and businessman.
Many became fine soldiers and farmers from this little band,
To give service to a special place of charm called Model Farm.

Donna T. (Buckley) Harriott 2005

Home and Happy Thought

This is a rhyme all of my own
That tells a story of my home
The length of it all will depend
On how far back you go from beginning to end.

The house on the hill stood with stately demand
Under the shade of elm trees, tall and grand.
A veranda to play and run upon
A great swing in the tree to go high on!

The fields stretched as far as a child could see
And were filled with many an adventure for me.
Frogs and tadpoles gathered in a bottle,
I'd tote them from the spring when I barely could toddle.

The elms were filled with birds in chorus.
The barn with animals and Dad at his chores.
It meant work had to be done is true,
But when all chipped in it was quickly through.

Hay from the hay loft, soft and sweet,
For Daisy and Molly had to eat.
The pig in the pen called Pinky
Was really cute but oh so stinky!

My heart was so joyful and glad
When Mother would say there's berries to be had.
With our sun bonnet and shiny lard pail
We'd head over the field toward the old style and rail.

Standing among the daises, clover and frond,
You'd hear in the distance a whistle sound.
A train must be coming, bringing to Dad's attention
Comin' through the cuttin' stop at Model Farm Station.

In winter the fields were piled high in snow.
The winds around our old home would blow.
The old stove in the kitchen named Happy Thought,
Would keep us cozy and hours of warmth it brought.

Christmas would be the talk for all.
Planning would start in early fall.
Mother would plan for the great day in December,
Sweet strawberry cookies and fruit cake to remember.

The smell of coffee and pancakes on the griddle.
Children laughing at some funny riddle.

Dad shining his shoes and wearing his railroad hat,
And the purring of Susie, Mom's favorite cat.

Remember gathering eggs and trying not to break.
Grandma would want her fresh morning egg to take.
She would stand at kitchen door in a great white apron clad,
Taking the eggs, "Thank you child dear" in a voice so glad.

School was only a mile to walk.
We'd gather together, cousins and friends to talk,
Passed the houses of friends and family known,
Over the rail road to Minnie's candy store and home.

Many are the memories of a home for all.
Loved ones, belles and beaus and later grand kids did call.
Childhood memories and Happy Thought,
God in His way wonderful blessings brought.

                    Donna T. (Buckley) Harriott 1998

Tea in the Parlor

It was a stately home shaded under the trees,
That had a great front door that welcomed you to please.
Through that door many would come
To visit grandma and a wonderful lady I called Mom.

The big old kitchen was busy and filled with sounds that delighted.
The fire crackled in the Happy Thought stove polished so bright.
The shinny old kettle hummed a familiar tune
For you see, special guests were to be calling soon.

Grandma in a white crisp apron

Rustled about in her long skirts, a stately matron.
Adding finishing light touches to a lovely lunch
To serve to ladies - a hungry bunch.

Mother laid out the table linen white
And with a sweet smile and a voice so light
Would say, "Now all is set ready you can see,
For the ladies as they come to tea."

The silver glistened and the cups of fine china
Colored in delicate patterns. Oh, no finer.
Napkins neatly pressed oh just right.
Made you think great things for one little mite.

For you see I was only a wee tot
And was very interested in what I sought.
For as my Mother and Grandma prepared,
I watched it all unfold before my eyes so rare.

Tiny sandwiches filled with many things,
Chicken salad, Cucumber and sweet cherry rings.
Cakes so delightful and delicate to taste,
I'd try to reach carefully then pull back in haste.

Then out from the kitchen, politely but clear,
Someone would call,"The water has boiled Mother Dear"
Out she would rush from the beautiful set table,
And take down her best tea set with English bone label.

Mind you the tea would be made just so.
Wash out the tea pot with clear hot water to and fro.
Measure the tea leaves carefully, that's right.
Pour hot water over them, oh what delight!

Now the tea would brew to color and flavor.
For no tea party would serve to a neighbor,
If not made in the proper way

For all the ladies who came that day.

In through the large front door the ladies would come,
Chattering and talking to greet each one
And admiring comments at all they did see,
As they sat in parlor chairs and brocaded settee.

After a friendly talk and greeting,
Manners were the utmost at this meeting.
Ladies waited for grace to be said
Then all waited for sandwiches and tea to be had.

The crisp white napkin folded in half
Covered carefully each ladies lap.
Mother carefully poured the tea, must not hurry or race.
She served her guests with such ease and grace.

I watched carefully as I peered over the old oak table
And listened and saw all I was able.
How Grandma and Mother gracefully served
These lovely ladies I carefully watched and heard.

Words of thanks in warmth expressed that day
When the ladies came to tea the old fashioned way.
Tea in the parlor was a delight, truthfully so.
But I thank God especially for all the things I learned and know.

For you see God uses all situations to show
His gracious ways for a child to know.
How appropriate a lesson a wise Mother taught me:
Take time for kindly service to others and serve a cup of tea.

Donna T. (Buckley) Harriott 1998

In Their Own Words

In this section you will find some of the recollections that older residents of the area have of the past. The first recollection in this section is an interview done by Valerie Evans with Elsie (Bishop) Marr for the Telegraph Journal on April 30, 1998.

Older residents recall the past
WITH VALERIE EVANS

Elsie (Bishop) Marr, 89, was 16 years old in 1925. That year, she came to Gondola Point where she still lives.

I always say, 'You have to cut the garment according to the cloth. If you don't have it, you don't need it.' My generation knew you didn't have things unless you worked really hard for them and if you didn't have them, it wasn't the end of the world. People were very generous and sharing. In 12 Romans, it says, 'Rejoice with those who rejoice and weep with those who weep.' We did that but now as long as you're all right, that is it.

I came here with my parents and siblings. We moved from the Sheffield area because my father was working in the construction of Vocational School, a marvelous building. I was terribly, terribly, terribly homesick and spent about three weeks when I felt the world had ended for me. But then I got acquainted with other young people.

Entertainment then was different from now. We never got bored and one of our favorite things in the evening was to walk up and go across on the ferry and maybe just wander around over there and come back. We used to go coasting a lot. Our favorite place was the church hill. Four or five would get on the sled up where the Anglican Church is now, come down and make the turn to stop.

I went to parties but I never danced. My father didn't approve of dancing and I didn't do anything that my father didn't approve of. I set myself some standards when I started out. I always said when a thing goes out of your mouth, it goes out of your control, so I was always very careful what I confided to other people. It never bothered me to see someone was doing something I didn't want to do. It didn't make me the most popular girl but anyway it worked for me. At an early age, I was pretty closely connected to my church and was involved in everything to do with it.

The roads out here were dirt and in spring the river came up over them. They had terrible mud holes and men who had teams made a bit of money hauling cars out of the mud. When we came here there weren't any buses. They started in 1926. The roads were paved about 1936 and they raised them but they didn't change them in any other way. In the winter, the roads were not plowed. The whole thing was quite different. This was a farming and summer community. One big milk farm down the road is now Hillhurst Subdivision. What used to be our garden patch is now half of Sherwood Park.

In 1929, I married Rob Marr. He was born in Quispamsis. The Marr Road is named after his grandparents. He was quite a bit older than I was. He mostly farmed and always dealt with teams of horses. He would have whatever work came available in the summertime, usually roadwork. He drove the school van for three or four years. He didn't have any profession or anything like that, which was the normal way then. I drove before I was married. Rob drove the mail out here for years. It didn't pay very much money so if he could get a job outside I would drive for him.

Robb Marr driving the Rothesay School van in 1925

Above is Mrs. Marr in 1928.

Above is Mrs. Marr in 1998.

For a long while, we burned wood. When we first had oil, I missed the wood very much. Then we had an electric stove and oil furnace. I wasn't sure if it was going to keep us warm or not. I never thought the day would come when I would push buttons and my washing would be done. I did it the hard way. When I was first married I used a washboard but eventually I had a wringer washing machine. You manhandled the wet clothes through the wringer, which you cranked. Then I had an electric wringer washer. We also had an icebox.

When I was expecting my first child, Marion, I made six sets of everything. I had her in the hospital. Very few women went to the hospital to have babies and my mother-in-law was very disapproving. She had had all of hers at home and some without even a doctor, but I wasn't on to that.

Johnny, my second child, was born 18 months later in Evangeline Maternity Hospital run by the Salvation Army. They catered to unmarried mothers but they took all cases and they charged the same for a room, as did the others. I had a private room for $4 a day. Those two children made my life. After they were born, that was the main thing in my life. I was so grateful to have those kids that I never begrudged anything that came up. You didn't go to the doctor every time your child was sick. Johnny would get so feverish it would practically burn you to touch him. I would give him Sweet Spirits of Nitre. It cut the fever down. He would be so sick; he would just lay like a dead fellow.

I never worked out until I was well into my 40's and then my husband did not approve of it. He had a bad accident helping a fellow building a house. The chap had made a staging but it broke while my husband was at the top of the two-storey house. He fell on a rock pile and smashed one arm up badly and that was when I went to work. I went to Phil Allison at M.R.A.'s, a great fellow he was. I told him I had never worked but it was necessary that I earn some money. Would he have any openings? He asked where I would like to work and I explained I wasn't fussy but I liked to sew. He took my name and wrote it on a scrap of paper and I thought he would throw it away when I got outside. I didn't hear anything from him for three weeks. Then I was back in town so I went in and asked if there was anything now. He looked at me and said, 'I called your house this morning. Can you come to work tomorrow morning in the pattern department? If you think you are not going to like it I would rather you didn't try.'

I said, 'I will like it.' My husband didn't know I had made the arrangements. When I came home, he told me, M.R.A.'s had called. He was totally shocked when I told him I was going to work there the next day. The first few weeks were murder. I never let anybody know how tired I was. I got $16 for 5 days per week, a dollar more than their usual starting salary. I stayed in the pattern department for two years until I stopped working full time. One Christmas, the head of the china department asked me if I would work in there and that is where I stayed until they tore the store down to get rid of me.

    Now I am not going to say that I have no regrets in my life because I don't think anyone can say that if they are honest with themselves but at the same time, I am quite satisfied with my life and I have been happy. I have been very lucky- but it was a little hard sometimes.

References used in compiling the history of the Town of Quispamsis

Bale, Gordon. *Chief Justice William Johnstone Ritchie: Responsible Government and Judicial Review.* Ottawa: Carleton University Press, 1991.

Canada & The South African War, 1899-1902. 2005. Canadian War Museum. 2006 Summer http://www.warmuseum.ca/cwm/boer/boerwarhistory_e.html

Cardwell. *Tales of The Kennebecasis A Resourceful People.* Saint John Regional Library and Old Time Diner. 1800's.

Cayo, Don. *Savage Civilization: The History of Native-European Relations.*

Dearborn, Dorothy. *An Anecdotal History of Kings County New Brunswick.* Saint John: Neptune Publishing, 2003.

Department of National Defense and Canadian Forces. Assistant Deputy Minister (Public Affairs). 2006. Canada. 21 May 2006. http://www.dnd.ca.

Dictionary of Canadian Biography Online. 2000. Library and Archives Canada. Summer 2006. http://www.biographi.ca/EN/ShowBio.asp?BioId=40517&query=

Gondola Point Community Hall. Quispamsis: Town of Quispamsis, 1967.

Jones, Eleanor (Nelly). (Past Local Historian) Her notes, newspaper articles, and research she gave to this project.

Kelbaugh, Peggy. Personal interview. Summer 2005.

Kings County Museum and Historical and Archival Society, Inc. Hampton, New Brunswick.

Kings County Retired Teachers' Association. Early Schools of Kings County, New Brunswick. Sussex: Royal Printing Ltd., 1985.

Linking the Past With the Present: THE LEGISLATURE AND THE OTTY FARM WHEN IT WAS A PROVINCIAL STOCK FARM. Fredericton: Provincial Archives of New Brunswick (Microfilm F11133 RS 184 C.3.a.). 1930.

MacManus, George E. *Post Offices of New Brunswick 1783-1930.* Toronto: Jim A. Hennock Ltd., 1984.

Mi'kmaq and Maliseet Institute, 2001. University of New Brunswick Fredericton. Summer 2005 http://www.unbf.ca/education/mmi/index.html

McLean, Lieut. - Colonel C.H., comp. *Prominent People of New Brunswick.* The Biographical Society of Canada Ltd, 1937.

Provincial Archives of New Brunswick, Fredericton Campus: University of New Brunswick.

Rayburn, Alan. *Geographical Names of New Brunswick.* Ottawa: Dept. of Energy Mines and Resources, 1975.

Roberts, Guilford. Personal interview. Summer 2005.

Robinson, J.F.H. *Village Historical Facts found in Town Records.* Quispamsis: Town of Quispamsis, April 1982.

Rothesay Regional Police. 2006. Powered by FCS. Online. Internet. Summer 2006 http://www.rothesayregionalpolice.com/history.cfm

Sabine, Lorezno. *Biographical Sketches of Loyalists of the American Revolution with a Historical Essay. Volume II.* Port Washington, NY: Kennikat Press Inc., 1966.

Smith, H. L. *A Rambling History of the Hammond River Valley.* Provincial Archives of New Brunswick, Fredericton. Nov. 24th, 1949

The Great Depression (1929-1939): historical context, economic impact and related links. 2006. Government of Canada. Summer 2006. http://canadianecon omy.gc.ca/english/economy/1929_39depression.html

The Great Depression of Canada. Porter Creek Secondary School in Whitehorse, Yukon, Canada. Summer 2005. http://www.yesnet.yk.ca/schools/projects/ canadianhistory/depression/depression.html

Welcome to Fundy Trail Parkway St. Martins New Brunswick. 2002. Fundy Trail Development Authority Inc. Summer, 2006. http://www.fundytrailparkway.com/welcome.htm

Wood, Robert. *River Boats Recollections By Robert Wood; Recollections Conjured up out of the past for the Entertainment and Edification of my niece Rosalyn Wood who arrived too late to be acquainted with River Boats.* Saint John: Saint John Regional Library (No. 387.243 W00.C.2)

Other useful sources and links:

Acadiensis, 1901-1908.

American Indian Tribal Lists: Native American Tribes and Languages. Summer 2005.
http://www.native-languages.org/languages.htm

Campbell, Patrick. *Travels 1791 and 1792.* Champlain Society, 1937.

Evans, Herbert G. *A Ferry Story.* Saint John: The Atlantic Advocate, 1966.

Hampton's King's County Historical Society.

Hampton New Brunswick. Tourism New Brunswick. Summer 2005.
http://new-brunswick.net/new-brunswick/hampton/

Hampton New Brunswick Information. 2006. Hampton. Summer 2005.
http://www.hometowncanada.com/nb/Hampton.html

Munro, Alexander. *New Brunswick.* Halifax: Richard Nugent, 1855.

Robinson, Charlotte Gourlay. *Pioneer Profiles of New Brunswick Settlers.* Canada: Mika Publishing Company, 1980.

Town of Quispamsis. 2006. Quispamsis Town Hall. Summer 2005 and 2006.
http://www.quispamsis.ca

Town of Rothesay. Rothesay Town Hall. Summer 2006. http://www.rothesay.ca/

Waterbury, David H. *A Chat on the Way From the City to Gondola Point on the Beautiful Kennebecasis.* Saint John: N.B. Historical Society (No. 12, Vol. IV.), 1928.

Webster, J. Clarence, Dr CGM MD. *Historical Guide to New Brunswick.* New Brunswick: New Brunswick Government, 1940.

Wright, Esther Clark. *The Loyalists of New Brunswick.* Moncton: Moncton Publishing Co. Ltd., 1955